Image and Meaning

Metaphoric Traditions in Renaissance Poetry

Don Cameron Allen is Sir William Osler Professor of English at The Johns Hopkins University. He is the author of *Doubt's Boundless Sea* and *The Harmonious Vision,* as well as of numerous journal articles on literature and poetry, and is the editor of *A Celebration of Poets.*

DON CAMERON ALLEN

Image and Meaning

Metaphoric Traditions in
Renaissance Poetry

New Enlarged Edition

Baltimore: The Johns Hopkins Press

Copyright © 1960, 1968 by The Johns Hopkins Press
Baltimore, Maryland 21218
Manufactured in the United States of America
Library of Congress Catalog Card Number 68–15444

Originally published, 1960
Revised edition, 1968

This book was brought to publication
with the assistance of a grant from
The Ford Foundation.

Contents

Introduction

The essays in this book are experiments in reading learned poems. Most of them have been publicly read before, and I return to them not out of dissatisfaction but only to offer readings made in a different way. There are probably many ways to read a poem; there is certainly not one way. I like to read poetry, when it is possible, in terms of its poetical antecedents. This method does not permit me to explain how the poet wrote the poem or how a contemporary of the poet read it. I once thought it possible to approximate one or the other of these critical ends. Now I am convinced that it is impossible to read a poem as a contemporary of the poet might have read it. One can explain lost references, one can annotate the poem from the historical remnants of its generation, but this is not giving it a contemporary reading. If we were told, "Let us read this poem as a contemporary," we might ask which contemporary the speaker has in mind. Since I cannot come close to reading an Elizabethan poem as an Elizabethan would, I can hardly have the bad taste to argue that I know how Spenser, Shakespeare, or Marvell wrote a poem. This volume is, then, a poor attempt of a modern who has read earlier poetry to read a later poem.

In general I have tried to use only poetical annotations in my commentary. Since my material is poems, I have not pushed them into another language. I have tried to suggest what they mean with a summary or a rendering of the necessary metaphor. I have not been so pedantic about the non-literary texts which I have translated because I could do them no harm.

I am grateful to the editors of *Comparative Literature* and *Studies in Philology* for permission to reprint the essays on Spenser and to the editor of the *Modern Language Quarterly* for the right to use the Lovelace essay. The explication of "Venus and Adonis" is reprinted with the permission of the Oxford Press from *Elizabethan and Jacobean Studies presented to F. P. Wilson,* and the study of Shakespeare's "Rape of Lucrece" first appeared in *Shakespeare Survey,* XV, published by the Cambridge University Press. For the Milton essay, which appeared in *Neo-Latin Poetry of the Sixteenth and Seventeenth Centuries,* the director of the William Andrews Clark Memorial Library must be thanked. The Herrick explanation is reprinted with the permission of the University of Texas Press and the editor of the Starnes' *Festschrift.* The Macmillan Company has kindly permitted me to quote the passage from Masefield, *Collected Poems,* New York, 1935, at the end of the Vaughan essay. I am also obliged to the editors of The Johns Hopkins Press who have endured me for so long and who have helped me see both versions of this book through the press.

Baltimore, 1967   D. C. A.

CHAPTER ONE

"The March Eclogue" of
The Shepheardes Calender

"The March Eclogue" of *The Shepheardes Calender* is the attempt of a young poet to understand the nature of love. The force of the passion, that expresses itself in smiles and snarls, that is weak when it should be strong, strong when it should be mild, was as yet hardly known to him. He had just reached maturity when he wrote this poem, but he already sensed, as Thomalin (the main character of this eclogue) does, the painful joy and the joyful pain of love. Thanks to poets who had spoken about these matters before, the youthful Spenser was able to talk maturely while he still felt only the first warm flashes of a life that had more passion and pain than he had ever imagined. The problem that he discusses in this eclogue is not a new one and to understand what he has to say we may listen first to Bion, who discourses on a similar theme in his poem about the young birdcatcher.

A bird-catcher yet a boy in a woody grove
Was hunting birds when he saw winged Eros
Perched on the young shoot of a box tree. When he saw it,
He rejoiced because to him it seemed a big bird.
At once he bound his reeds together, one on another,
To catch Eros, who kept hopping here and there and fled
                                                              him.
And the boy, being vexed that his task was endless,
Threw down his reeds and went to an old farmer
Who taught him the art, and told it to him,
And showed him Eros perching; but the old man,
Smiling, shook his head and spoke to the boy:
"Refrain from this hunting and stay away from this bird!
Fly far! This is a bad bird! You will be happy
As long as you do not catch him. But when you have man's
                                                          measure,
This thing which now flees and hops away of its own
                                                           accord
Will come suddenly and sit on your head."

Even when the graceful Greek of Bion is turned into a
dull, literal English translation, we have no difficulty in identifying this bird. He is the runaway Eros of Moschus,[1] still
fugitive, yet the mysterious center of Bion's idyll. In Moschus'
poem, his Cyprian mother describes him for lovers so that
"he might be known among twenty others"; but Bion never
gives him proportion because he sees him only with the eyes
of a boy on the edge of adolescence, a visual and psychological
station that is established by the opening phrase of the poem.
But the boy birdcatcher, who represents the anticipatory aspects of life as opposed to the old husbandman who has, to
use the Greek expression, "turned the page of love," is not
completely without experience. He has gone into the world
(the grove filled with trees) to hunt birds (symbols of mature
activities), carrying with him the engines necessary to man-

[1] *Eidyllion* I.

hood but for the moment inadequate for what he encounters. The boy of the idyll has speculated, perhaps, on the grown-up occupation with love; it has come before his eyes, but as yet he cannot understand it. It is, consequently, like a bird, singing and fluttering, but masked in its true and curious nature by the dense foliage of the wood of life.

To underscore the insufficiency of the boy's knowledge, Bion says that Eros lights on a "young shoot" of the box tree, and adds that to the boy it is a "big bird." This childlike descriptive phrase is attended by a childlike verb, for the boy "rejoices" at the sight. These are sophisticated attempts to reproduce an adolescent's verbal reactions to what he half perceives. The verb φαίνετο, which controls the fourth line of the poem, suggests the external; the boy sees only the bare outline of Eros. Because a Greek boy often sought the advice of his teachers, this young hunter turns quickly to the old man from whom he had learned his art. This youthful decision further demonstrates the boy's unworldliness.

The *senex* sees the "big bird" and ungraciously translates it into "κακόν . . . θηρίον" (wicked beast); in fact, when he uses the proper generic word, he distinguishes it with "τόδε" (*this* bird). He speaks at once; the bird must be avoided, not hunted. The old husbandman undoubtedly knows all that the Aphrodite of Moschus had said about her son. "If you catch him, he will lead you captive. He will betray you by weeping. His lips are poison." All of this the rural adviser, unwilling to state the alluring particulars, puts into blunt precept. More subtly, and perhaps sadly, he says that the time may arrive when Love, who now eludes him, will come of his own accord, a probability that the ambiguous "τὸν ἀπότροπον . . . Ἔρωτα" of the second line suggests. Love, "flying and to be fled," says the old man, will settle itself, not on the young shoot of the boxtree, but on *your* head.

The ploughman of the Greek idyll is a forbidding *magister*

amoris; he has taught the youth his arts, but he gives him no
real advice on the "τέχνη ἐρωτική." We must look to the Roman
elegiac poets, to Tibullus or Propertius, repeaters of the tropes
of Callimachus, or to Ovid, to find the full detail that illumi-
nates the taciturnity of Bion's old man. These poets tell us how
love is hunted with tears and wounds. Once it is caught, its
plumage is found to be as false as its eyes and heart. Fortunately, this sour attitude is not the only one because, when
Bion's poem is held up to the light, we see between its lines
another old teacher who is kinder and more joyous.

Three hundred years after the death of Bion, the *fabula*
of his delicate poem was repeated when Philetas, a rural Orpheus, told the story of Eros to the young lovers, Daphnis
and Chloe. It is the story of the old shepherd's experience, not
in the wood, but in a pleasant garden that he had made with
his hands.

> As I went in there today about noon, a boy appeared in the
> pomegranate and myrtle grove . . . [he was] white as milk and
> his hair shining with the glance of fire. . . . Naked he was,
> alone he was; he played and wantoned it about, and culled and
> pulled as if it were his garden. Therefore, I ran at him as fast
> as I could, thinking to get him in my clutches. . . . But he, with
> a soft and easy sleight, gave me the slip, sometimes running
> under the roses, sometimes hiding himself in the poppies.[2]

The little god, who is still Bion's elusive bird, refuses to be
questioned, but eventually he speaks with the voice of a wood
thrush to the old lover. "I may not be taken," he says, "though
a hawk or an eagle or any other swifter bird be flown at me,
I am not a boy though I seem to be one, but am older than
Saturn and all this universe." He informs Philetas that it was
he who managed that Philetas and his beloved wife Amaryllis
meet: "I was at her side, but you did not see me." Then he
adds, "Be glad, Philetas, that you alone of all mortals have

[2] Longus II.3–8.

seen this boy in your old age." Having said this, the boy Eros
skips from bough to bough like a nightingale, and the question
of Daphnis and Chloe about the nature of Eros, boy or bird,
is almost answered. The young couple never see the god although they are in his province; and the truth that emerges
and that seems to color Spenser's March eclogue is that Eros,
the feathered thing, manifests himself only to those who stand
on the threshold of maturity or to those others who have
passed out of love's limits and look back on its sunny counties
through the defiles of memory.

For the old shepherd Philetas, the recollection of love is
good, and he is truly a *magister amoris maximus* like Tibullus [3]
or Ovid.[4] It is, therefore, not without point that Eros describes
the flowers in the old man's garden as "poems," "τὰ φυτὰ ταυτα
τούτου ποιήματα." [5] The old husbandman in Bion's poem has, on
the other hand, shabby memories, which are shared by the old
woman who takes his place when Ronsard brings the whole
topic into French poetry. The old gentleman on whom both
the *presbyter* and the *saga* are fashioned is probably hoary
Cephalus, whom Socrates, no youth but an habitual bearer of
limed twigs, once consulted about the nature of passionate
love. "Never," said that old man, "lament the passing of love,
but say with Sophocles: 'Hush, to my great delight I have escaped it and feel free of a despot who was desperate and
angry.' " [6] It is this mood, rather than the playful one of Bion
or the happy one of Longus, that drifts like a cold mist
through Ronsard's poem.

The transition from Bion's sensitively conceived contrast

---

[3] "Vos me celebrate magistrum,/Quos male habet multa callidus arte
puer./Gloria cuique sua est: me, qui spernentur, amantes/ Consultent; cunc-
tis ianua nostra patet./ Tempus erit, cum me Veneris praecepta ferentem/
Deducat iuvenum sedula turba senem" (I.iv.75–80).

[4] "Inscribit spoliis, Naso magister erat" (*Ars* II.744).

[5] II.7.

[6] *Republic* I.329C.

between the attitudes of extreme youth and age in the revealed presence of the great god Eros to Ronsard's bitter
modification of the theme [7] can be made in part on the topic
of the *magister amoris*, who joins with the witch of the Latin
poets to make a new person for the gardens of love. The boy
in Ronsard's poem has been trying to catch birds for his cage
when suddenly he sees Eros "comme oyseau de mauvais
augure."

> Un enfant dedans un bocage
> Tendoit finement ses gluaux,
> A fin de prendre des oyseaux
> Pour les emprisonner en cage.
>   Quand il veit, par cas d'adventure,
> Pres un buys Amour emplumé
> Qui voloit par le boys ramé
> Comme oyseau de mauvais augure.

The "big bird" and the naïveté of the Greek poem are gone,
and, by direct intent, love is polluted with ill qualities; for the
winged God of Love has now become "l'oyseau de mauvaise
rencontre." On further inspection, the "enfant" discovers the
peacock colors of the bird's wings and that "sa face sembloit
un Ange/ Qu'on voit portrait en un tableau." This comparison
of Eros and an angel bothers us only until we remember that
Cupid was for some men of the Middle Ages a fallen angel.
Ronsard's "enfant" partly reproduces the experience of Bion's
boy; he also "rejoices" but it is in the hope of snaring "si grand
proye." The bird will not be surprised; and so in rage, the boy
drops his lures and

> Vint trouver une vielle mere
> Qui se mesloit de deviner.

[7] I follow Laumonier's 1934 text, VII.259–62. The description of Eros in
this poem comes from Moschus, I, via Poliziano's Latin rendering and
Baif's French version.

The *magistri* step aside so that Phryne, the witch who can fetch and dismiss love, may enter from another tradition.

It is clear that Ronsard's "mere" is not an old teacher of the boy; she is also no happy Amaryllis. She is gray-haired and sour-faced and as disillusioned with love as she is with life. She is Medea at sixty, and in literature she has many cousins. Propertius tells us that she is both instructress in the affairs of the heart and mistress of magic arts.[8] She is the witch of Atlas whom Dido remembered so well;[9] but she is best known to us through a poem by Tibullus, a poem that ends like a sorceress' incantation.

> Hanc ego de caelo ducentem sidera vidi;
>   Fluminis haec rapidi carmine vertit iter,
> Haec cantu finditque solum manesque sepulchris
>   Elicit et tepido devocat ossa rogo;
> Iam tenet infernas magico stridore catervas,
>   Iam iubet aspersas lacte referre pedem.
> Cum libet, haec tristi depellit nubila caelo:
>   Cum libet, aestivo convocat orbe nives,
> Sola tenere malas Medeae dicitur herbas,
>   Sola feros Hecatae perdomuisse canes.[10]

The "vielle mere" is a *verax saga amoris*, and Ronsard certainly thought, as he wrote, of her haunting song expressed by his beloved Theocritus:

> φράζεό μευ τὸν ἔρωθ' ὅθεν ἵκετο, πότνα Σελάνα [11]

This woman whom Ronsard displays in her dour and bitter years was once one of those lively young witches, a Simaetha who could beguile men's hearts, as Propertius [12] tells us, by charming the moon from the heavens. Now she has reached

[8] IV.5.
[9] *Aeneid* IV.478-91.
[10] I.ii.43-52.
[11] II.81.
[12] I.i.19-20.

the time in life when all seems stale. She is La Vielle of the *Roman de la Rose*, Dame Brysenne of the *Mort d'Arthur*, or, on a lower social level, Villon's Belle Heaulmière. Regnier writes about her in the seventeenth century; [13] and we shall see her again in Ronsard's "Contra Denise Sorciere," a poem that is founded on Horace's assault against Canidia and that shines with antique spoils. In all instances, she is a gray woman who scorns her recollections of love, and, like her predecessor in Bion, is a kind of Anteros, the half-brother of Eros, who saw to it in ancient times that love was reciprocated, but who had come to stand for his opponent, a violent Anti-Eros.[14] In both her person and her advice, the "mere" consulted by Ronsard's "garcon" is a personification of the enemies of Cupid. At one time she may have provided her clients with philtres to bring love, but she no longer practises fascination. Her charms and spells now effect the contrary.

Toward the center of her homily, she says to the youth:

> O que tu seras bien heureux
> Si tu le fuys toute ta vie
> Et si jamais tu n'as envye
> D'estre au rolle des amoreux.

"Stay off the register of lovers!" is the best advice that she can offer; then she goes on like Bion's old man, "in time, this bird that now eludes you will come without your thinking about it"—

> Comme une jeune et tendre queste,
> Et foullant de ses piedz ta teste,
> Que c'est que d'aimer t'aprendra.

She is correct in a way, for love swoops down on the unsuspecting. "Instat semper Amor supra caput," writes Proper-

---

[13] "Discours d'une Maquerelle," *Œuvres,* ed. Courbet (Paris, 1875), pp. 176-81.

[14] R. V. Merrill, "Eros and Anteros," *Speculum,* XIX (1944), 265-84.

tius; [15] and he complains that the passion is both "furor" [16] and "insanus." [17] So if love brings madness and insanity, it is quite right that the birds of Bion and Ronsard perch on the lover's head. But Ronsard's old woman uses the word *fouler* and adds "ses piedz." This is a far rougher landing than Bion's "καθιξειο." The reason for this is not far to seek. Black thinking about love had competed with the brightness of Hellenic joy. There is an Eros who tramples his victims; he is styled "saevus"; and his triumphs are in the literary annals.

The cruelty of Eros is described as early as the fourth chorus of Sophocles' *Antigone*, and the full brutality of victorious Love is recounted in Ovid's *Amores*.[18] Love is, indeed, a dire actor. He may do what he wishes. He is never punished except in the imagination of poets, and then only in another world. The "Cupido Cruciatur" of Ausonius and the "Amor Victus Somno" of Modestinus, poems that show Eros repaid in his own silver, are both dreams that take place in the birdless land of Avernus. Their importance rests in the fact that the *topos* of the *registre des amoureaux* begins with them. It is interesting, too, that the angry *martyres* who have it out with Love are all women—Phaedra, Scylla, Medea, Procne, Dido, Ariadne, Thisbe—and all ghosts in the dark realm. These unhappy ladies become part of the long procession of the *martyres d'Amour* and as such they are well known before the end of the Middle Ages. "Au fort martir on me devra nommer,/ Se dieu d'Amour fait mulz amoreaux saints," writes Charles d'Orleans. "And rad also ful often in my contemplatyff medytacons," says the author of *The Mass of Venus*, "the holy legende of Martyrs of Cupydo." [19] The register

---

[15] II.xxx.7.

[16] I.i.7.

[17] I.ix.16.

[18] I.ii.19–28.

[19] The French expressions are collected in I. Siciliano, *François Villon* (Paris, 1934), pp. 313-36. For the English, see *The Lay-Folk's Mass-Book*,

grew longer, the number of sad martyrs increased as each new
generation enrolled more broken lovers on the book. The
whole topic was enlarged and annotated for the Renaissance
by the truest of true lovers, Francesco Petrarch, in his "Trionfo d'Amore."

Petrarch's "Trionfo" looks back to the classics, to Dante,
and to his own *Africa* for many of its tropes and images. In
the *Africa*'s sixth book, Sophonisba, condemned to Hades as
a suicide but pardoned by the good offices of Aeacus, enters
the field of lovers and sees the martyrs wandering in the valley of shades. Her experience is repeated by the poet in the
proper language of Tuscany:

> Vidi un'vittorioso e sommo duce.
> Pur com'un di color che'n Campidoglio
> Trionfal carro a gran gloria conduce.[20]

The trampling triumpher of this poem is familiar—a young
man, proud and fierce of face ("garzon crudo"), who is nude,
winged, and weaponed. The martyrs of love surround him:
"parte occisi;/Parte feriti da pungenti strali." [21] The valley
through which he rides is the valley of the shadow, a dark circle of the Inferno; and all of us are certain where we are when
one of the chained prisoners, "un' ombra, alquanto men che
l'altre trista" [22] approaches the unknowing Petrarch and tells
him about Eros, "mansueto fanciullo, e fiero veglio." The line
of martyrs moves through the succeeding books of the poem,

---

ed. Simmons (London, 1879), pp. 394-95. In Hoccleve's "Letter of Cupid"
—a version of Christine of Pisa's "L'Epistre au Dieu d'Amours"—Cupid
uses the expression "In my legende of Martres" (*Works*, ed. Furnivall
[London, 1892], p. 85). The theme of Love as Death, which is also found
in Cavalcanti, is expressed by Ronsard and by Guillaume Alexis (*Œuvres*,
ed. Piaget and Picot [Paris, 1896], I, 24).

[20] "Triumphus Cupidinis" 1.13-15.
[21] *Ibid.*, 29-30.
[22] *Ibid.*, 40.

and, as they pass, the ghost "less sad than the rest" reads the *registre des amoureaux* and recites their fates. It is this book that the "vielle mere" (who is probably mentioned therein) has in mind when she warns the boy.

It must be confessed that when we reach the end of Ronsard's poem, our veins are less warmed and our sensibilities less charmed than when we had only Bion's poem in our emotional history. Love has become somewhat distasteful. It is associated with birds of ill-omen, with witchcraft, wounds, and bitter hearts. The delicate tradition invented by some of the Greeks is worn and tarnished. Eros has been expelled from the Christian Church; Cephalus has got a bishopric; and the terrestrial Cupid has made his bed in Hell.[23] But to return again to Anteros, the Renaissance "old ploughman" and "vielle mere" in one.

The little god Anteros, who plays an almost protective rôle in Ronsard's "Magie," appears also in the part of the cursed old man of Du Bellay's "L'Anterotique." His birth date was later than that of Eros, so the fact that the Renaissance thought of him as an old man may have had another sanction.[24] The classical conception of him as a *deus ultor*, who saw to it that the passion inspired by Eros was returned and who avenged the loving-unloved, was clear enough; but in his other nature, he was sometimes brought forward as a fighting opponent

[23] It is hardly necessary to prove the point that some mediaeval men could regard Cupid as a demon, but the texts are interesting. St. Isidore puts him sternly in Hell: "Est enim daemon fornicationis" (VIII.xi.80); and Theodulf, the "Pindar" of Charlemagne, follows the same theme: "Est sceleratus enim moechiae daemon et atrox / Ad luxus miseros, saeva barathra trahens" (*Carmina*, ed. Duemmler [Berlin, 1881], I, 543). In Gervais du Bus, *Le Roman de Fauvel*, Cupid and Venus are found in the company of "Fornicacion, Advoutire/ Viegnent la, tout sanz contredire/ Cupide vendra et Venus;/ De tel gent ne demeure nus" (ed. Langfors [Paris, 1919], p. 147).

[24] A figurine of an old man was identified as Anteros as early as the *Mythologia* of Gyraldus; it is published and discussed in Montfaucon, *L'Antiquité* (Paris, 1719), I, 184.

of Cupid, as a deity who preferred honor and virtue to love.
Alciati describes him as disarming and binding his passionate
brother,[25] and Marguerite of Navarre calls this violence an
act of purification.

> Amour, remply de pitié et de zelle,
> D'amour mourant toucha la legiere aille,
> Et l'arracha du corps tendre et beau:
> La trousse print, et ses traicts avec elle,
> L'arc impiteux et la corde cruelle,
> Aussi l'espais et ignorant bandeau.
> Le tout il mit en un feu si nouveau
> Que leur chaleur il convertit en glace;
> Sans oublier de Venus le flambeau,
> Dont ce sainct feu toute navrure efface.[26]

But Anteros as the chaste opponent of Cupid was capable of
disguises, and he assumes one of these in the "Cupido Conquered" of the subpoet Barnabe Googe.

Googe's poem, printed in 1563, is a vision poem in which
the classical past is expressed in familiar mediaeval *formulae*.
The poet, suffering from an amorous malady, wanders into
a spring garden and falls asleep by a pool. In his dream he
meets Mercury who escorts him to the Court of Diana, which
is filled with those who were formerly on the *registre des
amoureaux*. Then we learn that a hostile army is at the gates,
and we go out to see the Cupid of Petrarch ride by in his
chariot.

---

[25] In most editions of the *Emblemata* of Alciati, the CIXth emblem shows
Anteros looking very much like Eros but without his identifying attributes.
He is described as the god who draws men's minds on high. The CXth
emblem shows him tying disarmed Eros to a tree. In Belleau's "Contre
l'Amour," the poet assumes the part of Anteros and defies the god, saying of
love, "Il vient de nous, mais las! pour voiler mieux/ De nostre mal la trop
folle entreprise,/ Nous voulons bien que ce Dieu favorise/ Nostre malheur
d'un tiltre glorieux" (*Œuvres*, ed. Marty-Laveaux [Paris, 1878], I, 171–72).

[26] *Les Dernières Poésies*, ed. Lefranc (Paris, 1896), p. 301.

> The Captaine chyfe in Charyot ryde
> with Pompe and stately Pryde:
> With Bow in hand of glistering gold,
> and Quyver by his syde.
> Wher many a shaft full sharp doth ly:
> and many a mortall Darte,
> That hath with poysoned force destroid,
> Full many a yealdyng Harte.[27]

The army of Diana, commanded by "Hipolitus," takes the field, and the battle begins. Cannons blaze and arrows fly. Idleness, Cupid's Ovidian captain, is slain; then "Hipolitus" kills Cupid's charioteer and captures the god. At this point Googe wakes up, but once again Cupid is conquered in a dream. "Hipolitus" becomes Anteros in this particular action, but one must also recall that his Greek predecessor, Hippolytus, had a prominent place among the martyrs of love.

This is the poetical background to Spenser's March eclogue, and I should like to summarize it before I approach the poem. Bion provides us with graceful instruction on the nature of love as first seen by an adolescent boy, but he brings into the pleasant wood of birdsong the amused but cold voice of the old farmer. Among other Greeks and Romans, the god who is also a bird becomes fierce of claw and beak; he begins to resemble the feathered hawk described by Passerat, a French contemporary of Spenser:

> Cupidon me devore:
> Et ma chair, et mes nerfs, et mes os, et ma peau
> Sont tousiours deschirez par ce cruel oiseau.[28]

This other Eros is a destroyer and a trampler of lovers who can only work their revenge on him through wishful dreams. He is also a disease, as classical physicians testified, that re-

---

[27] *Eglogs, Epytaphes and Sonettes,* ed. Arber (London, 1910), p. 118.
[28] *Poésies,* ed. Blanchemain (Paris, 1880), I, 58.

quires witchcraft for cure or satisfaction. His insulting triumphs continue throughout the Middle Ages, and he makes martyrs by the score, but they hardly await beatification, for their god has descended to Hell. Much of this evil is gathered up in Ronsard's poem in which Love is a bird of prey, an angel with a dimmed aureole. From the whole literary tradition, not from two poems slavishly imitated, comes the March eclogue. This poem of Spenser's is a fragment of tradition as is the *Shepheardes Calender,* and unless we see it as part of the great whole, we shall never know its plain import.

We must first understand the timelessness posited by the poet for the whole work. It is not just a calendar for one year; it is a perpetual one. "Loe I have made a Calendar for every year," says Spenser in his epilogue. But though it is a calendar, it is also a compendium of a young poet's experience and thought. Spenser, a recent graduate of Cambridge, stands like the Renaissance Hercules at the choice of ways, but what had once seemed clear to him is now misted over by his first experiences with maturity. Like the boy birdcatcher, he, too, has glimpsed love as a life choice, but love, if the testimony of the whole poem may be believed, has played him false. "E. K.," the mysterious annotator of the *Calender,* makes this clear for us:

> Onely this appeareth, that his unstayed yougth had long wandred in the common Labyrinth of Love, in which time to mitigate and allay the heate of his passion, or els to warne (as he sayth) the young shepheards. s. his equalls and companions of his unfortunate folly, he compiled these xii. Æglogues. . . . [29]

The "unfortunate folly" of love dominates the eclogues for January, March, June, and August; and in the first and third

[29] *The Works of Edmund Spenser,* ed. E. Greenlaw, C. Osgood, F. Padelford, and R. Heffner (Baltimore, 1943), I (*Minor Poems,* ed. C. Osgood and H. Lotspeich), 10.

of these poems, Colin, who is at once both the hero of the whole poem and the poet himself, is the dominant speaker. March and August are, I think, special glosses on the other two poems that present the love tragedy of Colin and its consequent melancholia. The December eclogue echoes the tone of the eclogue for January and concludes with a renunciation of love: "Tell *Rosalind,* her *Colin* bids her adieu."

An anti-eroticism stains all the love eclogues. The poet is very young so he can talk of love as a passion with which he is finished. The god-bird has, indeed, trampled on his head. The experience of both Greek and French boys has been his, and the cynical advice of the "vielle mere" has proved correct. Even in the November eclogue, where the beloved Dido is the subject of his song, she is obviously a martyr of love, "Dead and lyeth wrapt in lead." For this reason, the love theme which begins in January, so that the rage of winter and the wasted world can be compared to the poet's heart, ends with December, when "The fragrant flowres, that in my garden grewe,/ Bene withered, as they had bene gathered long." Love-despair begins the poem and ends it. The January and December eclogues are soliloquies spoken by Colin-Spenser, but he also appears in November with Thenot, the traditional *senex,* who reproves the less sensitive Cuddie of February: "Thou art a fon of thy love to boste/ All that is lent to love wyll be lost." We see him again in June with Hobbinol, the contented middle-aged shepherd, who has found the Paradise "whych Adam lost." His attitude is reasonably constant; life is desperate, love fleeting, art unrewarding. In January he breaks his pipes; in December he forswears love. These were his immediate hopes; they are now his intense disappointments. The other eclogues examine at a distance the secondary problems of the young man's life.

When we turn to March, we discover, thanks to Professor

Spitzer,[30] that Bion's old man and Ronsard's "mere" have become the second story, the lesser story that is told offhandedly.
When Eros was a young bird, Willye's father,

> him caught upon a day,
> (Whereof he wilbe wroken)
> Entangled in a fowling net,
> Which he for carrion Crowes had set,
> That in our Peeretree haunted.
> Tho sayd, he was a winged lad,
> But bowe and shafts as then none had:
> Els had he sore be daunted.

Willye's father seems to have escaped, to have had a better
fate than Thomalin; but is he really free? There is at home,
according to Willye, "A stepdame eke as whott as fyre."
It seems as if the "vielle mere" has crossed the waters from
France to be the second wife of the ploughman, who has lost
his Amaryllis. Eros has been "wroken." It is the case—not
unknown in literature—of the bird and the birdcatcher re-
versing rôles, a theme which begins with Petrarch's

> Amor fra l'erbe una leggiadra rete
> D'oro e di perle tese sott'un ramo
> Dell' arbor sempre verde ch' i' tant' amo,
> Ben chè n'abbia ombre più triste che liete.[31]

But it is Thomalin who is the major character of the March
eclogue, and, in spite of the parallels, his is a totally new story.
In some ways he is a fitting center because, as we learn in the
July eclogue, he is a young man of high religious sensitivities,
who suffers as much over the wounds of the shepherds' church
as he does over those of love.

[30] "Spenser, *Shepheardes Calendar*, March ll.61–114, and The Variorum
Edition," *SP*, XLVII (1950), 494–505.

[31] *Le Rime*, ed. Mestica (Florence, 1896), p. 260. On the theme of the net-
layer caught, see Lorenzo d'Medici, *Opere*, ed. Simioni (Bari, 1913), I, 163;
Baif, *Œuvres*, ed. Marty-Laveaux (Paris, 1881), I, 97; O. de Magny, *Souspirs*,
ed. Courbet (Paris, 1874), p. 8.

The March eclogue begins on a day with a hint of spring in it; and Willye and Thomalin, who have been noticing the evidences of the new life—the starting grass, the nesting swallow, the clearing skies—ponder the end of "winters sorowe." The accumulated suggestions of the gay season are made into an aria by Willye.

> *Flora* now calleth forth eche flower,
> And bids make ready *Maias* bowre,
> That newe is upryst from bedde.
> Tho shall we sporten in delight,
> And learne with Lettice to wexe light,
> That scornefully lookes askaunce,
> Tho will wee little Love awake,
> That now sleepeth in *Lethe* lake,
> And pray him leaden our daunce.

The "little Love" whom Willye talks about is not the devastating Eros, who destroys the body and the mind; he is the sort of love that invests the body during the warmer weather for a day. Neither of the shepherds is exactly an innocent adolescent; they are more mature than Bion's "κυρος" and Ronsard's "enfant." Willye has had some previous experience with this sort of love; he calls it "sport" and adumbrates the remarks that Milton's fallen but inexperienced Adam makes to his facile consort Eve. Lettice is for him a charming animal; now she looks "askaunce," but her season will come. The fleshly nature of his springtime infatuations is supported by "E. K's" gloss on the subject of Flora, once a Roman harlot, who was made by the Latins into a "Goddess of floures."

Thomalin, we can imagine from our insight into his puritan nature, began as an opponent of love. He, too, may have once thought of passion as a seasonal matter—it came when the sap rose—and this attitude may have put him off guard. Now he knows better: "lustie love still sleepeth not,/ But is abroad at his game." He has gone into the wood, into the field of life;

but he has not gone as a boy birdcatcher. He has entered the
world as an aggressive hunter, bearing bow and quiver. He
sees a bush move and discharges an arrow. He knows that the
quarry is not a nightingale or a wood thrush, but greater
game, "faerie, feend, or snake." When the god shines forth,
he needs no old man nor sullen ancient hag to warn him. He
knows whom he faces. There is also no question of catching
the bird, of securing another specimen for his aviary. Thomalin assumes the nature of the Renaissance Anteros; he "levelde
againe/ And shott at him with might and maine,/ As thicke,
as it had hayled." His purpose is clear; he is the avenger of
the martyrs of love; he will strike Eros down. The nature of
this god is also plain. He is not a bird on the bough; he has
grown too large for the pear tree (the lecherous perch) where
Willye's father bagged him. He is now of man's size, and he
appears among the "lasciva hedera," the "wanton ivy" that
we know so well.[32]

Thomalin's darts are swiftly exhausted, and he throws

[32] The "wanton ivy" is a definite symbol for Spenser. When Venus in-
vades the dream of the Red Cross Knight and brings the false Una, Flora
crowns the phantom with "yuie garland" (I.1.48). The Bower of Acrasia
is "Framed of wanton Yuie, flouring faire" (II.5.29), and her phallic fountain is covered with a golden vine of imitation ivy, which "Low his lascivious armes adown did creepe" (II.12.41). The covert in the Garden of
Adonis where Venus meets her paramour is shaded by trees that are knit
together "with wanton yuie twine entrayld athwart" (III.6.44). It is hardly
surprising to meet Lust clad only in "a wreath of yuie greene" (IV.7.1-2).
Ivy patronized by Bacchus and hence associated in Spenser as in antiquity
with drunkards and gluttons was made wanton when Theocritus transferred it to Priapus. The god is represented, his head bound with ivy and
crocuses, creeping round the bed of the sleeping Daphne (*Epigrammata*
3). Catullus shows us a lover going to his nuptial bed with love chaining
his mind as the ivy winds about a tree (*Carmina* LXI.31-35), and Horace
gave Spenser the proper adjective: "Omnes in Damalin putris/ Deponent
oculos, nec Damalis novo/ Divelletur adultero,/ Lascivis hederis ambitiosior"
(*Carmina* I.36.20-23). It should also be noted that the mouth which makes
the entrance to Alma's House is "cast" over with a "wandring vine/
Enchaced with a wanton yuie twine."

"pumie stones" with little effect. Suddenly he knows that he is lost, that flight is his only safety. He ends his career as Anteros and assumes the crown of a martyr. Eros does not trample on him; this is a special honor reserved for Love's servants. The fate of Thomalin is to be worse because the arrow that Cupid shoots hits him in the heel and not in the heart. This strange change of target would perplex us, indeed, if "E.K." did not supply us with an enlightening gloss, the spiritual reading, as a mediaeval man might say, of Spenser's literal text. The shot that Paris, the ancestor of lascivious Paridell, fired at Achilles and the inflicted wound are, "E.K." writes, expressions of lustful love. But, as he explains, the head of the arrow cut those veins that lead "to the previe partes" and hence "the partie straighte becommeth cold and unfruiteful which reason our Poete wel weighing, maketh this shepheards boye of purpose to be wounded by Love in the heele." When Eros is opposed, he can become Anteros. He can transform, by a pull on his bowstring, a young hunter into an old ploughman. Thomalin, wounded by Love at the entrance to spring, lives still in "the winter sorowe."

There is no question that Spenser's March eclogue abandons the simple charm of Bion's poem and embodies the melancholy sickness of Ronsard. The "enfant" has reached manhood; the dire predictions of the witch have matured in a frightening way. The sensitive shepherd has learned a great deal about the nature of love, and what he has learned is both a poetic explanation of the malady of Colin-Spenser and an apologia for his cold Decemberish rejection of love.

CHAPTER TWO

Edmund Spenser

"Muiopotmos, or The Fate of the Butterflie"

The tradition that helps in the reading of the March eclogue enables us to discover a moral meaning in the "Muiopotmos." When the poem is read literally, it is delicate in fancy, suggesting an Alexandrian intaglio in which the elaborateness of execution makes up for the slenderness of theme. But when we read Spenser's poem for a second time, we are convinced that it has a meaning more serious than it seems to have; and though some early readers of the poem described it as an imaginative exercise in the mock-heroic mode, a charming predecessor of Drayton's "Nymphidia," others saw behind the literal screen a serious purpose. One critic saw in it a Keatsian contention between Youth and Death; another thought it a poem about "the fate of a dreamer"; others contend that it is an allegory of the poetic nature and that it is associated in some way with Spenser's notions of his own poetic powers.

More recently the poem has been anatomized by historians who have found in it some fragment of Tudor history, something about court or political rivalry, some morsel of backstairs gossip. We are informed by them that the poem is a secret account of the relations between Spenser and Lady Carey, Raleigh and Essex, Spenser and Burghley, Sidney and Oxford, or Burghley and Essex. All of these historical interpretations are hung like delicate but withering garlands on the seemingly confusing implications of the first and second stanzas. Now the first stanza informs us that we shall hear of "deadly dolorous debate. . . . / Betwixt two mightie ones of great estate," who were drawn into "armes, and proofe of mortall fight" through hate and ambition. Neither of the two antagonists, Spenser continues, could endure the scorn of the other, and hence "from small iarre/ Their wraths at length broke into open warre." The second stanza, which is probably disconnected from the first, is used by Spenser to ask the Muse Melpomene to "reveale" to him the "roote" and "tragicall effect," and to "detect" the "meanes," through which Clarion declined "to lowest wretchednes." To these opening stanzas Spenser seems to have appended a poem of more than four hundred lines that completely forgets (unless an historical fact is read into the literal) all of the first stanza.

My own reaction to the first stanza is to ask whether or not Clarion or Aragnoll have the necessary attributes to be "mightie ones." And I am unable to discover that Clarion ever realizes that Aragnoll is his mortal enemy. As a matter of poetic fact, the very opposite of this is flatly stated a moment before the butterfly falls victim to the spider.

> Suspition of friend, nor feare of foe,
> That hazarded his health, had he at all. (377–78)

There is certainly no combat between the two symbolic
insects, no "small iarre," no "open warre," no "wraths" except
that of Aragnoll. We are told that Clarion is Aragnoll's
"hated foe" (254), and Spenser supplies a pair of myths to
expound this hate; but nowhere in the poem is it openly announced that Clarion, the hero, knows anything about the
potential danger to himself. In fact, Aragnoll seems not too
busy about his personal revenge; shortly before he saw the
butterfly in the garden, he was impartially contemplating
"How he might anie in his trap betray" (248). A particular
revenge on Clarion is really not his primary intent; he is
ready for any victim he can snare. Quite plainly, almost
everything that Spenser says in the first stanza is flatly denied
by the poem as a whole.

Spenser, as we know, is a forgetful poet; yet it is hard to
believe that, having written the first stanza, he would immediately put it out of his mind. Because of the troubling
nature of these opening lines, the whole poem has been read
by several critics as recreation in the manner of Vergil's
"Culex"; and though we might wonder whether Spenser
read Vergil's poem in this fashion, it is not impossible that
he intended a playful meaning for the "Muiopotmos." The
mock-heroic is not, however, an Elizabethan literary fashion.
Spenser did not know the literary rules laid down for it by
Boileau, Le Bossu, and Scarron. This mode was only popular
after his time and was founded, I think, on a calculated mis-
reading of the opening lines of the *Iliad*.

Should Spenser have wanted to write a mock-epic, he
would probably have recalled the straightforward introduc-
tion to the "Culex": "Lusimus, Octavi, lusimus . . . ut historiae per ludum." Here is no pretense to grandeur; it is all
fun, as Vergil honestly remarks; it is a vacation from the
Muses of serious poetry. "Doctrina, vaces licet." A glance at
the opening phrases of "Virgil's Gnat" will suggest how

closely Spenser heard the Roman voice. A second model that
would come to his mind is the pseudo-Homeric "βατραχο-
μυομαχια." At the beginning of this poem, the Muses are summoned to sing a theme fit for Mars, to tell the giant deeds of
frogs and mice, deeds comparable to those of the Titans:
"μιμούμενοι ἔργα Γιγάντων." This induction is rightly ironic,
but the poem that succeeds it fits the promise of the preface
even though the fit is tight. With the opening lines of these
two ancient mock-epics, the "Muiopotmos" has nothing in
common; for this reason and because of what I read in the
poem, I am ready to believe that the key stanza was solemnly
intended.

The second stanza, on the other hand, is more closely
adjusted to the action of the poem, and it probably should not
be read as a continuation of the first stanza. "The roote
whereof and tragicall effect" does not necessarily conjoin
"open warre," although it is usually read as a poetical ap-
pendage. It could, in fact, be grammatically self-contained and
its purpose might well be the exposition of Clarion's tragedy.
The grammatical unity becomes clearer, and typographical
blurring may be avoided, if the difficult stanza is rewritten with
a transposed line:

> Vouchsafe, O thou the mournfulst Muse of nyne,
> That wontst the tragick stage for to direct,
> In funerall complaints and wayfull tyne,
> Reveale to me, and all the meanes detect
> The roote whereof and tragicall effect,
> Through which sad *Clarion* did at last declyne
> To lowest wretchedness; and is there then
> Such rancour in the harts of mightie men?

In this form the stanza is aloof from its predecessor; and since
we have difficulty in thinking of either the butterfly or the
spider as "mightie ones," there could be some other opponents

implied whose traditional quarrel brought on the murder
of Clarion. Rancor is a trait of uncontrolled passion that fits
the nature of Aragnoll, but the whole statement is also a
kind of afterthought that reduces to the human level a mental
disturbance experienced on a higher plane.

There are two well-known classical myths brought together in the "Muiopotmos," and by scanning them we
may find the moral translation of "mightie ones." The poem
itself depends to a great degree on these myths, and so we
cannot regard them as simply ornamental. The first myth
is that of Venus and Astery, a legend that Spenser invents by
combining the story of Cupid and Psyche with that of Jupiter
and Asteria. The myth that Spenser remakes from these is
that Astery, the most charming of Venus's nymphs, made her
companions so jealous they complained to the goddess that
Cupid had aided the girl in a flower-gathering contest. When
she heard of this aid, Venus gathered old fears as Astery
gathered "the children of the spring,"

> Not yet unmindfull, how not long agoe
> Her sonne to *Psyche* secrete love did beare,
> And long it close conceal'd, till mickle woe
> Thereof arose, and manie a rufull teare. (130–33)

She gave the girl the form of the butterfly, a pleasanter
metamorphosis than that of the classical Asteria. The second
important myth, with necessary innovations, is the more
familiar one of Minerva and Arachne; it blends with the first
legend to explain the difficult stanza and weave the subtle
web of the "Muiopotmos."

The Venus of the first myth, recalling her former domestic
difficulties with Psyche, whom she persecuted because the
innocent beauty of the girl brought about a decline in her
own cult, decides on this occasion to take no risks, for she
has a "iealous feare" of a repetition of the old disaster. She

promptly transforms her erstwhile favorite, who had gathered
flowers so well, into a butterfly infatuate of blossoms. The
butterfly comes into being because of the goddess's fear and
envy. In the second myth, Arachne is changed into a spider
through her own impious pride, but Minerva effects this
metamorphosis, not because of jealous fear but out of reasonable pity. The pity of the wise goddess is thus contrasted with
the jealousy of the sensual one. Clarion flits between the two
myths when Spenser revises the Ovidian legend by making
Minerva a patroness-general of butterflies. The goddess, according to his invention, places a butterfly among the leaves
of her peaceful olive when she ties the final knots in her
weaving. The butterfly begotten of Venus's jealousy and the
unjust punishment of an innocent nymph is adopted by
Minerva as the supreme symbol of her skill in her art; it
seems to flutter and shine and is almost alive in wool. When
the competing Arachne sees it, she knows that she is beaten.
This is the reason for Aragnoll's hatred of Clarion, according
to the Spenserian text; the spider sees in the butterfly the
ensign of his mother's defeat. Since their competitions with
mortals (Psyche and Arachne) recall it, we also may remember that the two goddesses were ancient rivals.

The mythographers whom Spenser read take us back to the
famous contest between Juno, Minerva, and Venus for the
golden apple of Eris (daughter of Nemesis of the first stanza),
a legend well known in the Renaissance but one that Spenser
never retells. From this contention and the decision of
Paris came the war between the Greeks who were favored
by Juno and Minerva, and the men of Troy who were supported by Venus. If it is a reasonable act of interpretation to
pass by association from clear myths to hidden ones, we
may have the meaning of the bothersome first stanza. The
names of Venus and Minerva may be substituted for "the
two mightie ones of great estate." They were certainly drawn

into arms and mortal strife "through prowd ambition and hart-swelling hate." The "small iarre" produced by Jar at the marriage feast of Peleus and Thetis becomes the "open warre" between the Greeks and the Trojans. A minor footnote to this epic conflict is the "Muiopotmos," for, as Spenser's composed myths suggest, the butterfly is favored by Minerva as the symbol of her triumph; but it is also the sign of Venus's irrational jealousy. The links of the chain of causes bind the death of Clarion to the apple of Eris. Stanza one may contain the great antecedents; stanza two, the proposition of the immediate poem.

The literal reading of the "Muiopotmos" may now be made with a certain assurance. The butterfly Clarion, unaware of his symbolic history and of the great cause between Venus and Minerva, is slain by the spider who is well tutored in traditional antipathy. A conflict on high affects the humble ones below. The moral may be pondered: when great men or goddesses quarrel, lesser innocents suffer. This may be all that the poem means; but I am inclined to think that it has a higher seriousness than this, that it is an allegorical account of the eternal struggle between Good and Evil, and, on a subordinate plane, between Wisdom and Pleasure as partisans of these great forces. To discover this seriousness we can make an excursion into the history of the legend of Cupid and Psyche to which Spenser alludes.

The legend of Cupid and Psyche came to the Renaissance through the *Metamorphoses* of Apuleius, but it had first passed through the Middle Ages where it was converted into an allegory of the human soul. The apotheosis of Psyche attracted Martianus Capella,[1] who states that Psyche was born divine because she was the daughter of Entelechia and Apollo; he adds that she was endowed with the diadem of immortality

---

[1] *De Nuptiis Philologiae et Mercurii*, ed. Dick (Leipzig, 1955), pp. 6–9.

by Jupiter, given a fillet by Juno, a robe by Minerva, and other symbolic gifts by other divinities. She was denied as a bride to the postulant Mercury because she was already wed to Eros. The handsome story first told by the Platonist Apuleius was thus made into an Aristotelian legend.

The pseudo-Fulgentius (thought by the Renaissance to be a contemporary of Martianus) gave the story Christian meaning for "those who do not read it falsely." His account is as follows:

> Those who read rightly will consider the city in which Psyche lives as the world, and they will see in her parents, the King and Queen of the city, God and Matter. They will also assume that Psyche and her two elder sisters are Flesh, Liberty (or Free-Will), and the Soul, for the Greeks call the soul *Psyche*. They will also want Psyche to be the youngest, because, as we know, the body is made first and then the soul is added. She is naturally the most beautiful of the three sisters, because she is superior to Liberty and more noble than Flesh. Venus or Libido envies her and sends Cupid to destroy her. But there is a desire (cupiditas) of good as well as of evil, so Cupid is charmed by the Soul and mingles with it in union, persuading it not to look at his face, that is, not to learn the delights of desire. So Adam, though he saw, did not see that he was nude until he ate of the tree of desire. So the Soul did not agree at first with her sisters, Flesh and Liberty, in their wish to learn Love's face, but, finally, moved by their continuous demands, she uncovered the lamp, which is the hidden flame of desire burning in the breast. Seeing that his face was comely, she loved beyond reason, The droppings of the lamp are said to have burned him, because all desire, the more it loves, the more it burns and stains the flesh with the mark of sin. So, desire made bare, the Soul is deprived of her powerful fortune, cast into dangers, and expelled from her royal house.[2]

[2] *Expositio Sermonum Antiquorum*, in *Auctores Mythographi Latini*, ed. Van Staveren (Leyden, 1742), pp. 715-20.

After these allegorical readings, the legend of Cupid and Psyche slept soundly during most of the Middle Ages,[3] to come wide awake in Boccaccio's *Genealogy of the Gods*. Boccaccio admittedly read an ancient myth as if he were a mediaeval theologian.[4] With a sense of the four interpretations to sustain him, Boccaccio retells the story of Cupid and Psyche and summarizes Martianus's reading; then, lifting the literal cloth, he finds the moral meaning on the bare boards of the story. Psyche is without question the human soul, the daughter of the Sun, of God, who is the true light of the world and the creator of the rational spirit. Her two sisters

[3] M. Kawczynski, "Ist Apuleius im Mittelalter bekannt wesen?" in *Bausteine zur Romanischen Philologie* (Halle, 1905), pp. 193–210. Apuleius came to the Renaissance with an impressive testimony behind him. His Renaissance biographers, Beroaldus and Wowerius, describe his reputation as a magician, which had earlier been emphasized by Lactantius in the *Divinae Institutiones* (*PL*, VI, 558) and by Augustine in letters to Marcellinus and Deogratias (*Epistolae* [*PL*, XXXIII, 383, 583]). In the *De Civitate Dei*, Augustine elevates Apuleius to the ranks of the Platonists and describes him as the best philosopher in Greek and Latin (VIII.12.14). He is commended by Bessarion for defending Plato, in *In Calumniatorem Platonis* (Venice, 1516), pp. 4–4v. He was read by Ficino and cited in the *Symposium*, in *Opera* (Lyons, 1548), p. 280. The only Renaissance mythographer, as far as I know, to record the legend of Cupid and Psyche besides Boccaccio is Gyraldus. See his *Historiae Deorum*, in the *Opera* (Leyden, 1696), I, 406. For histories of the myth in western literature and art, see: Harriet Blake, *Classical Myth in the Poetic Drama of the Age of Elizabeth* (Lancaster, Pa., n.d.), pp. 49–60; Alice Nearing, *Cupid and Psyche by Shakerly Marmion* (Philadelphia, 1944), pp. 11–95; B. Stumfall, *Das Märchen von Amor und Psyche in seinem Fortleben in der französischen, italienischen, und spanischen Literatur bis 18. Jahrhundert* (Naumberg, 1907); U. de Maria, *La Favola di Amore e Psiche nella Letteratura e nell' Arte Italiana* (Bologna, 1899); J. M. de Gossio, *Fábulas Mitológicas en España* (Madrid, 1952), pp. 257–70; H. LeMaistre, *Essai sur le Mythe de Psyché dans la littérature française des origines a 1890* (Paris, 1950).

[4] *Della Genealogia degli Dei* (Venice, 1585), p. 8. Boccaccio here argues that pagan myths must be read according to their literal, moral, allegorical, and analogical senses. The same view was put forward by Ficino (*Opera* [Basel, 1576], p. 1370), and approved by Pico in *Heptaplus*, ed. Garin (Florence, 1942), I, 188.

are the vegetative and sensitive parts of the soul; consequently, Psyche is the youngest of the three because the rational soul is the last to develop. Her marriage to Cupid portrays the honest love of the soul for God, and she is carried to this love by Zephyr or the Vital Spirit. The prohibition of her lover against her seeing his face really expresses the unwisdom of attempting to learn the mysteries of theology. Now the two sisters—the lower two parts of the soul—are able to arrive at the lower limits of the rational soul's knowledge; but when they can go no further, they envy it. This is natural, for sensuality never accords with reason. The sisters now urge Psyche to look on her lord's face; they want her to use natural reason instead of the knowledge supplied by faith. They wish, also, to turn her from contemplation, to sow those seeds that bring weariness and no satisfaction. When she yields, she sees only the form of her lover; she sees the extrinsic works of God but not divinity, for no one can see God. Thus offending with her pride, she becomes disobedient and descends to the senses. The good of contemplation is totally lost; the divine marriage is dissolved. Penitent at last, Psyche wisely wishes the destruction of her sisters and sees to it that they have no power over reason. Purged of pride and disobedience, she comes once again to divine love and contemplation, is brought to eternal glory, and bears Love the child Pleasure, who is timeless beatitude.[5] In this fashion Boccaccio reads morally the story told by the old woman to Apuleius.

The myth of Cupid and Psyche, hallowed by the Platonic associations of its author, was read during the Renaissance as an allegory of the rational soul bound in marriage to Divine Love but disturbed in its marital duties by the lower levels of the mind. Martianus seems to have inaugurated the reading; the pseudo-Fulgentius elaborated it; and Boccaccio

[5] *Ibid.*, pp. 90v–92.

converted it to a spiritual narrative. None of these under-
standings of the myth lived in isolation from the others, for
with the *editio princeps* [6] of the *Metamorphoses* the wide
meadow of annotations surrounding it informs the reader
that the story has other meaning than the literal, and the
exegesis of these three allegorizers is either referred to or
reprinted. If Spenser had read Apuleius in an original text, he
would have learned from the margins what it meant in a
spiritual sense. It is not impossible, therefore, that this myth
is the key to a possible allegory hidden beneath the literal
text of the "Muiopotmos." The fate of the butterfly could
be the fate of the rational soul in a world where Evil and
Good contend for domination. Spenser's *fabula* can be a revision of the Psyche story. To make all of this a bit clearer,
I shall pass from Psyche to Clarion, the butterfly.

The Psyche legend, like that of the Phoenix, was one of
the few pagan myths accepted by early Christians. The
myth is represented on many Christian monuments, grave-
stones, catacomb frescoes, and sarcophagi; and the Christian
Psyche is usually painted with the wings of a butterfly.[7] The
reason for these symbolic wings is that the Greeks represented
the human soul as a butterfly. Now probably none of this
artistic tradition was known to Spenser, and the literary tradition that carries it to him is very thin. There are two poems
by Meleager in which that poet compares the enamoured soul
to a butterfly,[8] but I cannot believe that Spenser knew them.
When Dante describes the soul of man as a butterfly: "angelica
farfalla,/ Che vola alla giustizia senza schermi," [9] the older

[6] *Apuleius cum commento Beroaldi* (Venice, 1510); see the discussion of
the allegory on p. 80v.

[7] M. Collingnon, *Essai sur les Monuments Grecs et Romains relatifs au
Mythe de Psyché* (Paris, 1877).

[8] *Anthol. Pal.*, V, 57; XII, 132.

[9] *Divina Commedia, Purg.* X.121–29.

scholiasts immediately recognize the symbol and explain it; [10] but there is no reason to believe that Spenser read Dante or his commentators. Though poets of the Italian Renaissance liked to compare lovers to butterflies circling a lamp,[11] I can find no evidence that they ever thought of the human soul as a butterfly. I do not think that the literary tradition is necessary in this instance to establish a connection; Spenser had only to look up the word for "soul" in any Greek lexicon such as the 1586 edition of Scapula's dictionary to read: "ψυχή, spiritus, flatus . . . Item papilio: apud Plut. symp. 2, prob. 3, & Aristot. hist. an. 1, 5, c. 19." I expect that any Renaissance man with "lesse Greeke" would have discovered this equivalence in the latter years of grammar school. So with this item of information we may attempt to explain the meaning of the "Muiopotmos." The poem is possibly about the rational soul, Clarion, the clear, the bright one. The butterfly hero may not be chosen by whim; the poem is no vacation from the Muse of serious verse.

Critics who have expounded the "Muiopotmos" in terms of "Virgil's Gnat" might do better to think in terms of the early books of the *Faerie Queene*, because the "Muiopotmos" could be an allegory of the wandering of the rational soul into error. The title, then, is not so ironic as it seems, for "πότμος," as Spenser surely knew, was reserved by the Greeks for the fatal destiny of great heroes: "πότμον ἐπισπεῖν," as Homer is accustomed to say. On the literal level there is irony, but it

---

[10] See the commentaries of Landino and Pietro di Dante in the edition produced by Biagi, Passerini, and Rostano (Turin, 1931). Benevenuto de Imola's commentary reads: "L'angelica farfalla, id est, papilionem, per quem intelligit animam rationalem, qui videtur de natura angelica celesti, quia immortalis, incorruptibiles, levis et pura" (*Comentum super Dantis Comoediam*, ed. Vernon [Florence, 1887], *ad loc.*).

[11] See the collection in Picinelli, *Symbolicus Mundi* (Cologne, 1687), I, 531–34.

washes away as the allegory unfolds. The clear soul, faultless
and sinless, sponsored by piety and wisdom (Minerva), yet
ballasted and weighed down by the senses (Venus), can come
through spiritual heedlessness into the web of evil. For this
tragedy, "πότμος" is an exact term and Melpomene the proper
Muse.

Clarion, when first we know him, is, while "heaven did
favour his felicities," no earthbound creature like Aragnoll;
he possesses the "Empire of the Aire." He is superior to all
other butterflies, the favorite of his father, who, we are told,
hopes that in time Clarion will be worthy of his paternal
heritage, "as should be worthie of his fathers throne." He is
not slothful, but joys to fly

> Through the wide compas of the ayrie coast,
> And with unwearied wings each part t'inquire
> Of the wide rule of his renowned sire. (38–40)

His flights of admiration above the clouds to the "Christall
Skie" in order to "vew the workmanship of heavens hight"
are counterpoised by his inspection of the watery surfaces
below. In Spenser's description of Clarion's active career of
admiring wandering there is a note of warning—Clarion
sometimes dares to "tempt the troublous winde." This is the
biography of Clarion before the tragedy begins, and it not
only contains certain suggestions of the flight of the rational
soul through the realm of creation but also hints at the
prospects of the spiritual inheritance of Christians who do
not succumb to curiosity.

This suggestion of an *hubris* in Clarion may mean no more
than the literal reading admits, and when I go beyond it,
I may be overreading; nonetheless, the enticing phrase, "troublous winde" has in it the suggestion of a traditional symbol.
If Spenser read an interpreted Bible, he would have found

the "wind" of Psalms 1:4 equated with inner temptation and the "wind" of Proverbs 11:4 with "spiritus malignus." [12] The "great wind from the wilderness" that smote the house in which Job's sons and daughters were eating and drinking (1:19) was clearly of diabolical origin, and glossators enlarged on the matter. When, for example, Garnerus wrote his chapter on the allegory of winds, he drew his first exemplary text from Job, but his summary heading for the essay makes the point clearer: in the Scriptures when "wind" is used in the singular, it means "the devil, hellish temptation, transitory good fortune, or pride"; in the plural "winds" means the souls of the holy.[13] Spenser uses the word in the singular. So Clarion's reckless tempting of the wind and the "ungracious blast out of the gate/ Of *Aeoles* raine," one of the possible causes of his fatal fall, may mean more than the letter states.

With the seventh stanza of the "Muiopotmos," we are present on a special summer day, a day so pleasant it seems impossible that any evil can blight its English charm. It reminds us of the day when the Red Cross Knight, proud in his new-found Christian virtues, met the windy Orgoglio. Clarion is about to venture forth, but the cautionary expression "with vauntfull lustie head" speaks disaster, for heedlessness, a false sense of security, and a failure to bridle the two lower sisters of the soul, will purchase his ruin. Before he goes forth, Clarion puts on his armor, and it is not unlike the gear recommended by St. Paul and rehearsed by Spenser in his letter to Raleigh. The breastplate is "pure substance"; and faith is "the substance of things hoped for." The helmet is of metal too rare for the metallurgists of this world, not Bilbo steel, not Corinth brass, not Orichalum. It is magically

---

[12] Rabanus Maurus, *Allegoriae in Sacram Scripturam* (PL, CXII, 1073–74).
[13] *Gregorianes* (PL, CXCIII, 51–56).

spiritual armor that can protect the wearer from bodily wounds too. When Clarion is finally armed, he puts on Psyche wings. The butterfly, or the soul, is ready.

The first flight of Clarion and the pleasures that the flight brings are totally natural and Christianly decorous. Spenser, by saying of them "That none gainsaid, nor none did him envie" (151), stamps them with spiritual approval. By mid-stanza, Clarion wavers from the true course and his tragic flaw becomes apparent.

> The woods, the rivers, and the medowes green,
> With his aire-cutting wings he measured wide,
> Ne did he leave the mountaines bare unseene,
> Nor the ranke grassie fennes delights untride.
> But none of these, how ever sweete they beene,
> Mote please his fancie, nor him cause t'abide:
> His choicefull sense with everie change doth flit.
> Ne common things may please a wavering wit. (153–60)

With the last four lines of this stanza our fine estimate of Clarion changes. The lower levels of his soul, the two gross sisters of Psyche, take over; his flight of admiration becomes a flight of idle curiosity.

The butterfly's "unstaid desire" now takes him to the "gay gardins" where Art contends with Nature in an ominous lavishness.[14] We know the garden that now attracts Clarion from the world of legitimate natural pleasures; it is a sub-division of Acrasia's Bower:

>   whose faire grassy ground
>   Mantled with greene, and goodly beautifide
>   With all the ornaments of Floraes pride,

---

[14] One recognizes these gardens as Renaissance replicas of those sensual pleasure places that the Middle Ages associated with the cult of Venus. We recall *Le Roman de la Rose* (1323–1424), the poem of Flora and Phyllis in the *Carmina Burana* (92.59–60), and the well-known witches' gardens in Ariosto and Tasso.

> Wherewith her mother Art, as halfe in scorne
> Of niggard Nature, like a pompous bride
> Did decke her, and too lavishly adorne.[15]

Patterned after this garden of the fleshly way of life, the "gay gardins" where Clarion wanders are those in which Art aspires

> T'excell the naturall, with made delights:
> And all that faire or pleasant may be found
> In riotous excess doth there abound. (166–68)

The permissible world of experience is left behind, and Clarion yields to the senses. As yet he has not sinned, but his spiritual weakness will carry him into the web of evil. Spenser now begins to warn the reader, to suggest by adjectives that the butterfly-soul is in trouble. Clarion has a "curious busie eye" (171); he attempts to satisfy "his glutton sense" (179); he preys "greedily" (204) on the flowers, and then he rests in "riotous suffisaunce" (207). The hero, in spite of his Christian armor and the good hopes of his "Sire," is slipping into heedlessness. He is becoming more and more like Dante's "l'angelica farfalla."

> L'anima semplicetta, che sa nulla,
> Salvo che, mossa da lieto fattore,
> Volontier torna a ciò che la trastulla.
> Di picciol bene in pria sente sapore;
> Quivi s'inganna, e dietro ad esso corre,
> Se guida a fren non torce il suo amore.[16]

The poet Spenser, having suggested by plain statement that the butterfly-soul is curious, greedy, and uncontrolled, pauses in the direct narrative for an ironic excursion into the hedonist's doctrine.

[15] *The Faerie Queene* II.xii.50.
[16] *Purg.* XVI.88–93.

What more felicite can fall to creature,
Than to enjoy delight with libertie,
And to be Lord of all the workes of Nature,
To raine in th'aire from earth to highest skie,
To feed on flowres, and weed of glorious feature,
To take what ever thing doth please the eie?
Who rests not pleased with such happiness,
Well worthie he to taste of wretchednes. (209–16)

If this stanza stood by itself or if we did not read it with some
care, we might feel that Spenser approved of Clarion's conduct in the "gay gardins." To the Christian reader, however,
the whole passage is a meditation on destruction; it is almost
a paraphrase of Satan talking to a rather simple victim. The
worldly emphasis of the first line is seconded by the "delight
with libertie" of the next. The butterfly-soul that cannot distinguish between "flowres" and "weed of glorious feature"
will easily succumb to the eye-sins that hide behind "what
ever thing doth please the eie." The Christian implications
of this stanza are immediately bulwarked by the following
one that comments on the transitoriness of existence, the
mutability of all things, and the absurdity of fragile pleasures
unless one is guided by "a God, or God." So Spenser warns
against the lower life of the senses, and the phrase "a God,
or God" establishes a religious tone on the foundations of
both pagan and Christian morals.

It is just at this point, too, that Clarion is doomed, for
we are instantly informed that Jove has woven the fate of
the butterfly. "Heavens avengement," "πότμος," is at hand.
Both Destiny and Providence are aware that the butterfly
must fall. "Careles Clarion" (375) flutters sinward while
Spenser provides us with two passages that comment on his
"unstaid desire" and the heedless independence that is mutually
possessed by the butterfly and the Red Cross Knight. Directed

by desire, reckless Clarion feeds hither and yon in the garden of sensation,

> And whatso else of vertue good or ill
> Grewe in this Gardin, fetcht from farre away,
> Of everie one he takes. (201–203)

His inability on this fair morning to distinguish between good and evil, his love of foreign pleasures (any normal Englishman would see the fault in this), his eagerness to possess all that the spring brought forth comes, perhaps, from the spiritual vanity that ruined the Red Cross Knight. This suggestion is strengthened by a suite of lines that ushers in the actual tragedy,

> [Clarion] walkt at will, and wandred too and fro,
> In the pride of his freedome principall:
> Litle wist he his fatall future woe,
> But was secure, the liker he to fall.
> He likest is to fall into mischaunce,
> That is regardles of his gouvernaunce. (379–84)

This is a poetical restatement of the advice given by St. Paul to the men of Corinth, when he reminded the Church of the pride that brought Lucifer down and would overthrow them, too. "Let him that thinketh he standeth take heed lest he fall." Through heedlessness as much as through the "troublous winde," through pride of self-surety as much as through the hate of the spider, Clarion, brightest and fairest of souls, descends to the realm of the senses. With this fall, we return to a Christian reading of the Psyche myth.

It is time now, since the cue has been heard, for Aragnoll, son of Arachne and foe by tradition of Minerva's butterfly, to enter. Thanks to Job 8:14 (His trust shall be like the spider's web) and Isaiah 59:5 (They have eaten the eggs of asps and woven the webs of spiders), Aragnoll and his house embodied a Christian symbolism that associated them with impiety, heresy, hypocrisy, worldliness, and the very Devil himself. The web of the spider, says that great analogist Gregory,[17] "is like trust in hypocrites." Jerome [18] identifies the heretic with the spider, and Cyrillus [19] states that all impiety is like a web hung by a spider in an empty house. Origen [20] writes that the spider is the symbol of the sinner, and Petrus Blesensis [21] compares the insect to the foolish man of the world. An early commentary on the eleventh century *Physiologus* of Theobaldus combines all of these meanings into a spiritual discourse on the nature of Aragnoll.

> The Devil catches us as if we were flies; he is always putting traps, nets, and loops in our way so that he can take us through sin. When he takes someone in mortal sin, then he eviscerates and deprives them of grace unless the sinner is rescued by confession and penitence. So the chief snare of the devil is man's own will and it is only by repentance that he can avoid it. The spider fears the sun just as the devil fears the Holy Church and the just man, who can also be compared to the sun. Usually the spider weaves his web at night; so the devil weaves his when the just man is less watchful.[22]

Thus Aragnoll, the destroyer of the butterfly-soul, is unmasked.

What we now know about Aragnoll, we could have read out of his mother's legend. The ancients who knew her story saw it as another parable of a mortal who was foolish enough to challenge the power of the divine. When Spenser calls

---

[17] *Moralia in Job* (PL, LXXV, 845); echoed in the *Glossa Ordinaria* (PL, CXIII, 779–80).

[18] *Epistolae* (PL, XXII, 1174–75).

[19] *In Isaiam* (PG, LXX, 1308).

[20] *Commentarius in Psalmos* (PG, XII, 1408–1409).

[21] *Epistolae* (PL, CCVII, 60).

[22] Auber, *Histoire et Théorie du Symbolisme Religieux* (Paris, 1884), III, 496.

Arachne a "presumptuous Damzel," who "rashly dar'd" to compete with Minerva, he is simply carrying out the dictates of a long tradition. The fourteenth century *Ovide Moralisé* takes a similar attitude toward the story.

> Pallas, qui bien le veult gloser,
> Note devine sapience,
> Araigne fole outrecuidance,
> Qui ou dyable regne et maint,
> Et dou dyable l'ont or maint
> Qui ensivent sa discipline.
> Pallas, sapience divine,
> Fu corroucie et despit ot
> Dont Araigne la despitot,
> C'est li mondes musars et nices,
> Plains d'outrecuidance et de vices,
> Qui contre Dieu se vait ventent,
> N'a riens de cest siecle n'entent
> Fors aus oeuvres de vanité
> Et a confondre verité.[23]

This moral comment on the nature of Aragnoll's mother and her act of impiety was accepted by the later commentators, Giovanni del Vergilio[24] and Thomas Wallensis,[25] whose remarks were sometimes incorporated in editions of the *Metamorphoses* printed in the Renaissance. The dynasty of spiders had a moral and spiritual equivalence that Spenser could not avoid.

Spenser covers Aragnoll, at the very beginning of the poem, with satanic epithets. He is "a wicked wight," "foe of fair things," "author of confusion," "slave of spite." He builds a "hateful" mansion in which he lurks to "betray." He is

---

[23] Ed. de Boer, *Verhandelingen der Koninklijke Akademie van Weten-schappen, Afdeeling Letterkunde*, XXI (N.S., 1920), 298.

[24] For an account of his moralized Ovid, see Wicksteed and Gardner, *Dante and Giovanni del Vergilio* (Westminster, 1902), p. 321.

[25] *Metamorphoseos libri moralizati* (Lyons, 1513), *ad loc.*

filled with "poison." He has "malice" and a "false hart." He
is "deceitful" and plots "treason." At no point in the poem
is anything pleasant ever associated with this spider-Satan,
and this fact alone spoils the historical theories that identify
Aragnoll with some grand personage of the Elizabethan court.
Spenser fills his *Faerie Queene* with feckless knights, but there
is no reason to believe that he approved of fecklessness for
himself.

When Aragnoll is almost sunk under this freight of damna-
tion, two familiar similes are made with reference to him,
and once more he is associated with creatures of low moral
repute. We are told that he is like the fox stalking lambs, or
"a grimme Lyon rushing with fierce might." The first figure
is clear enough for any Christian reader, whereas the second
comes neatly from Psalm 21:22 (Save me from the mouth of
the lion) and I Peter 5:8 (because your adversary, the devil,
ranges round, a roaring lion). The Christian symbolists,
when it was fitting to do so, associated the lion with Hell.
"Evil spirits are called 'lions' because of their pride," [26]
writes Alanus de Insulis, an author not unknown to Spenser.
Faultless until then except for his heedlessness and his failure
to keep his lower senses in restraint, the butterfly-soul finally
falls into the web of impiety with Satan at its center. Spenser
has plotted the steps toward this fall, but he eventually gives
us the exact causes.

Clarion, Spenser says, is entangled in the web of impiety
because of "cruell Fate," "wicked Fortune," or an "ungracious blast out of the gate of *Aeoles* raine" (417–20). On
the Christian level, Fate, as Milton's God observes, can be
equated with Providence; and Fortune and the wind combine
to make the means by which Providence works. The wind
from "Aeoles raine" is a particularization of the "troublous
winde," which possessed a possible moral meaning. The moral

[26] *Elucidatio in Cantica Canticorum* (PL, CCX, 80).

interpretations of Vergil may make Spenser's meaning more clear. The story of Aeneas's experience with the winds of Aeolus is, of course, a major event in the *Aeneid,* and the humanists, who saw in Aeneas the pattern of the perfect man, made moral use of it. In a letter to Aretino, Petrarch announces that Aeneas is the human reason, and the winds that assail him are passions that afflict reason and that reason must control.[27] The philosopher Landino, who wrote a moral interpretation of the *Aeneid,* describes the epic as an allegory of the soul in search of divine wisdom or the Venus Urania. To this end, he writes, Aeneas or the soul flees from Troy (the vulgar Venus) and from its own sensuous nature (Paris) and embarks on a sea (life) fretted and disturbed by the storms of passion and desire.[28] It is not impossible that Spenser knew these moral equivalents of the wind symbol, and he may have expected us to read them into his literal statements.

It is not improper to read the "Muiopotmos" as a moral poem, as an account of the soul caught in the eternal struggle between reason and sensuality, between Good and Evil. The butterfly Clarion may exist to warn Spenser's readers about the nature of pleasure and self-confidence. The myth of the two insects is on a lower level than that of Cupid and Psyche but its ultimate purpose is probably the same. The universality of the moral is indicated by one of the final couplets that introduces the fate of the butterfly in tones recalling the greatest of tragedies.

> For loe, the drerie stownd is now arrived,
> That of all happiness hath us deprived. (415–16)

[27] *Opera* (Basel, 1554), p. 868.
[28] *Disputationes* (s.l., n.d.), fol. 4.

CHAPTER THREE

William Shakespeare

"Venus and Adonis"

It is possibly an error to think of Shakespeare's "Venus and Adonis" as a legitimate child of the tenth book of the *Metamorphoses* even though some of its elaborate wit is plainly fathered by twists and turns in the Latin text. When the poem is broadly regarded, it is rather certain that in tone, purpose, and structure the two poems have little to share. To begin with, the true poet of the Latin poem is by artistic pretense not Ovid at all but widower Orpheus, whose personal tragedy quietly informs each one of the songs that he sings on his Thracian hill to an assembly of wild beasts and birds. We can also be sure that the literate Roman was perfectly aware of the alternate myth of Adonis in which Pluto's queen contended with Venus for the love of the

young hunter,[1] for this knowledge must certainly have been
assumed by Ovid to be in the possession of his readers and to
make plainer than plain the connection between the short
life of Orpheus' bride and that of Venus' minion. The wind-
flower which fragilely makes the lesson sets this forth: "brevis
est tamen usus in illo."

In Shakespeare's version none of this pathos comes through,
and the Ovidian music that the annotators have heard is ghost
music. True enough, the Latin poet's description of Venus
in the role of a rustic Diana is the germ of Shakespeare's finished caricature of the frustrate lady, flushed and sweating.
Her advice on hunting to the rumpled Adonis, tersely expressed in Latin, becomes a sportsman's lecture in English.
But, in the main, the two poets saw the myth differently.
Shakespeare's Adonis, contrary to the whole tradition, scorns
love. In the sonnets of *The Passionate Pilgrim*, if these be
Shakespeare's, the boy is mocked for missing his chance, but
the longer poem takes, I think, a different position. The
legend of Atalanta and Hippomenes, which Ovid relates as
a harmonious part of the central legend, is also omitted by
Shakespeare and replaced by an animal diversion between
Adonis' stallion and an eager mare. Actually Shakespeare's
intent and plan are as different from those of Ovid as his
Venus—a forty-year-old countess with a taste for Chapel
Royal altos—is from the eternal girl of the Velia.

"Venus and Adonis" is clearly the work of a young and
unfinished artist, but there is no question about his independence. When we read previous poems based on the myth,
we see at once that something very new is being ventured.
Parabosco has the goddess come down from a cloudy reach
and exhibit herself naked to the little hunter. Unused to the
sensation of passion, he falls at her feet, and the text is then
Italianly expanded as a warm prelude to the cold Roman con-

[1] Apollodorus *Bibliotheca* III.14.3-4.

clusion.[2] Ronsard's "L'Adonis"[3] is a virtuoso conflation of Ovid's narrative and Bion's lament. The French poet, who was as curiously fearful of women as Shakespeare's Adonis, writes in warning terms. Venus may mourn passionately for Adonis, but almost at once she will find consolation in the young Anchises. For Ronsard the scattering anemone is a symbol of the faith of women. Now no one knew more about the thinness of certain kinds of love-sorrow than Shakespeare; but, in this poem, he stresses vagaries of ladies that are beyond the intellectual reach of the French poet; in fact, his goddess is far more seductive—at least to men of the north—than even those conjured up by his Italian predecessors. We must read Shakespeare's poem for its differences from its predecessors to learn what it is about.

Orthodox commentaries have regularly observed that "Venus and Adonis" is an epyllion like "Hero and Leander," and, consequently, it is possible to point to a few similar poems before it and a good many after.[4] This measurement tells us very little about the poem, under the surface of which one hears the faint murmur of an inverted *pastourelle*,[5] of a mythological satire,[6] and of a poetic discourse on the nature

[2] *Delle Lettere Amorose* (Venice, 1568), pp. 306–21.

[3] *Œuvres*, ed. Vaganay (Paris, 1924), V.43–52.

[4] R. Putney, "Venus and Adonis: Amour with Humour," PQ, XX (1941), 533–48; "Venus Agonistes," *University of Colorado Studies, Language and Literature*, IV (1953), 52–66.

[5] The usual manner of these seduction poems is to present the effects of knightly or scholarly blandishments on a simple shepherdess. The one *pastourelle* that is a kind of ancestor of "Venus and Adonis" is "L'autre jour en un jardin" (K. Bartsch, *Altfranzösische Romanzen und Pastourellen* [Leipzig 1870], II, 75), which describes the assault on a knight of a strong and vigorous young girl who reverses the usual technique.

[6] In Venus, Shakespeare satirizes women who pursue young lovers and who are fairly scatter-brained—Erasmus gets the same ladies in his "Laus Stultitiae"—but he is also mindful perhaps of the anti-Venus literature of the Renaissance, which begins with Bebel's five-book hexameter poem, "Triumphus Veneris" (Tübingen, 1501), a treasure of motifs that are enhanced by the learned annotations of Joannes Altenstaig.

of the decent Venus. Rising above these mutes are the silver
horn calls of an English *cynegeticon*, for "Venus and Adonis"
can be partially explained in terms of a timeless hunt. Venus,
the amorous Amazon (both Plautus[7] and Shakespeare say
that she manhandled Adonis) hunts with her strong passions;
the hunted Adonis lives to hunt the boar; and the boar is
death, the eternal hunter. The text, if one is needed, hangs
on a common theme, succinctly expressed by an Italian of
Shakespeare's generation:

> Questo mondo è una caccia, e cacciatrice
> La Morte vincitrice.[8]

The metaphors and epithets that adorn the Shakespearean text
come, if I may be permitted a metaphoric pun, from the lexicon of venery. The great goddess is an "emptie eagle," given
to "vulture" thoughts; whereas the young hunter is a bird
"tangled in a net," a dabchick hiding in the waves, a "wild
bird being tamed," a protected deer in Venus' "parke," a
"yeelding pray," a roe "ty'rd with chasing," and an escaped
quarry that "runs apace" homeward "through the dark
lawnd." The omitted Ovidian parenthesis of Atalanta and
Hippomenes reminds us that in the other half of her legend
the runner was a huntress and that her lover-conqueror dissolved his first disappointments in love by hunting.[9]

So it is the larger literary scheme of the hunt that controls
the first four scenes of this poem, from the sunshine morning
of the first day to the dismal gray of the second, and the
whole notion was passed on to Shakespeare through the means
of a long symbolic tradition. The Middle Ages, for instance,
had laid it down that Venus, in her pursuit of Adonis, had
proved herself the mistress of the chase. "Apri dentibus ex-

---

[7] *Menaechmi* I.ii.35.
[8] V. Belli, *Madrigali* (Venice, 1599), p. 43: "This world is a hunt, and
Death the inexorable hunter."
[9] Propertius I.i.11–12.

tinctum Adonidem deflet Venus, habens semper cum vena-
tione vel robusta commercium." [10] Men who could subscribe
to this conclusion naturally agreed that Ovid, archpriest of
Venus, was also a mighty hunter of both beasts of venery and
of the chase.[11] The Middle Ages, which stood so close to
antiquity as to think of its goods as its own in a way that the
Renaissance never could, knew its uncles of Greece and Rome
and rightly bestowed this title on him who told Cupid that
a good hunter pursued only *fugaces*,[12] who put hunting terms
in the mouth of amorous Apollo,[13] and who describes women
as fit to be hunted, likening the lover to the skillful *retarius*
spreading his nets.[14] He who knew Ovid, knew that love was
a hunt.

But Ovid did not invent this simile to which he gave so
much currency. Plato, who discovered most of what we
know, was the first to call Eros "the mighty hunter," [15] and
to classify the "lovers' chase" (ἡ τῶν ἐρώντων θήρα) as a sub-
division of the great hunt.[16] In addition to this philosophical
metaphor, the lover in antiquity is often a hunter and the
hunter often a lover. We remember in this connection the
poetess Eriphanis, who fell in love with the hunter Menalcas,
and, as the old phrase goes, "hunted him in turn." [17] The
god Dionysius, tamer of animals, pleads in another Greek
text with the famous huntress Nicaia that she make him companion of her hunt.[18] The deserted Oenone reminds Paris that

---

[10] John of Salisbury, *Policraticus*, ed. Webb London, 1909) I.21-22. "Venus,
herself a businesslike huntress, wept Adonis killed by the boar's tusks."

[11] Richard de Fournival, *La Vielle ou les derniers amours d'Ovide*, ed.
Cocheris (Paris, 1861), pp. 45-52.

[12] *Amores* II.9.9.

[13] *Metamorphoses* I.505-7.

[14] *Ars* I.45-46.

[15] *Symposium* 203D.

[16] *Sophist* 222D; see Musaeus, 146-56.

[17] Athenaeus XIV.619C.

[18] Nonnos *Dionysiaca* XVI.75-87: see Virgil *Eclogues* III.74-75.

in the days of their love she showed him where to place his nets and send his dogs.[19] The Roman elegiac poets transformed these myths into rhetorical figures and combined them into charming song. Tibullus, in his elegant last book, shows us Sulpicia begging the boar to spare Cerinthus, whose days in the forest and rocky wastes might more properly be spent in her bed.[20] And, finally, Propertius, forsaken again by Cynthia and made effeminate by love, turns for comfort to the soft hunt, the hunt that Shakespeare's Venus praises to the boy Adonis:

> Ipse ego venabor: iam nunc me sacra Dianae
> Suscipere et Veneri ponere vota iuvat.
> Incipiam captare feras et reddere pinu
> Cornua et audaces ipse monere canes;
> Non tamen ut vastos ausim temptare leones
> Aut celer agrestes comminus ire sues.
> Haec igitur mihi sit lepores audacia molles
> Excipere et stricto figere avem calamo.[21]

The continued imagination of the Greeks and Romans is found again when Nicolette sends messengers to Aucassin. "Tell him," she says, "that there is a beast in the forest (greater in worth than deer, lion, or boar) that he should come to hunt." [22] What the Middle Ages knew so well did

---

[19] *Heroides* V.17-20.

[20] IV.3.

[21] II.19.17-24: "I myself shall go out to hunt; my vows to Venus put aside, I shall do the rites of Diana. I shall begin to take wild beasts and fasten their horns to the pine and to urge on the brave dogs. I should not dare to attack the great lions or go quickly to face the boars of the field. It is daring enough for me to snare a tender hare or shoot a bird with an arrow."

[22] *C'est d'Aucassin et de Nicolete*, ed. Bourdillon (1887), p. 42. In the Middle Ages the theme of the hunt was sometimes used religiously as the hunting of the human soul by demons, or, in the case of the "Minnejäger," one of whom has the lead in the twelfth-century "Jagd" of Hadamar

not pass unknown in the generations that came afterward. Like Shakespeare's Adonis, the hero of Poliziano's "La Giostra" scorns love, "the soft insanity," and plunges into the woodland gloom after a wild deer because he does not know, as the hero of Marie de France's "Guigemar" learns, that white deer are uncertain beasts. So Julio, thanks to his ignorance, hunts the deer to the gate of the palace of Venus, misled by the nymph who masqueraded as a creature of the chase.[23] The theme of the love-hunt undoubtedly lies behind the flight of Lorenzo de' Medici's Ambra through the dark forest of the world;[24] it inspires Valvasone's praise of the hunting Cupid [25] and Francisco Berni's amusing "Caccia di Amore." [26] For the benefit of French lovers, Marot describes the companions of Cupid hunting rabbits, hare, and deer, blowing

---

von Laber, in the chase of the beloved. Von Laber's hunter is aided by his familiar dogs: Gelück, Lust, Liebe, Genade, Fröude, Wille, Wunne, Trost, Staete, Triuwe, and Harre. After difficulties with the wolves, Auflaurer and Angeben, the pack finds the hunter's beloved. Schmeller, the editor of this tedious poem (Stuttgart, 1850), has found a number of similar poems in German manuscript collections (p. xx). The three-day hunt in *Gawain and the Green Knight* has certainly something to do with the greater and lesser hunts. It is also interesting to discover that the medieval hunting lover, like his classical prototypes, begins with a reluctance to love. Sir Degrevant hunts by night and day, but "Certus, wyff wold he non,/ Wench ne leman." This attitude changes when he meets Mayd Melidor: "Now hym lykeys no pley./ To honte ne to revey (hawk)" (ed. Casson [1949], pp. 5, 35). The hero of *Ipomedon*, ed. Kolbing and Koschwitz (Breslau, 1889), is another mighty hunter with an initial antipathy to women (p. 19); and so is Robert de Blois of *Flores et Liriope* (ed. Von Zingerle [Leipzig, 1891]), p. 42. The medieval lover, like his predecessors in Tibullus and Propertius, hunts for consolation and to ease his troubled soul; see *Guy of Warwick* (ed. Zupitza [1888]), E.E.T.S., XLIX.399, and *Metrical Romances* (ed. Weber [London, 1810]), III, 124.

[23] *Op. cit.*, ed. Carducci (Bologna, 1921), pp. 259, 274ff. In Chretien de Troyes's "Erec," there is some connection between love and the Easter hunt of a white deer.

[24] *Poesie Volgari*, ed. Ross and Hutton (1912), II.81.

[25] *La Caccia* (Milan, 1808), p. 148.

[26] *Le Rime*, ed. Palazzi (Genoa, 1915), pp. 165–69.

horns and trumpets, gaining and losing trophies of the chase.[27]
Baif takes up the theme in "L'amoureux est chasseur, l'Amour
est une chasse";[28] and Ronsard uses the love-hunt as the main
scheme of his political allegory, "Eurymedon et Callirée." [29]
Across the Channel, a poet of the court of Henry VIII was
writing, "Who list to hount, I know where is an hynde," a
line that must have eventually pleased the poet whose Duke
Orsino could "hunt the hart" and whose Rosalind could
sharply remark: "Her love is not the hare I do hunt."

But the love-hunt, dangerous and valiant as it may be, does
not on the lower venerian level ennoble the soul; hence, the
classical pedagogues did not recommend it to young men for
whom life had a grander course. Plato much prefers the hunting of the "sacred hunters" (ἱεροὺς θηρευτάς),[30] an assembly
of brave youths, similar to those described by Philostratus,[31]
who take the great land animals with little aid beyond that
of their own physical and mental powers. In the same section,
Plato condemns "the hunters of men," but for many Greeks
hunting was the hero's preliminary education. To the grave
end of testing and training heroes, Apollo and his sister Diana,
the legend runs, taught hunting to Chiron, who, in turn, imparted this wisdom to a great register of demigods and noble
men.[32] Both the Middle Ages and the Renaissance knew this

---

[27] *Œuvres*, ed. Grenier (Paris, n.d.), I.17. In his "Epigrammes" he
describes love as the hunter of virtuous men as well as of beasts.

[28] *Œuvres en rime*, ed. Marty-Laveaux (Paris, 1881), I.312.

[29] *Op. cit.*, II.176–91; see also I.132, 177 and III.121. A parody of the love-
hunt appears in the next century in the "Advice to the Young Hunter
Lysidor," *Variétés historiques et littéraires*, ed. Fournier (Paris, 1855), I,
66.

[30] *Laws* 823D.

[31] *Imagines* I.28.

[32] Xenophon *Cynegeticon* I.1–2. This list of Chiron's alumni was later
revised and increased; see Ronsard's "La Chasse" (IV.191–97) and Bargaeus'
Cynegeticon (Rome, 1585), pp. 27–28. The latter author says that hunting
began when Venus, lamenting Adonis' death, went to Diana for help. See

myth by heart, and so hunting became first the proper preparation for knighthood and, later, for the forming of a gentleman.

At the age of twelve the great King Alfred had yet to learn to read, but he was, nonetheless, of "incomparable skill and success in his incessant hunting." [33] Child Horn, according to his poem, was especially tutored in the art,[34] and King Alisaundre of romance was likewise a mighty boy hunter.[35] It is plenteously clear, too, that Tristram knew more at fifteen about hunting than about good manners.[36] But, while most knights were skilled hunters and the hunt was widely commended by men of the Middle Ages, it was not for everyone, nor for every hunter were all kinds of hunting.[37] "God," according to the precepts of the *Livre de Chasse du Roy Modus*, "has given each man different tastes and desires, and so he authorized several hunts accommodated to the nature of one's virtues and station." [38]

Thanks to poetical texts from antiquity, from the Middle Ages, and from the Renaissance itself, we can now sit before Shakespeare's "Venus and Adonis" with something better than a blank understanding. We know that love is a hunter, that the seduction of the beloved is a kind of chase, and that it is all the soft hunt, which is essentially improper. On the other hand, the hard hunt, the work of the sacred hunters, is the honest training of those who would be heroes. But there are hunts available to some and not to others, and the best that one can do is to see, as Bruno suggests, that all of life is a hunt and to hope that one has the implements helpful

---

also Xenophon *Cyrop.* I.6.28–29; Aristotle *Pol.* 1256B; Cicero *De Nat. Deor.* II.161; and Silius Italicus *Punica* VIII.515–16.

[33] Asser, *De rebus gestis Aelfredi*, ed. Stevenson (London, 1904), p. 20.

[34] *King Horn*, ed. Hall (London, 1901), p. 75.

[35] *Metrical Romances* I.32.

[36] *Sir Tristram*, ed. McNeill (London, 1886), p. 9.

[37] *L'Escoufle*, ed. Michelant and Meyer (Paris, 1884), p. 96.

[38] *Op. cit.*, ed. Tilander (Paris, 1931), p. 4.

in its conduct.[39] The poem fits this doctrine as well as any poem fits any doctrine. Venus hunts Adonis; Adonis hunts the boar. The first hunt is the soft hunt of love; the second is the hard hunt of life. But in this simple exposition, there are some interesting implications that I should attend to before I return to the nature of the two hunts.

The myth of Atalanta and Hippomenes, which is the center of Ovid's poem and explains the goddess's hatred and fear of the bitter beasts, is replaced in "Venus and Adonis" by the episode of the horses, which is a love chase on a bottom level. Shakespeare's Venus produces this event as a burning incitement to the adolescent Adonis and as a living text for her sermon on lust to the more mature readers. Actually, it can be interpreted as an animal allegory springing from the race described by Ovid and setting the tone for Venus' wooing. It is at once love among the beasts and a satire on courtly love, for the stallion is a noble earl and the jennet a maid-in-waiting. But before we understand the moral meaning of the episode, we should ponder the reason for Shakespeare's substitution of it for the older legend. Without doubt Shakespeare felt that the lengthy tale of Atalanta and Hippomenes was a dramatic distraction that threw the central story out of focus and that for this reason should be omitted. I also suspect that an associative process led him to add the mating of the horses.

Shakespeare's Adonis is, after all, a remaking of the notoriously chaste Hippolytus. The son of Theseus is on every list of heroic hunters, but his similarity to Shakespeare's Adonis does not end here. His chaste resistance, his death through Venus' agents, his connection with horses make him a member of Adonis' set.[40] The ancient poets and mythographers some-

---

[39] *De gli Heroici Furori* in *Opera*, ed. Lagarde (Göttingen, 1888), pp. 722–23.

[40] The commentaries on Shakespeare's poem usually mention the story of Hermaphroditus and Salmacis, but I expect that the more familiar one of Hippolytus is the real basis.

times said that a jealous Mars or an avenging Apollo sent the
boar that killed Adonis, but Passerat, a French contemporary
of Shakespeare's, invented a new and perhaps more congenial
legend. Diana sent the boar to revenge the killing of Hippolytus. "Soeur de Phaebus, tu le voulus ainsi/ De longue
main courrouces et despite/ Contre Venus, pour la mort
d'Hippolyte." [41] In addition to this, there is a hint in the
names. Hippomenes ($\iota\pi\pi o$- $+\mu\epsilon\nu os$: passion or strength of a
horse) has a connection with Hippolytus and with Adonis'
stallion that one with "small Greek" would notice. So the
episode of the stallion and the jennet slides into the poem by
normal associations. But why is it there?

With the exception of Robert Miller,[42] no critic has seen
much in the episode of the horses beyond a splendid testimony to Shakespeare's knowledge of livestock. It is always
pleasant to discover that Shakespeare knew about as much
as the average man, but it is possible that on this occasion he
knew more. Perhaps the poet who shortly would write

> But you are more intemperate in your blood
> Then Venus, or these pamp'red animals
> That rage in savage sensuality,

had something else in mind. If one could read with Venus
and Shakespeare the book of creatures from which both of
them took this animal *exemplum*, one would find some very
interesting classical footnotes about the love madness of stal-
lions and the libidinousness of jennets.[43] Of course, any pas-
ture would hold suggestion; but, as Miller observed, this stallion breaks his reins and crushes his bit with his teeth, "Con-
trolling what he was controlled with." He is a creature of
virtue, but he lacks "a proud rider on so proud a back." It is

[41] *Les Poésies françaises*, ed. Blanchemain (Paris, 1880), I.24.
[42] "Venus, Adonis, and the Horses," *E.L.H.*, XIX (1952), 249–64.
[43] Oppian *Cynegetica* I.158–65; Virgil *Georgics* III.250–54; Horace *Satires*
II.7.47–50; Lucretius *De Rerum Natura* V.1073–77.

Shakespeare who makes this complaint. When it is the turn
of Venus to speak, the horse's rebellion is praised:

> How like a iade he stood tied to the tree,
> Servilly maistred with a leatherne raine,
> But when he saw his love, his youths faire fee,
> He held such pettie bondage in disdaine:
> Throwing the base thong from his bending crest,
> Enfranchising his mouth, his backe, his brest.

For Venus, lust equals freedom, but when we, tutored by a
longer tradition than she knew, view the chase and hear these
words, we recognize the horse.

Plato, who first supplied us with the doctrine of the hunt,
returns to give us the correct annotation on the horse. "Now
when the charioteer sees the vision of Love and his whole soul
is warmed throughout by the sight and he is filled with the
itchings and prickings of desire, the obedient horse, giving in
then as always to the bridle of shame, restrains himself from
springing on the loved one; but the other horse pays no attention to the driver's goad or whip, but struggles with uncontrolled leaps, and doing violence to his master and team-mate,
forces them to approach the beautiful and speak of carnal
love." [44] Yes, here he is;

> Imperiously he leaps, he neighs, he bounds,
> And now his woven girthes he breaks asunder,
> The bearing earth with his hard hoofe he wounds,
> Whose hollow wombe resounds like heavens thunder,
> The yron bit he crusheth tweene his teeth,
> Controlling what he was controlled with.

Adonis' stallion is certainly Plato's horse, but Venus' little
lesson is sadly blunted by Shakespeare, who describes the mare
as a "breeding jennet." Venus had used her animal parable to

Phaedrus I.254A.

argue that Adonis should reproduce himself (a curious obsession of Shakespeare's at this time), but Adonis, a youth learning the hard hunt, spoils her moral.

> You do it for increase, o straunge excuse!
> When reason is the bawd to lusts abuse.

It is clear that Venus' strategy was first to get Adonis dismounted so that she could demonstrate her powers. Her second task is to make the soft hunt with its meaningful ease so attractive that he will abandon the hard hunt, the preparation for the heroic life. Venus knows that Adonis is not yet ready for her kind of love: "The tender spring upon thy tempting lip,/ Shewes thee unripe." In spite of this knowledge, Venus, who is rich with experience, tries her blandishments on Adonis; she even transforms him into a deer and accords him the luscious grange of her body. But Adonis knows allegory when he hears it, and so he rushes to remount his horse at the exact moment that it smells the jennet, "sees the vision of Love." The adolescent hunter, the sullen morning boy of "lazie sprite," "heavie, darke, disliking eye" loses his temper; he is angry with the older woman who has cost him his horse, who has hindered his natural duties. From this anger grows a partial kind of love, but it is not the sort Venus would have. Adonis is a child with her. When she swoons, he fusses over her as a boy might fuss over his mother. He will readily kiss her good night when it is time for bed. The goddess takes advantage of this filial-maternal relationship which is really all Adonis wants. Then the horse-metaphor returns: "Now is she in the verie lists of love." But Adonis will not manage her; he will only hunt the boar. Venus equates the boar with Death, and, as becomes an otiose goddess, returns to the problem in hand and praises the soft hunt.

In Venus' venery, the soft hunt is the pursuit of the *fugaces*, of those timid animals that never turn and stand—the hare,

the cony, the fox, and the deer, but especially the hare. This
is the hunt for which, we will remember, Propertius was bold
enough. Ovid, himself, describes the god Apollo bounding
after the flying Daphne like a French hound pursuing a hare
in an open meadow.[45] It is, of course, by no artistic accident
that Venus who could describe the grazing of the deer so
sensuously, now paints the hunting of wet "wat" so well. The
whole section, like that on the horses, has been vastly admired
by the Shakespearean lovers of nature, and I do not doubt
that Shakespeare, like any country lad, sent his dog after
rabbits. But the landscape over which "poore wat" tours, the
"farre off" hill upon which he stands erect with "listning
eare," is not too different from Venus' "parke"; moreover,
the creatures among which he seeks to lose himself—"deare,"
"sheepe," "conies"—were not without female counterparts
among the Elizabethans. There is no doubt that little Will
Shakespeare watched the hare run, but this "wat" is probably
more than a "deaw-bedabbled wretch."

It was not unusual for artists to show Venus accompanied
by the hare; its unbelievable fecundity, for it was said to con-
ceive while it was gestating,[46] made it a symbolic companion
for the generative mother. The ancients thought that hares
could exchange sex,[47] and an aggressive masculinity was attributed to the females[48] that suits Shakespeare's impression of
Venus. The lubricity of the hare was also long the subject of
human comment,[49] but the symbolism of the Shakespearean
hare probably goes beyond this. In the *Satiricon* of Petronius,
the witch who has undertaken to heal the impotence of the
hero turns at the proper moment and remarks to her assistant:

[45] *Metamorphoses* I.533-34.
[46] Pliny, *Nat. Hist.*, XXXVIII, 248; Athenaeus IX.400; Pollux *Onomast.*
V.12.
[47] Varro *De Re Rust.* III.12.
[48] Vincent of Beauvais, *Speculum Naturale* (Douay, 1624), p. 1360.
[49] Oppian, *op. cit.*, III.514-25.

"You see, my Chrysis, you see; I have raised a hare for others." [50] The hunting of the hare can probably have only one meaning; but Shakespeare, as only Titian[51] before him, alters Adonis from the soft hunter of hares, who meets death when he turns to the harder hunt, to a youth whose whole intent is on the hunting of the boar.

If the boar meant something to Shakespeare's generation besides the hard hunt, the proper education of the sacred hunter, and, as Venus herself names him, Death, I have not been able to find it. In the legend Adonis always dies at the tusk of the boar, and in the more orthodox accounts of the story the commentators had no trouble with the meaning. In the medieval annotations, the boar was lechery.[52] Horologgi, who explained an Italian translation of the *Metamorphoses*, puts the boar down as jealousy,[53] and, interestingly enough, in Shakespeare's account Venus is strangely jealous of the boar. For the more sophisticated Sandys the ancient weather

---

[50] *Op. cit.*, p. 131. This passage probably explains Ovid's *Ars* III.662: "Et lepus hic aliis exagitatus erit."

[51] Borghini reproves Titian for changing the myth, and making Adonis reject the advances of Venus, observing that this is beyond his rights as an artist: *Il Riposo* (Milan, 1807), I, 72–73.

[52] *Ovide Moralisé*, ed. De Boer (Amsterdam, 1936), p. 100.

[53] Andrea dell'Anguillara, *Le Metamorfosi di Ovidio* (Venice, 1584), p. 388. The notion that the boar is death is supported by scores of literary texts. Lucretius describes the struggles of primitive men against boars, and the exploits of Hercules and Meleager make the boar the beast against which heroes test their might. The great boar hunt is an important moment in many medieval romances of chivalry, and the heroes of these pieces are sometimes likened to boars. In *Brut*, ed. Madden (1847), Edwin urges his men to have "boars' hearts" (III.220) and Merlin predicts that Arthur will become a wasting boar (II.250). The vision of danger that Venus has in the poem is reminiscent of the boar dreams that warned the heroes of romance of either their impending deaths or an almost fatal disaster; see *Nibelungen Lied*, ed. Bartsch and De Boor (Weisbaden, 1956), pp. 155–65; *Horn et Rimenhild*, ed. Brede and Stengel (Marburg, 1883), p. 225; *Ogier de Danemarche*, ed. Barrois (Paris, 1842), pp. 333–34; and *Gaydon*, ed. Guessard (Paris, 1862), p. 11.

myth holds valid, so his Adonis is destroyed as the summer is when boarish winter comes.[54] At this time in his poetic life, Shakespeare, one should observe, may have had boars in his head because he had only recently been looking through the life records of Richard III, "the wretched, bloody, and usurping boar," and he was also fascinated, as young men often are, by innocent and unmerited death in youth. He needed, I imagine, no goddess to expound any of this to him, but, nonetheless, he brings Venus back in the later part of the poem to discourse foolishly on love like a fluttery and apprehensive Doll Tearsheet of forty. As for his Adonis—since all Adonises must die—this one, the invention of Shakespeare, gets off with a cleaner biography than any.

[54] *Metamorphosis Englished* (1632), p. 367.

CHAPTER FOUR

William Shakespeare

"The Rape of Lucrece"

Lucrece, the heroine of Shakespeare's second brief epic and the human opposite of his foolish and frustrated Venus, had long been for men, and hence for their wives, a gracious yet tragic example of married love. During most of the Middle Ages, she was placed on the short list of wives and widows celebrated for their chastity and faith; sometimes she was bracketed with the patriotic Judith, whose established purity helped to disestablish a tyrant.[1] In Chaucer's "Legend of Good Women," she takes her place in the assembly of the virtuous, but Chaucer was only presenting in English a directory of ladies already consecrated in decency by the master poets across the Channel. If we want to see her on parade, we have only to turn through the books of Eustache Deschamps:

[1] Jacobus Bergomensis, *De Claris Mulieribus in De memorabilibus et Claris Mulieribus* (Paris, 1521), p. 42v.

> Car de Dydo ne d'Elaine,
>   De Judith la souveraine,
> Ne d'Ester ne de Tysbee
>   De Lucresse la Rommaine,
> Ne d'Ecuba la certaine,
>   Sarre loial ne Medee
> Ne pourroit estre trouvee
>   Dame de tant de biens plaine.[2]

This is an impressive procession even though one may have his doubts about the credentials of some of the marchers. But no matter what our reservations, Judith is here and so is Hecuba, the queen whose tragedy softens the despair of Shakespeare's Lucrece.

Deschamps concludes his poem by remarking that all these women are like "stars shining beyond the mountain in the dawn." They are aloof, unearthly ideals of femininity lost in the dark folds of history. Though men of the Renaissance knew from Livy that Lucrece had been dead for two thousand years, she seemed, thanks to their nostalgia for antiquity which shortened chronological distances, to be near at hand. "There is no one so stupid," the Italian critic Sperone Speroni writes, "who has not heard of her by hearsay or through his reading."[3] Shakespeare underlines this statement when he tells us that Aaron, a Moor, and Olivia, a lady of Illyria, knew about her almost as much, perhaps, as he did himself. But Shakespeare's age was also one that trusted in monuments, that felt the presence of illustrious dead as it surveyed the marble aisles and floors of churches. If one doubted the testi-

---

[2] *Œuvres Complètes,* ed. De Queux de Saint-Hilaire (Paris, 1880), II, 336. Further lists are found at III, 294, 303; VII, 14, 289, and in Guillaume Alexis, 'Le Blason de Faulse Amours,' *Œuvres Poétiques,* ed. Piaget and Picot (Paris, 1896), I, 214, as well as Charles d'Orléans, *Poésies,* ed. Champion (Paris, 1924), p. 191. Gower places Lucrece between Penelope and Alcestis in the *Confessio Amantis* III.2632–9.

[3] "Dialogi primo sopra Virgilio," *Opera* (Venice, 1740), II, 187.

mony of the ancients, one had only to go to Viterbo to read
the plaque erected to a noble wife by her sorrowing husband:

D.M.S.
COLLATINUS TARQUINIUS DULCISSIMAE CON-
IUNGI ET INCOMPARABILI LUCRETIAE PUDICI-
TIAE DECORI, MULIERUM GLORIAE. VIXIT ANN.
XXII. MEN. III. DI. VI. PROH DOLOR QUANTUM
FUIT CARISSIMA.[4]

But there was another reason why men remembered Lucrece
and why her tragedy attracted the attention of the young
poet; she was not only a Roman heroine but also the center
of a Christian controversy.

A decade after Shakespeare's poem was in print, the Vice-
Chancellor of Altdorf attended the production of a play about
Lucrece at his university.[5] As he left the theater he met some
of the faculty arguing heatedly about the true nature of the
lady's virtue. Her advocates quoted Ovid, Vergil, Florus,
Valerius Maximus, and many other ancients in her cause; the
serious negative was supplied with cartridge by St. Augustine.
Being a man of pompous moderation, the Vice-Chancellor
spread oil on the flames by quoting, as he says, a Latin version
of a Greek poem. The poem was actually first written in
Latin by a Frenchman, and the Vice-Chancellor merely established his right to office with this blunder; but the poem,
which presents the essential paradox, was widely known and
I shall make do with a later English version:

> Were that unchast mate welcome to thy bed,
> *Lucrece*, thy lust was justly punished.

[4] Probus, *De Notis Romanorum Interpretandis*, ed. Tacuinus (Venice,
1525), p. lxxixv.
[5] Possibly the popular *Lucretia und Brutus* of Bullinger described in H.
Galinsky, *Der Lucretia-Stoff in der Weltliteratur* (Breslau, 1932), pp. 76–80.

> Why seek'st thou fame that di'dst deservedly?
> But if foule force defil'd thine honest bed,
> His onely rage should have bene punished:
> Why diest thou for anothers villanie?
> Both wayes thy thirst of fame is too unjust,
> Dying, or for fond rage, or guiltie lust.[6]

The personal feeling of the Vice-Chancellor toward Lucrece was, I am happy to say, kinder than that of the poet, who simply echoed the saintly opinion of St. Augustine.

To stern Tertullian and austere Jerome,[7] Lucrece was a splendid example of pagan domestic virtue, a woman whose actions might well be countenanced by Christian ladies possessed of the inner light. With the views of these mighty predecessors, St. Augustine, who was inclined to condemn even the worthiest heathen when he was making a case against the spiritually unredeemed, heartily disagreed. In the *City of God* he attacks the conduct of Collatine's poor wife: "This case is caught between both sides to such a degree that if suicide is extenuated, adultery is proved; if adultery is denied, the conviction is for suicide." There is no way, he thinks, to resolve the problem. "If she was adulterous, why is she praised? If she was chaste, why was she killed?" If she had been a Christian, she would have eschewed "Roman pride in glory" and found another way "to reveal her conscience to men." [8]

For the sixteenth century the tragedy of Lucrece was a kind of casuistic problem, a matter of legal gamesmanship

---

[6] P. Camerarius, *Operae Horarum Subcesivarum, sive Meditationes Historicae* (Frankfurt, 1609), p. 292. The poem, according to Bayle ("Lucretia"), was written by Renatus Laurent de la Barre; it is printed in Latin and French in Estienne's *Apologie pour Hérodote;* the English version is from *A World of Wonders,* trans. Carew (1607), p. 101.

[7] Tertullian, *Ad Martyres*, PL, I, 698–99; *De Exhortatione Castitatis*, PL, II, 929; *De Monogamia*, PL, II, 952, and Jerome, *Epistulae*, PL, XXI, 1051; *Adversus Jovinianum*, PL, XXIII, 294.

[8] I.19.

for canon lawyers.[9] From controversy of this nature the case
got into the writings of the humanists, and we find Speroni
remarking that Lucrece was of "imperfect chastity" or she
would have held fort against the assaults of Tarquin. A truly
chaste woman, he assures us, would have died before surrender; but Lucrece abandoned her virtue just as a distressed
ship jettisons its cargo. Her compliance with the desires of
Tarquin was, in fact, an act midway between the forced and
the voluntary.[10] With this view the French humanist, Henri
Estienne, agrees: "poore *Lucretia* did not judge aright of her-
selfe and her own estate." Suicide is no revenge. "Be it that
her death were Vindicative, yet it were but a revenge of the
injury done to the defiled body, and not of the wrong done
to the undefiled mind, which is the seate of chastitie." [11] The
story of Lucrece was, I expect, made important for Shakespeare by this ancient yet current controversy; and without
the benefit of this knowledge, we are nonplussed by the tenor
of certain areas of his poem.

One may comprehend Shakespeare's consideration of the
great argument by watching his Lucrece after the departure
of Tarquin. She recites arias on Time, Night, and Occasion;
then, looking at her sharp-nailed fingers, she blames them for
not defending their "loyal dame." A few stanzas later (1149–

---

[9] According to Camerarius, Bartolomi di Saliceto and Guillaume
d'Oncieux, sixteenth-century jurists, excused Lucretia of any legal blame.
The conventional position on her suicide is expressed by Justus Lipsius,
Manuductiones ad Stoicam Philosophiam in *Opera* (Antwerp, 1637), III,
525. In the Constantius and Marsus edition of Ovid's *Fasti* (1527) the im-
possibility of Lucretia's fighting, flying, or crying for aid is emphasized
(p. lxxxvii).

[10] "Orazione contra le Cortigiane," *Opera*, III, 208–11.

[11] *Op. cit., loc. cit.* A comparison of Lucretia with the wife of Origiacon,
who brought her husband the head of her ravisher, is the subject of John
Dickenson's Latin poem "De Lucretia Romana," in *Speculum Tragicum*
(Leyden, 1605), pp. 234–35.

76), the notion of suicide crosses her mind, and she recalls what Augustine has said, or, in a historical sense, is going to say: " 'To kill myself,' quoth she, 'alack, what were it,/ But with my body my poor soul's pollution?' " The moral dilemma is made almost emblematic when Lucrece—almost her own symbol—lies dead in "rigols" of pure and corrupt blood (1737–50); the Christian rather than the Roman lesson is to be read in this stylized *cul-de-lampe*. The living nature of the questions about Lucrece's action is also italicized when Brutus, who fails to speak the lines of the historians, says to the hysterical husband:

> Is it revenge to give thyself a blow
> For his foul act by whom thy fair wife bleeds?
> Such childish humour from weak minds proceeds:
> Thy wretched wife mistook the matter so,
> To slay herself, that should have slain her foe. (1823–27)

We must, I think, face the fact that Shakespeare read the story of Lucrece in its Christian context. There was no question in his mind about its tragic import, but he felt that it must be glossed in terms of Christian options. Lucrece should have defended herself to the death, or, having been forced, lived free of blame with a guiltless conscience. Her action was rare and wonderful, but a little beyond forgiveness.

Shakespeare's recognition of the double understanding of the Lucrece story explains, I think, the symbolic mileposts that guide us through this poem as they lead us through Spenser's *Faerie Queene*. His successors cling to the literal, and, as a result, Heywood's *The Rape of Lucrece* is simply a jolly exercise in dramatic bad taste, whereas Middleton's (?) *The Ghost of Lucrece*, while clinging to Shakespeare's text and superficially appearing to recognize the problem, fails to understand the ultimate lesson of Shakespeare's poem. If one

looks across the Channel to the play on the legend by Nicolas
Filleul, to the anonymous *Tragedie sur la Mort de Lucresse*,[12]
to Chevreau's *La Lucresse Romaine Tragedie*, or to Du
Ryer's *Lucrece Tragedie*, one discovers that only the last play
takes notice of the question, tacking it on in an annotating
speech of two dozen lines[13] that is a limping intruder in the
neoclassic scene. But if Shakespeare's poem cannot be interpreted in terms of its English successors, it can only be partially understood when read under the light of its predecessor
"Venus and Adonis."

The conventional statements about the relation of these
two poems need not be rehearsed; it is almost enough to say
that they are no more in opposition to each other than are
"L'Allegro" and "Il Penseroso," with which they are sometimes compared. Milton's poems, I think, represent a progres-
sive course of thinking about the preparation of the poet-
prophet; Shakespeare's poems are a similar sequence of
discourses on the nature of human love. The poems are
continuations rather than contradictions. In "Venus and
Adonis," love, though veiled by courtly compliment, is discussed mainly on the basis of animal heat and placed outside
the limits of a proper definition of the reasonable life. The
animal theme returns in "Lucrece," but in this second poem
(a rougher Venus taking one part) the opposition comes from
a different aspect of love: the devotion of a wife to her
fleshly honor. The problem, as in subsequent plays, has something to do with *honor*, but it is also concerned with a total
estimate of chastity on a higher level.

In "Venus and Adonis" the animal metaphors that point
toward the ultimate theme depend to a degree on the hunter
and the hunted; the same type of metaphor controls the first

[12] L. E. Dabney (*French Dramatic Literature in the Reign of Henri IV*
[Austin, Texas, 1952], pp. 198–200) describes this manuscript play.
[13] *Op. cit.* (Paris, 1638), pp. 76–77.

third of "The Rape of Lucrece," but here the hunt is less equal than that of the other poem. Tarquin is not a proper hunter pitted against an equal quarry. He enters in the night when only owls and wolves are heard because he is the "night owle" that will catch the sleeping dove. In due course, he is compared to a serpent, a "grim Lion," a "faulcon towring," a "Cockeatrice," a "rough beast," a "night waking Cat," a vulture, and a wolf. After his crime is done, he changes into a "full-fed Hound, or gorged Hawke," and then slips away like a "theevish dog." Lucrece is naturally an innocent thing of nature: a "white Hind," a mouse, a doe, a lamb, but more commonly a dove, a "new-kild bird," a lesser fowl crouching under the shadow of the hawk's wings. She continues to be conscious of her metaphoric identity and eventually compares herself with the birds and with her mythological similar, Philomele. In the end, a "pale swan," she sings before she dies.

These comparisons are plain enough and certainly to be expected, but whereas in "Venus and Adonis" there are several real animals—a stallion, a jennet, a hare, and a boar—in the cast of characters, "Lucrece" has only one. As Tarquin creeps to the bed of Lucrece bearing the "lightless fire," "Night-wandering weasels fright him, yet he still pursues his fear." We know from the annotations on this passage that "especially among the British" it is inauspicious to meet a weasel,[14] but the British were not alone in this superstition, which was widely enough held in the sixteenth century to produce the axiom "Quidquid agis, mustela tibi si occurrat, omitte: Signa malae haec sortis bestia prava gerit." But the weasel was more than a warning; it was a sign "of evil to those

---

[14] T. F. T. Dyer, *Folklore of Shakespeare* (London, 1883), p. 189. The notion begins with Theophrastus *Characteres* XXVIII.5; see Erasmus *Adagia* I.173; Alexander ab Alexandro, *Geniales Dies* (Paris, 1965), p. 275v.; Carolus Figulus, *Mustela* (Cologne, 1540); C. Gesner, *Historia Animalium* (Frankfurt, 1603), I, 759–61.

whose houses they infest." [15] The literal weasel not only warns Tarquin but foretells the evil that awaits Lucrece. But the literal weasel is more than a weasel. The poet who was going to make us see the spider Iago without saying "spider" can make us see who the weasel, well-known as a bird-nester, is; and we can annotate the concealed metaphor with a stanza from one of the great Renaissance Latin poets.

> Tu fera passeribus pestis sturnisque fuisti,
> Quos trahere e nidis ars tibi summa fuit.
> Teque suis visae pullis timuere columbae,
> Et magnis avibus parvulae terror eras.[16]

But Tarquin, who is evil on the animal level, sins against his creed when he attains human shape. Long before he commits his rape, he denounces himself: "O shame to knighthood, and to shining Armes." He is a warrior in arms but not in love, because he carries over the violence of battle to the tents of love. The animal metaphors that bring Shakespeare's two poems momentarily together change when Tarquin crosses the threshold of Lucrece's bedchamber; and, as befits a poem laid against a background of war and siege, love and battle make the terms of the analogues. "Love," says the quiet poet George Herbert, "is a man of war," and Shakespeare knew this trope only too well. He may have learned it from the *Aeneid* (XI.736–37) or from the Latin elegiac poets;[17] but

---

[15] A. Alciati, *Emblemata* (Leyden, 1593), CXXVI.

[16] *Strozzi Poetae Pater et Filius* (Venice, 1513), II, 71v.–72v. U. Aldrovandus mentions poems on the same subject by Reusner, Mantuanus, and J. C. Scaliger (*De Quadrupedibus Digitatis* [Bologna, 1637], pp. 313, 319, 326). The weasel quite fittingly turns up in the pseudo-Ovidian "Philomela."

[17] The earliest example is the πρῶτον μὲν στρατευτικωτάτους recorded by Athenaeus, 13.562. In Latin there are Propertius II.12.9–16, III.5.1–2, 6.40–42, 8.31–34, 20.19–20, and Tibullus I.1.75, 3.64, 10.53–56. Almost all classical examples have been gathered in Alfons Spies, *Militat Omnis Amans* (Tübingen, 1930).

his probable master was Ovid, who gave him in the *Fasti* the basic material of his poem, and whose great pattern poem, "Militat omnis amans et habet sua castra Cupido," is in the first of the *Amores*. From this book of the heart we learn that lovers and soldiers are the same except that the comrades of "Frater Amor" are never demobbed.[18] The wars that they fight under the erotic banners are, however, seldom bitter and never violent.

From the texts of the Roman poets the troubadours,[19] the goliards,[20] the stilnovists,[21] and the only begetters[22] of Renaissance French and Italian poetry took their lessons. As a consequence of this long tradition, Shakespeare cannot avoid these comparisons when he writes about soldiers and their women.

[18] *Amores* II.9.1–4; *Ars* I.36–37; II.233–38, 671; III.3–4; *Rem.* I–II.158. See also Statius *Silvae* I.2.61–67; Plautus *Persa* II.2.49–50; *Truc.* II.1.18–19. One of the more famous tropes is in Horace's recall to the colors at the age of fifty (IV.1.1–2). The theme appears in the later Latins: Ausonius, *Opuscula*, ed. Schenkl (Berlin, 1883), p. 253; Venantius Fortunatus, *Opera poetica*, ed. Leo (Berlin, 1881), p. 125; Dracontius, *Romulea*, in *Opera*, ed. Vollmer (Berlin, 1905), VI, 17–21, and X, 338–39.

[19] *Peirol d'Auvergne*, ed. Aston (Cambridge, 1953), p. 107; Aimeric de Peguilhan, *The Poems*, ed. Shepard and Chambers (Evanston, 1950), p. 101; *Piere Vidal*, ed. Anglade (Paris, 1923), p. 37; C. Appel, *Der Trobador Cadene* (Halle, 1920), p. 44; Arnaut de Mareuil, *Les Poésies Lyriques*, ed. Johnston (Paris, 1935), p. 72; Bernart de Ventadornt *Seine Lieder*, ed. Appel (Halle, 1915), pp. 23, 77–78, 199.

[20] *Carminà Burana*, ed. Schmeller (Stuttgart, 1847), pp. 126–28, 135, 146, 184, 188, 198, 214.

[21] See the poems of Lapo Gianni and Cino da Pistoia in *Rimatori del Dolce Stilnovo*, ed. Di Benedetto (Turin, 1925), pp. 95, 163.

[22] Petrarch gives the story of Lucrece political emphasis in the third book of his *Africa* and places the lady in the "Trionfo della Pudiciza" (131–36) and in the sonnets (pp. 357, 504 of the Mestica edition [Florence, 1896]). He uses the love-war motif in his sonnets (pp. 41, 141, 154, 156, 183–84, 203, 225), a theme common among his successors. Aretino, for example, can hardly write a sonnet without it, and it is popular among the French: see Louise Labé, *Œuvres Complètes*, ed. Boutens and De Grave (Maestricht, 1928), pp. 88–89; Guy de Tours, *Premières Œuvres*, ed. Blanchemain (Paris, 1879), pp. 70–71; Ronsard, *Œuvres*, ed. Vaganay (Paris, 1924), I, 4, 62, 96; III, 136, 352.

Tarquin says that "Affection is my captain" and follows the metaphor through three stanzas as he follows the passageway to Lucrece's chamber. His lusts obey their "Captain," too; and as he stands beside the sleeping young woman, his pulsing veins are "like straggling slaves for pillage fighting." But these figures are all ironic when applied to Tarquin. He is not a soldier of love fencing with his dear enemy or sharing her field bed as an amorous companion; even when the metaphors turn to those of siege and assault, they are improperly in his company and exhibit him for what he is.

The theme of love as a siege comes also from Ovid's comparison between the soldier battering at the walls of an armed camp and the excluded lover weeping outside his beloved's locked door: "Ille graves urbes, hic durae limen amicae Obsidet: hic portas frangit, at ille fores." In the age of chivalry, when the taking of fortified places was a high military science, the metaphor of the capture of love's castle is fairly common. "Que ja castels frevols qu'es assatzatz," writes the troubadour Ponz de Capduelh, "Ab gran poder." [23] Raimon de Toulouse, an expert in both the arts of love and war, says that castles and towers are of no avail when love attacks. "Ja castels ni tors No us cugetz que s'tenha, Plus gran forsa 'l venha." [24] Le Roman de la Rose[25] ends with a great siege in which the beloved is rescued; and "Le Hault Siege d'Amours" of Jean Molinet[26] plays on the theme of the amorous but gentle war. It is, of course, in this classical-medieval tradition that ardent Tarquin gallops from the siege of Ardea to the ravishing of Lucrece, but there is no indication that he has read its literature rightly.

Romeo driven back from Rosaline's walls can only com-

[23] E. Wechssler, "Frauendienst und Vassaltät," Zeitschrift für französische Sprache und Literatur, XXIV (1902), 176.

[24] K. A. F. Mahn, Die Werke der Troubadours (Berlin, 1846–79), I, 6, v.

[25] Op. cit., ed. Langlois (Paris, 1914–24), V, 76–78.

[26] Les Faictz et Dictz, ed. Dupire (Paris, 1937), II, 569–83.

mend her for not staying "the siege of loving terms, Nor bide
th'encounter of assailing eyes." The "false lord" Tarquin runs
furiously like an enraged captain at the breaching of a wall;
and, as Shakespeare sees him charge, "Honour and beauty, in
the owner's arms/ Are weakly fortress'd from a world of
harms." Lucrece's husband is likewise unaware that "This
siege . . . hath engirt his marriage." The unknightly ravisher
—his heart beating like a drum—lets his hands "scale" the
"round turrets" of the lady's breasts, and by this action informs her that she "is dreadfully beset."

> His hand, that yet remains upon her breast,—
> Rude ram, to batter such an ivory wall!—
> May feel her heart—poor citizen!—distress'd,
> Wounding itself to death, rise up and fall,
> Beating her bulk, that his hand shakes withal.
> This moves in him more rage and lesser pity,
> To make the breach and enter this sweet city.   (463–69)

In keeping with the traditional tropes, Tarquin sounds "a
parley," and the pale face of Lucrece appearing over the
turret of her white sheets seems a flag of surrender. "Under
that colour I am come to scale Thy never-conquer'd fort."
Lucrece, like a damsel of the romances, defends herself with
words, but the situation is once again ironic. She is no coy
and half-persuaded girl refuting the kindly arguments of her
decent lover. She cannot prevail, and the fortress of her
chastity is overcome not by favor but through force and
duress. But though the castle of her virtue falls to an exterior
force, the walls of Tarquin's soul are also demolished by interior revolt. "Her subjects with foul insurrection/ Have
batter'd down her consecrated wall." One of the central paradoxes of "Venus and Adonis" is that of the hunter hunted; in
this part of "The Rape of Lucrece" the ruiner is ruined.
Tarquin goes off with his spotted soul, bearing Lucrece's

honor as his "prisoner," and leaving the girl behind "like a late-sacked island"; then Lucrece writes her series of poems to Night, to Opportunity, and to her mythological predecessor, Philomele. A modern reader could object that all this rhetoric is hardly in keeping with the events, but he must remember that these early poems are barns in which the young poet is storing up themes and metaphors for the future. They are virtuoso performances in which Shakespeare like a good musician is demonstrating both his repertoire and his skill with his instrument. The Troy cloth which follows them and occupies such a large section of the poem is possibly in the same tradition, but it may also have a deeper meaning.

The painted spectacle of the war before Troy that Lucrece studies and that Shakespeare describes has struck many critics as simply another rhetorical description that slows the movement of the poem until Collatine arrives and that gives the reader a chance to meditate on the tragedy. There have been various comments on whether or not Shakespeare had a real picture in mind; and if he did, the Italian painter, Giulio Romano, who painted Troy scenes, has been nominated as the most likely artist. The ecphrastic poetry of ancient and modern poets has been brought forward to account for Shakespeare's lines, and it has even been asserted that Shakespeare is attempting in this episode to distinguish in an aesthetic fashion between the task and skill of the artist in paint and verse.[27] All of these observations have been helpful in their ways, but the main questions are why the idea occurred to Shakespeare and what would a sixteenth-century reader see in the picture.

T. W. Baldwin has pointed to the commentaries of Marsus and Constantius on the Lucrece story in Ovid's *Fasti*[28] as the

[27] *The Poems*, ed. Rollins (Philadelphia, 1938), pp. 224–27.

[28] *On the Literary Genetics of Shakespere's Poems and Sonnets* (Urbana, Ill., 1950), pp. 144–45. A connection between Lucrece and Sinon is made by Fabrini in his *Opere* (1588) at *Aeneid* II.79 when he observes that good

text that carried Shakespeare from Rome to Troy. In these commentaries, Lucrece is not only defended against the charges of St. Augustine, but Tarquin is compared obliquely, by a quotation from the *Aeneid*, to Sinon, the betrayer of Troy. One hardly knows how a poet's imagination works, and Baldwin may be completely right; however, a few other matters might have brought this idea into Shakespeare's mind. Lucrece was, of course, a Trojan by ancestry, and the destruction of Troy was the greatest tragedy that she knew. She was also regularly associated in lists of noble women with Hecuba, that other faithful and suffering wife. There is finally the fact that the Renaissance attributed, until Goldast argued otherwise,[29] a poem on Philomela and a "De Excidio Trojae" to Ovid and that Shakespeare could have found these now rejected poems in the *Opera*. But we shall probably never know exactly how Shakespeare got from the rape of Lucrece, that fallen fortress of chastity, to the destruction of Troy.

Though we cannot explain the turns and halts of Shakespeare's imagination, we most certainly know that the Trojan episode in "The Rape of Lucrece" came from the first two books of the *Aeneid*: the "pictura inanis" from the first book, the fall of the city from the second. If we now think in terms of the Renaissance Vergil, we may be able to read a meaning into this section that may not be Shakespeare's but that suits the moral trend of his poem and may represent what a certain type of Renaissance reader saw in it. To introduce this last point, we must simply remember that the sixteenth century regarded Vergil as a superb moral poet and his hero as a man

---

and evil done under duress do not count and uses Lucrece as the counterexample. Jacobus Pontanus in his *Symbolarum libri XVII* (Augsburg, 1599), col. 837-38, compares Sinon to Zopyrus and Tarquin.

[29] Both poems were regarded as genuine until the publication of the *Erotica et Amatoria Opusculi* (Frankfurt, 1610) in which Goldast assigns the "Philomela" to either Albus Ovidius Juventinus or Julius Speratus and the "De Excidio" to Benigne of Fleury.

of high human perfection. In this regard they had, as we know, no quarrel with the Middle Ages; but, even with this knowledge, we sometimes forget that a man of the Renaissance could read with the help of the experts the great allegory of the career of Aeneas. It is, then, not so much a question of how the Troy painting got into "Lucrece," or why it is there, as what consonant meaning a man of the Renaissance might find in it.

Petrarch is always a good figure to stand at the door of any study of Renaissance intellectual attitudes, and in one of his letters he informs Frederico Aretino that the city of Troy is a symbol of the human body deep in sleep. Its gates are opened by sins that kill the defenders of the soul on the threshold. "Relicta tergo mollitie, & antiqua coniunge ibi amissa, hoc est consuetudine voluptatum a prima aetate copulata, animo solus primum, sed virtute armatis." "Now all this tumult, this ruin, this destruction in which the voluptuous city, victim of its own passions, struggles between the fires kindled by libidinousness and the sword of anger occurs fitly at night to denote the darkness of human error and the blackness in which our life, buried in sleep and drenched in wine, is ignorantly and drunkenly immersed." This is the tone of Petrarch's reading and he continues to match the poetry to the moral. The great horse is made by the evils of youth; and Laocoön or reason being overthrown, the "infausta machina" is admitted conveying into the town Odysseus or "wicked cunning," Neoptolemus or "pride and vindictive ardour," and Menelaus or "revenge." [30]

Boccaccio, Petrarch's friend, always looked under "the fitting veil of the fable for hidden truth" (sotto velame di favole appropriato, nascondere la verità),[31] and in his *Genealogy of the Gods*, he illustrates what he finds under this covering with

[30] *Opera* (Basel, 1554), pp. 872–73.
[31] *Della Geneologia* (Venice, 1585), p. 233.

a moral reading of the story of Perseus. He would obviously have approved of the letter to Aretino because, as he informs us, he looked into "the core or literal sense" for the other allegorical significances.[32] The apparently medieval practices of both these poets were also followed by the humanist Collucio Salutati, who insisted on searching for "the allegorical meanings in the traditional stories of the poets." [33] A century later, the Florentine humanists, Ficino and Pico della Mirandola,[34] both recommend that the classical poets be read in terms of the four-fold exegesis of the twelfth-century theologians; and a member of their society, Landino, took it upon himself to provide such a reading of the *Aeneid*, a poem in which "Vergil hid the most profound knowledge." His "In Virgilii Opera Allegoria" was printed either in the Quaestiones *Camaldulenses* or as an appendix to the *Aeneid* at least twenty times between 1480 and 1596.

For Landino, Troy is the youthful life of man when reason slumbers and the senses rule; it is what philosophers call the "natural state" and in this state the body reigns among fleshly pleasures. But some men discover, as they near maturity, that there is a road leading to the right which they must follow. To make plainer this notion of the divided way, Landino states that both Aeneas and Paris lived in Troy but followed separate courses. Paris preferred pleasure to virtue and perished with Troy; Aeneas, impelled by his mother, the higher Venus, left Troy to seek the truth and came eventually to Italy or divine sapience. One may object, Landino acknowledges, that Aeneas fought for Troy, but one must also admit that even though the night of passions surrounded him, he foresaw the fall of

[32] *Ibid.*, p. 8.
[33] R. H. Green, "Classical Fable and English Poetry," *Critical Approaches to Mediaeval Literature* (New York, 1960), p. 120.
[34] E. H. Gombrich, "Icones Symbolicae," *Journal of the Warburg and Courtauld Institutes*, II (1948), 163–92.

the city. For Aeneas was son of flesh (Anchises), but he also had a soul (Venus), and it is the death of his father as well as the wisdom of his mother that brings him in the end to perfection.[35]

We have only to remember Spenser's allegorical presentation of portions of the Troy story or Chapman's remarks on the Homeric allegory in the epistle to the *Odyssey*, to realize that Landino's formal symbolic reading is not a unique medieval retention. This impression of a strong sense of allegory in the Renaissance's interpretation of classical poets (aided, perhaps, by the discovery of some of the ancient moral and physical glosses on Homer) is given further emphasis by Fabrini's edition of the *Aeneid* in 1588. In this edition the Latin text is surrounded by the usual morass of an *apparatus criticus*, but the editor adds to the customary comments on syntax, history, and so forth a separate "allegorical exposition" that draws heavily on Landino's method and results. When, for instance, Venus pays her son a nocturnal visit (II, 489–504), Fabrini observes that this is the celestial Venus described by Plato, Pythagoras, Empedocles, and St. Paul. She comes, he writes, to lead Aeneas away from Troy, the body of man besieged by pleasures and passions, in order that he may follow a divine course. Anchises (the flesh) naturally refuses to leave because he would rather die than give up his sensual desires, and so he must be carried off by force on the shoulders of the soul.[36] Fabrini's moral commentary omits

---

[35] Vergil, *Aeneidos*, ed. Hostensius (Basel, 1577), pp. 3001, 3004–8, 3011. Allusions to Vergil as an allegorist are found commonly at this time in prefaces to editions of the various works of Vergil and in some of the Italian critics. One of the most interesting is Celio Calcagnini, a contemporary of Landino's, who not only discusses the allegorical interpretation of ancient poetry (*Lectiones Antiquae* (Lyon, 1560), II, 555–59), but also criticizes Landino and argues that Troy is not youth or the body but the world from which Aeneas rises on a three-scale Neo-Platonic ladder (II, 429).

[36] I have used the Venice edition of 1615.

much that is in Landino's, but what it accepts is elaborately annotated, and its basic conclusion is the same. Troy is the body which must be destroyed and abandoned so that the ideal man can gain the profits of a higher life.

Now there is absolutely no reason to believe that Shakespeare had any of Spenser's liking for overt allegory, but it is quite probable that he could allude to matters that had intrinsic allegorical value for his readers. The garden scene in *Richard II* connects symbolically with John of Gaunt's "This other Eden"; and Falstaff, the "old white-bearded Satan," takes us promptly to the Pauline "homo vetus." Neither of these suggestions is allegorical in the strict sense; but granted the intellectual inclinations of the audience, one cannot feel that corn was being sown on stony ground. I am moved to suppose, considering the nature of the central discussion and the symbolic signposts, that "The Rape of Lucrece" (although it is not an allegory in the same sense as Spenser's "Muiopotomos") has certain sub-literal possibilities.

I cannot assume that Shakespeare knew the moral readings of Landino and Fabrini, but Lucrece, who compares the ravishment of her body with the fall of Troy—"so my Troy did fall"—seems to have intimations of this nature. Like the allegorizers of the *Aeneid* and, of course, in keeping with her historical utterances, she makes a careful distinction between her flesh and her soul:

> My body or my soul which was the dearer,
> When the one pure, the other made divine?
> Whose love of either to my self was nearer,
> When both were kept for heaven and Collatine?

But the house of her soul is "sackt," her mansion "batter'd," her temple "corrupted." There is but one thing left to do: she must leave. "If in this blemisht fort I make some hole,/ Through which I may convay this troubled soule."

In the allegories, Aeneas' Troy is equally ravaged by sins
and sensations from without; and so, on the advice of his
mother, he departs to find divine wisdom. Lucrece's decision
is similar, but, like Tarquin's amorous soldiership, morally improper. Her Troy is ruined by Tarquin-Sinon, and she believes that it must be annihilated to preserve the purity of her
mind. Unfortunately she does not aspire to divine sapience
but to pagan honor. Unled by the celestial Venus, her maculate body appears to control her decision more than her im-
maculate soul, which, according to her own statement, only
endures in "her poyson'd closet." So while Brutus seems to
have the last word in the pagan sense, it is really St. Augustine
(whose words fitted to Lucrece's tongue have earlier taken
their place in the poem) who wins, in spite of Shakespeare's
obvious sympathy for the lady, the debate between the classical and the Christian worlds.

CHAPTER FIVE

William Shakespeare

The Tempest

Though *The Tempest* is a play, it is also a complicated masque or a narrative poem with lyric intervals. It is difficult to compare with Shakespeare's other plays, for it is briefer, more elaborate in fantasy, and in some respects more intensely personal than they. During the last century, it was thought to be confessional and Prospero's final speeches were associated with Shakespeare's retirement from the theater. The play does not permit this conclusion. Shakespeare is not forsaking his art. If *The Tempest* is to be read biographically at all, it must be seen as a poetical summary of the poet's life and its satisfactory achievements, as the poetic rendering of that bright moment at the end allowed to men of special favor, a moment that assures them that what they have loved will endure. *The Tempest*, like *Pericles*, *Cymbeline*, and *The Winter's Tale*, is one of a series of warm afternoons in the late autumn of Shakespeare's life. It is mellow with the ripeness of knowledge, for its maker has discovered the right ritual for the marriage of the inner and the outer world, of the real and the ideal, the experienced and the imagined, the dream and the actuality.

With the writing of *Hamlet* Shakespeare begins to experiment with darkness, and the sun does not come again until Pericles, who is "music's master," hears, like no other character in Shakespeare's plays, the harmony of the heavenly spheres. This is the same harmonious end toward which Prospero looks: "When I have required/ Some heavenly music—which even now I do." It is plain from the tragedies that an awakening from idealism into cold reality is the required preliminary experience to the search for celestial harmony. The distaste for life expressed by Hamlet, a distaste that helps to shape the succeeding tragedies, has been associated by biographical critics with the poet's private experience, with his increasing boredom with life and art, with an obsessing puritanical temper, with a disappointment in love or friendship, and with some sort of neurotic illness. None of this can be proved. All we know is that Shakespeare experimented with tragedy and tragic despair; then, using the same sets of tragic circumstances, he led his creatures out of the world of darkness into eternal day.

In each of the three plays written before *The Tempest*, the dramatic premise is tragic, although the poet always forfends "the promised end." Pericles, a Hamlet-like seeker of truth, begins his search in a place evil with the reek of incest and carnage. He wanders through storm upon storm over the wide map of the great lost world of antiquity. In the end, he hears the divine music, sees the vision of the celestial "goddess argentine," and finds at last his lost wife and child. The play follows an established legend, but the bareness of myth is made a living reality through the poet's restored belief. *Cymbeline*, which is drawn from the truth of history, shuns history so that Cymbeline may see the consequence of wrong, that Imogen may triumph in her love, that the lost princes may be found, that Posthumus, cured and forgiven, may have his dream made real, and that Iachimo, weak son of Iago, may be pardoned. With *The Winter's Tale* the miracle increases, for Greene, father of the story, could not believe in the resurrection of Hermione or the redemption of Leontes. Shakespeare, the poet, is alone able to distract the current that flows toward tragedy. The end is so miraculous that we, too, like the healed King Leontes, may say, "If this be magic, let it be an art/ Lawful as eating." The ritual of restoration, the magic that transforms the stale world into the "brave new world," is presented to us in the last play, which interprets the mode of all these romances. We must go to *The Tempest* for this information and then we may understand what the wise, young poet Keats meant when he said that Shakespeare lived the life of allegory.

The Tempest, like the other last plays, is separated from the world of the Elizabethans by an imaginative reach that is greater than the finite measurements of space and time. It is remote in time and it is out of time. The imaginative distances are enhanced by the mortal chronology of the text: the precise three hours of the action and of the twelve-year island sojourn of Prospero and Miranda. Because of these exact statements the interior distance between us and the island is closer than are the external distances of time and space. We can almost find the island in the atlas of literary tradition: it is on or off the direct course to Carthage or Tunis, the capes where Aeneas, swept by storm, came into the realm of "widow Dido." The time may be any time, but it is more truly a constant present. All of these distinctions are made certain by the past, for it is not just that Shakespeare was

an Englishman or read the sea adventures of Jourdan that put
the island on the chart of his imagination.

We stand, at the play's beginning, watching a storm that
we also see through the eyes of Prospero, the stormmaker,
and of the admirable Miranda. It is a fairy storm, real only
to the men returning from Carthage and to the spellbound
girl. It is a storm similar to the one that Prospero may have
known inwardly when twelve years before he and his infant
daughter crossed the same waters on "a rotten carcass of a
butt."

> There they hoist us,
> To cry to the seas, that roared to us; to sigh
> To the winds, whose pity sighing back again
> Did us but loving wrong.[1]

The storm that was then in Prospero's mind was not unlike
the one that drove Lear mad, but now, except for occasional
ripples of anger or impatience, it has blown itself out. Prospero
has been tested and educated in his island; he has learned to
control his passions' weather and so he can make storms in
semblance. When Miranda asks how they came ashore,
Prospero, grateful for the experience, can give her a serene
answer, "By Providence divine." To reach this emotional
shelter, one must pass through stormy weather to an island,
and it is on the island, outside of known reality, that a
symbolic miracle can occur.

To come across broad waters in a helpless boat and to
find haven at last in a magic island is a symbolic motif that
has found a place in the history of heroes since literature
began. The storms that drove the Argonauts are poetically
recorded; [2] we know in the same way the wracking tumult in

---

[1] I.ii.148–51.

[2] Apollonius of Rhodes, *Argonautica* IV.1228–1304; Valerius Flaccus
I.574–607.

which Ceyx drowned [3] and the monstrous gale that brought
Aeneas to Carthage.[4] The accounts of the poets are sustained
by the romantic historians, one of whom, Diodorus Siculus,
gives us the tale of Iambulus, storm-driven for months in the
Erythraean Sea and brought at last to an island where men
lived happily in the earliest of Utopias.[5] The same romancer,
in his book of islands, sets down a legend congenial with that
of *The Tempest*. He writes that sailors from Carthage, ex-
ploring the sea beyond the Pillars of Hercules, were carried
by strong winds far into the ocean. After many days, they
were driven onto an island filled with springs, rivers, and
beautiful orchards but unknown to men. Its climate was so
felicitous that "it would appear . . . that it was a dwelling-
place of gods." [6] But the master of storm, of shipwreck, and
of enchanted islands is the wise son of Laertes, Odysseus of
many counsels. To understand part of the tradition behind
The Tempest, we should rehearse his Mediterranean journeys
and understand what they mean.

The whole course of Odysseus from Troy to the high hall
of King Alcinous is related by Homer in the central section of
the epic. It is placed in the mouth of the great adventurer,
who takes on himself a kind of "minstrelsy" ($\dot\rho\alpha\psi\omega\delta\iota\alpha$), as he
words it, in order to offer the listening Phaeacians his real
story as a counterwork to the artful myth recited by Demodocus. The storm begins to blow after the boats leave the
beach at Ismarus; for nine days the ruinous winds carry the
hero past Malea and Cythera to the Land of the Lotus-Eaters.
Even when the son of Hippotas gives the wanderers a wallet
containing the ways of the winds, a triumph of ill-counsel
brings the tempest again until further smash and bluster drive

[3] *Metamorphoses* XI.481–534.
[4] *Aeneid* I.81–141.
[5] *Bibliotheca* II.55–60.
[6] *Ibid.*, V.19–20. The same tale appears in the pseudo-Aristotle, *De
Mirabilibus Auscultationibus*, in *Opera*, ed. Bekker (Berlin, 1831), II, 836.

Odysseus with his single ship to the island of Circe. After she frees Odysseus and his companions and the dreaded rocks are avoided, the storms crash again, destroying all but the hero, who is carried after nine days to Ogygia "where dwelt Calypso of the braided hair." His release from this island at the request of the gods and his long and stormy voyage on the raft of his own making to the kingdom of Alcinous end the mighty story that he relates to the king and his white-armed wife, Arete. This is the way the topic begins: The hero crosses watery wastes impelled by power beyond his will; he arrives on islands or strands beyond the reach of the real; and there he finds a perfection of soul that makes actuality, when he returns to it, endurable. This is the ancient understanding of the travails of Odysseus, and it was not unknown to the Elizabethans. It seems possible to me that the story of Odysseus and its moral meaning may have colored for them the dramatic procedure of *The Tempest*.

To an Elizabethan who had the Greek and the stomach for the task, a number of commentaries explained the meaning that Homer hid beneath the literal fiction of Odysseus' wanderings in the islands. Armed with the popular notion that noble doctrine should be sugared with story, the Elizabethan might come to the labor of reading the Homeric commentaries of Heraclitus, Eustathius, Porphyrius, and the pseudo-Plutarch with more interest than these ancient exegetes can beget in us. The *De Vita et Poesi Homeri* of the pseudo-Plutarch argues that the Homeric poems are philosophical accounts of the physical nature of the world as well as ethical expositions of the vices and virtues.[7] Heraclitus demands that both epics be read as allegories. Only the ignorant, says he, who do not understand the language of allegory, who are incapable of recognizing truth, and who reject analogical interpretation, cling to the appearances of fiction. As a consequence, these

---

[7] Plutarch, *Opera*, ed. Dübner (Paris, 1875), V, 104.

ignoramuses are deaf to the voice of philosophy; but the wise, who hear the voice, go forward, accepting the *Iliad* and the *Odyssey* as guides to holy truth.[8] Some samples of this truth are apropos.

"All of the wanderings of Odysseus," writes Heraclitus, "if one regards them closely are great allegories. Homer invented this man in order to expound the nature of virtue and to serve the teaching of wisdom, because he detests the manifold vices that consume men." [9] The lotus is, consequently, a symbolic plant; it represents those pleasures and delights that cause men to forget their true home. The fact that Odysseus passes close to slaves of exotic and barbarian pleasures and is not tempted makes a shrewd moral point.[10] His temperance is further illustrated when he refuses, though starving, to eat the cattle of Helios. The temptations of Circe's island are obvious, but the reader must also understand that Hermes, who aids Odysseus in subduing the goddess, is a symbol, not a god in presence. Hermes is reason and dwells in Odysseus. When they seem to be talking, it is Odysseus reflecting or conversing with himself. The magic moly is the sign of reason; hence, it has black roots to represent the hard first steps in knowledge, but it terminates in a bright flower.[11] Such is the pagan reading; now we can continue this knotty explanation of Odysseus' wanderings by turning to Bishop Eustathius for the Christian message.

The island goddess Calypso, says Eustathius, is literally "the fair goddess," but she is also two abstract ideas. She is the body that confines the soul; and Odysseus, aided by Hermes-Reason, gives her up in order to return to Penelope, or Phi-

[8] *Quaestiones Homericae,* ed. Oelmann (Leipzig, 1910), p. 4.
[9] *Ibid.,* pp. 91–92.
[10] *Ibid.,* pp. 94–95.
[11] *Ibid.,* pp. 96–97; Alcinous is equated with the Epicurean philosophy; and hence, his kingdom has no charm for the Platonist Odysseus. Cf. pp. 105–106.

losophy. There is a second meaning. Calypso is the child (the thought) of Atlas, so she is clearly the science of astronomy and astrology. Odysseus, we know from other places in the epic, was well versed in starlore; but after Calypso has furthered his education in this science, he, realizing that it is only a minor branch of learning, returns to his wife, whose daily weaving and unweaving of her web shows that she is Philosophy.[12] So Eustathius finds moral readings here and in other episodes in the epic to support his conviction that the poem is a treatise on the education of men.[13]

There is no question that the sixteenth century saw these moral meanings in the stormblown ventures not only of Odysseus but also of his Latin reflection, Aeneas. When Chapman inscribed his translation of the *Odyssey* to the Earl of Somerset, he stated that a moral reading of the poem was a requirement. The *Iliad*, he writes, begins with the word "wrath," the *Odyssey* with "man"; the latter poem is, consequently, superior in moral instruction.

> In one, Predominant Perturbation; in the other, overruling Wisedome; in one, the Bodie's fervour and fashion of outward Fortitude to all possible height of Heroicall Action; in the other, the Mind's inward, constant and unconquerd Empire, unbroken, unaltered with any most insolent and tyrannous infliction. . . . Nor is this all-comprising Poesie phantastique, or meere fictive, but the most material and doctrinall illations of Truth, both for all manly information of Manners in the yong, all prescription of Justice, and even Christian pietie, in the most grave and high-governd. To illustrate both which in both kinds, with all height of expression, the Poet creates both a Bodie and a Soule in them—wherein, if the Bodie (being the letter, or historie) seemes fictive and beyond Possibilitie to bring into Act, the sence then and Allegorie (which is the Soule) is to be

---

[12] *Commentarii ad Homeri Odysseam* (Leipzig, 1825), I, 16–17
[13] *Ibid.*, II.4–5; Odysseus listens to the sirens because it is good for a philosopher to hear the poets.

sought—which intends a more eminent expressure of Vertue, for her lovelinesse, and of Vice, for her uglinesse, in their severall effects, going beyond the life than any Art within life can possibly delineate. Why then is Fiction to this end so hatefull to our true Ignorants? [14]

Heraclitus comes to life in the last sentence, but the tone of the whole passage implies that he was never really dead.

If Odysseus' journeys to the storm-set islands were allegories of the moral testing and education of men, we can, perhaps, assume that the voyage of Prospero and that of his enemies might have the same intent. We must notice at the start that the islands of the Greek epic and that of *The Tempest* are not exactly alike. The Greek islands are fantastic garden spots, direct mirrorings of the Isles of the Blest; they are not unlike the one that Diodorus' sailors found in the broad ocean. The Renaissance had not forgotten the Homeric islands, and we have only to turn to Ronsard's poem on Calypso to recapture their charm.

> Terre grasse et fertille,
> Lieu que les Dieux avoient pour eux esleu,
> Pour tes forests autrefois tu m'as pleu,
> Pour tes jardins, pour tes belles fonteines,
> Et pour tes bords bien esmailles d'areines.[15]

Prospero's island, like Perdita's Arcadia, suffers intrusions from reality. In most instances we see the island through the eyes of Caliban, the only animal survivor now that its Circe (Sycorax) is dead. Through these banal eyes, we see that the island has fresh springs, brine pits, barren and fertile places, bogs, fens, flats. We learn through other eyes that there are desolate spots where there is "neither bush nor shrub." But it also has grassplots, "lush and lusty"; it produces berries,

[14] Homer, Chapman transl., ed. Nicoll (New York, 1956), II, 4–5.
[15] *Œuvres,* ed. Vaganay (Paris, 1924), IV, 218.

pignuts, crabapples, filberts, and limes. It is, however, no
thornless Eden, for—once again Caliban tells us—it has
"toothed briars, sharp furzes, pricking goss, and thorns."

When Prospero set foot on the island, it was not unlike
Circe's Aeaea, not honored "with a human shape." The blue-
eyed witch Sycorax (a true half-sister of the daughter of
Helios), whose antiquity is attested by her ability to "control
the moon," ruled the island with "earthy and abhorred com-
mands." The child of this earthy enchantress is naturally
earthy, an animal bent on animal pleasures, filled with animal
desires, haunted by animal fears. Odysseus broke the spell of
Circe; but Prospero, although he can undo the black magic of
Sycorax, is unable to raise Caliban to human estate. The island
has also some colors of Ogygia; but of Calypso, who sang with
sweet voice while she wove on her loom with a golden shuttle,
only the music and the knowledge are left. It is this music that
Ferdinand hears—the singing of the invisible Ariel—before
he sees Miranda, and so he speaks as Odysseus may have
spoken when, fresh from Hell and sea-peril, he saw the hu-
mane goddess "who took him in and treated him kindly."

> Most sure, the goddess
> On whom these airs attend. Vouchsafe my prayer
> May know if you remain upon this island,
> And that you will some good instruction give
> How I may bear me here.[16]

The music that diabolic magic imprisoned in a tree, heavenly
magic released, and now it has charms even for beast-hearted
men. "The isle is full of noises," says Caliban, "sound, and
sweet airs, that give delight and hurt not." [17] The two clowns,
made beasts by wine, "lifted up their noses/ As they smelt
music." [18] If in these respects the island has recollections of

[16] I.ii.420–25.
[17] III.ii.144–45.
[18] IV.i.177–78.

Ogygia, there are reminders of Calypso in both Prospero and Miranda: her wisdom in the father, her beauty in the girl. In Miranda there is a further quality of the Greek woman—the pity that only a goddess can have for men. "For I have a proper mind," says Calypso as she walks to the beach with Odysseus, "and my heart is not iron but as pitiful as yours." [19]

Prospero's island also brings to mind other literary islands of later date. Honorius, who wrote two thousand years after Homer, tells about the Island Perdita, charming, fertile, unknown to men. "Once you have found it by chance, if you leave it, you will never find it again." [20] This island like all lost islands—Atlantis, the island of the sybil who prophesied the birth of Christ, the islands of Delos unknown before the Flood—haunted the imagination of many generations. Sir John Mandeville knew many of these islands, and we can follow his sail from Crues to Lamary to Silha to the Isle of Bragman. [21] But the most popular legend which brought together saints, men of sin, and visions, is the story of Brendan, the Irish Odysseus, who found Island Perdita (lost by Honorius), the Island of Sheep (where the kine of the Sun are remembered), and the "Paradisus Avium" (where a great white tree was filled with Ariels). [22] He who has visited the islands of antiquity and of the Middle Ages has no difficulty in finding his way to those of the Renaissance.

When we visit the islands of the sixteenth century writers of romances, we sometimes find that they are also inhabited

[19] V.190–91.

[20] *De Imago Mundi* (PL, CLXXII, 132–33).

[21] *The Travels*, ed. Pollard (London, 1915), pp. 108–15, 119–39, 192–98.

[22] *The Anglo-Norman Voyage of St. Brendan by Benedeit*, ed. Waters (Oxford, 1928), pp. 23, 28–29; see also *St. Brandan*, ed. Wright (London, 1844); *Sanct Brandan*, ed. Schröder (Erlangen, 1871); *Les voyages merveilleux de Saint Brandan*, ed. Francisque-Michel (Paris, 1878); *Die altfranzosische prosaübersetzung von Brendans Meerfahrt*, ed. Wahlund (Upsala, 1900); *An old Italian version of the Navigatio Sancti Brendani*, ed. Waters (Oxford, 1931).

by women who stand in the ranks of magic between Sycorax
and Circe. Ariosto's Alcina and Tasso's Armida are superb
island enchantresses; but a better link between the experiences
of Odysseus and Prospero is supplied by Francesco Bello's
Mambrino, who sailed from France in fair weather and was
overtaken by storm.

> Con sì gran furia allor mugghiava il mare,
> Che se il patron commanda non è inteso;
> Più non si può col timon governare,
> Col qual gran pezzo già s'era difeso
> Il cìel altro non fa che balenare;
> De la tempesta ognor duplica il peso,
> E sopra il legno in modo balzan l'onde,
> Che ognun in sè medesimo si confonde.[23]

Flung into the sea, Mambrino swims to the Isle of Monte Fag-
gio, a place charming in palace and gardens and ruled by Car-
andina, who is described as a woman more gifted in magic
than Zoroaster, Circe, and Medea. The hero and his companion, bewitched by her arts, live a luxurious life until they
are reminded of their forgotten duties by a divine vision. This
island miracle is suggestive but the experiences of Ariosto's
Ruggiero are even more helpful for the moral interpretation
of *The Tempest*.

The sea storm during which Ruggiero's conversion begins
was mentioned in the last century as Shakespeare's literary
model. This artistic relationship is probably untrue, but the
career of the hero after the storm may enable us to add meaning to Shakespeare's play. Until he was swept into the sea,
Ruggiero was a pagan; but as he swims, he remembers his un-
fulfilled vows and the loss of time. It occurs to him that he is
being baptized in bitter salt water because he refused the
sweet water of Christ's mercy. He makes a vow. By miracle,

[23] *Mambriano,* ed. Rua (Turin, 1926), I, 8.

"miracol fu," his swimming becomes easier and, like Prospero, he arrives at a providential island: "Nel solitario scoglio uscì Ruggiero, / Come all' alta Bontà divina piacque." Climbing a hill of juniper, laurel, myrtle, palm, and clear springs, he comes to the hermit's cell at the summit. Here the holy man greets him with the words that blind Saul heard on the Damascus road; [24] and Ruggiero's penitence, conversion, and religious education begin. These qualities of vision, conversion, penitence, and education—the archetypal influence of Patmos and the exiled St. John cannot be avoided—[25] attach themselves to the Christian island and may be transferred to the island that Shakespeare made in the Middle Sea.

The island of *The Tempest* is one in which pagan magic has been replaced by Christian miracle, and the maker of these miracles is a man who resembles to some degree an island saint. When we first encounter Prospero, he is "master of a full poor cell," not of the splendid palace surrounded by vast gardens of rare plants that once he may have possessed. The hermit who converted and instructed Ruggiero set fruit-bearing palms about his hut; and Prospero, equally modest, defends "this mouth o' the cell" with a grove of lime trees. In this

---

[24] *Orlando Furioso*, ed. Caretti (Milan-Naples, 1954), pp. 1061–64.

[25] Though Erasmus had questioned whether or not St. John the Apostle was also the writer of the Book of The Revelation and was followed in this position by Sebastian Castellio, who called him "Joannes Theologus" as did some of the Fathers (see his *Biblia* [Basel, 1565], p. 486), the post-Trent Vulgate and the Protestant scholars thought of the two Johns as one man. The nature of their arguments is summed up by Beza in the prolegomena to the Apocalypse in the *Biblia* (Hanover, 1602). The usual legend read that John was exiled to Patmos by Diocletian and there not only preached the faith but had his vision: see J. Camerarius, *Historia Jesu Christi . . . Itemque de Apostolis* (Leipzig, 1581), p. 124; and Surius, *De Probatis Sanctorum Historiis* (Cologne, 1575), VI, 1013. The notion of an island saint is not too uncommon. In *Le Roman en Prose de Tristan* (ed. Löseth [Paris, 1890]), Sadoc is thrown overboard during a storm and swims to some rocks where he is saved by an eremite and where he lives for three years (pp. 4–5).

place, the banished Duke lives and meditates; there are even periods when he shuts himself off, like an anchorite, from all human conversation. But this is credible because Prospero was something of an eremite before his scheming, worldly brother deprived him of the dukedom:

> I thus neglecting worldly ends, all dedicate
> To closeness, and the bettering of my mind.[26]

"Closeness" is a word that explains the Prospero whom we know; he is an aloof man, who stands apart or rises above (as if he were a playwright) the other characters in the drama that his secret powers have made.

On Shakespeare's lost island, Prospero was first his daughter's schoolmaster; it is here that she had her only education.

> Here in this island we arrived, and here
> Have I, thy schoolmaster, made thee more profit
> Than other princess can, that have more time
> For vainer hours, and tutors not so careful.[27]

The admirable and sympathetic Miranda has attempted, in turn, to teach Caliban the Italian language; but her lessons have been partially wasted, because, like so many poor linguists, the man-brute has only an ear for profanity. Prospero, too, has tried unsuccessfully to give lessons to the son of Sycorax. But while he was teaching others, Prospero taught himself, learning, first, about his own nature and, next, how to predict and control his inner weather. In this control, he surpasses his old foe Alonso, who is "cloudy" over the loss of Ferdinand until he, too, is educated by the man he helped to depose. There are occasions when the lightning still flashes in the sky of Prospero's anger, but he never inflicts, as he was quite able to do, another tempest on his storm-driven enemies.

[26] I.ii.89–90
[27] I.ii.171–74.

> Though with their high wrongs I am stuck to th' quick,
> Yet, with my nobler reason 'gainst my fury
> Do I take part. The rarer action is
> In virtue than in vengeance. They being penitent,
> The sole drift of my purpose doth extend
> Not a frown further.[28]

Though education is preliminary to conversion, it is only a preparative requirement, and Prospero, whose real change of heart may have begun when his raft reached the island, knows about that process, too.

Before the hapless wedding party arrived on the island—we should notice the difference between Prospero and Alonso as matchmakers—Prospero tried to dissuade Caliban from the worship of Setebos; but it is useless to attempt the conversion of those who are guided by the lowest levels of the soul.

> A devil, a born devil, on whose nature
> Nurture can never stick; on whom my pains,
> Humanely taken, all, all lost, quite lost,
> And as with age his body uglier grows,
> So his mind cankers.[29]

With the newcomers his task is easier, because they are supposedly Christians from a Christian land. Actually, only Gonzalo is a real Christian, who testifies to his faith on all occasions. He joins the King in prayers; he believes in "the miracle" of preservation; he comforts the suffering King; he plans, to the amusement of the scoffers, a Christian state; he trusts heaven; he calls on "the name of something holy"; he requests the guidance of "some heavenly power"; he asks the gods "to look down"; and his last speech in the play is "Be it so, Amen." There is plain piety in almost every word he utters, and everything he does explains his earlier act of dangerous charity to Prospero and the infant Miranda. Gonzalo has grace enough

[28] V.i.25–30.
[29] IV.i.188–92.

for sainthood, but he is associated with men whose need for spiritual rehabilitation is obvious.

The clowns, Trinculo and Stephano, are almost too stupid for salvation. They will run down the primrose path to the eternal bonfire, forever boisterous, forever drunk, forever singing the libertine's song: "Flout 'em and scout 'em, and scout 'em and flout 'em; / Thought is free!" Paired with them are the freethinking and worldly cynics, Sebastian and Antonio. The atheism of Antonio is made clear when he is asked, after proposing murder, about the state of his conscience.

> But I feel not
> This deity in my bosom. Twenty consciences
> That stand 'twixt me and Milan, candied be they,
> And melt ere they molest.[30]

It is only by a kind of angelic intervention through the miracle of music that the crime of murder is avoided. Conscience finally comes to Antonio, as it does to the other "men of sin," and it comes, as we might expect, because of the nature of islands, through a vision. In this case the vision is that of a banquet served by mysterious ministers. With the appearance of these harmonious servants, the doubting sinners begin to believe. Religious words fill the mouth of Alonso; the sceptical Sebastian and Antonio, smitten dumb by the spectacle, find their tongues with the word "believe." Gonzalo, true to his pious nature, thinks that he sees the realization of his Christian community, that he has arrived on Mandeville's Island of Bragman.

> For certes these are people of the island—
> Who, though they are of monstrous shape, yet note,
> Their manners are more gentle-kind than of
> Our human generation you shall find
> Many, nay, almost any.[31]

[30] II.i.277–80
[31] III.iii.30–34.

Then, as speculation gives way to hunger, Ariel appears in the form of a harpy and the banquet vanishes like a dream.

To understand Ariel's appearance as a harpy and the nature of the banquet, we must go, as Shakespearean annotators have gone, to the third book of the *Aeneid;* but we must apply the speech of Celaeno, as it has not been applied, to the lecture of Ariel. "I, the eldest of the Furies," says the harpy Celaeno, "reveal it to you." "Vobis Furiarum ego maxima pando."[32] Harpies are Furies; they both bring divine vengeance. Valerius Flaccus affirms the testimony of Vergil when he writes that the harpies thrust the earned anger of the gods on men.[33] But harpies are more than this. Hesiod says that they are "beautiful creatures of the wind and air";[34] whereas Homer, who does not mention their beauty, identifies them with "the spirits of the storm." In the fourteenth book of the *Odyssey,* Eumaeus gives us a key text: "νῦν δέ μιν ἀκλεῶς ἅρέπυιαι ἀνηρείψαντο" (371). So Ariel, the beautiful spirit of the air, who made the storm of the first scene, is also a Harpy-Fury who troubles the minds of the three sinners. "Holy" Gonzalo, who observes the change in the countenance and manner of the three, cannot withhold his observation: "Their great guilt . . . 'gins to bite the spirits." The effect of the lecture of Conscience is greater than biting; Antonio and Sebastian, who thought they had the power in pocket, twist in its mighty grasp.

> Thou art pinched for't now Sebastian. Flesh and blood,
> You brother mine, that entertained ambition,
> Expelled remorse and nature, who, with Sebastian—
> Whose inward pinches therefore are most strong—
> Would here have killed your King.[35]

[32] III.252.
[33] IV.428–61.
[34] *Theogonia* 265.
[35] V.i.74–78.

Faithful to tradition, the island of education, saints, and visions, is also a place of repentance and conversion; but the visions do not end with one that produces a change of heart.

For the troth-plight of his daughter and Ferdinand, Prospero makes a pleasant, yet visionary, masque of spirits who are borrowed, except for the realistic British harvestmen, from the mythological records. To point the difference between the two kinds of visions, Shakespeare makes Ferdinand say in the middle of the second:

> This is a most majestic vision, and
> Harmonious charmingly. May I be bold
> To think these spirits? [36]

Prospero admits that they are spirits, whom he has called forth to act his "present fancies." His fancies are worth noticing because they reveal the ultimate Shakespearean resolution of the fate of man. The theme of the masque is fertility in marriage, a theme annotated for us by Ferdinand's vow of prenuptial chastity. Such a condition is impossible for Caliban, the rapist, and his new-found human gods; they accept propagation, but sacraments are not for them. Because their sort of love is excluded from the idealism of the island, Venus and her son are omitted from Prospero's cast of characters. Iris informs us that the heroine of *Venus and Adonis* has departed with her son for Paphos.

> Here thought they to have done
> Some wanton charm upon this man and maid,
> Whose vows are, that no bed-right shall be paid
> Till Hymen's torch be lighted.[37]

So the goddess of marriage, Juno, and the goddess of fertility, Ceres, are the principal actors in this blessed vision, which concludes with the symbolic August scene of harvest and gar-

[36] IV.i.118–20.
[37] IV.i.94–97.

ner. The masque, it must be noticed, is structurally bound to the play through the character of Iris, who, in her mythological guises, is the messenger of the goddesses, a virgin,[38] and, better still, sister to the Harpies.[39] It is a part that Ariel could and did play with great skill.

The masque is one of the dramatic centers of the play, and in its simple theme of immortality through generation we have again the doctrine that lighted most of Shakespeare's days on earth. Though I shall return to this, I want first—now that the island is for the moment so plainly a place of vision—to ponder the secondary emphasis in this play, as in previous ones, on the world of vision and dream. This emphasis is finely stated when Prospero speaks his famous lines concluding the revels.

> These our actors,
> As I foretold you, were all spirits, and
> Are melted into air, into thin air;
> And like the baseless fabric of this vision,
> The cloud-capped towers, the gorgeous palaces,
> The solemn temples, the great globe itself,
> Yea all which it inherit, shall dissolve,
> And like this insubstantial pageant faded
> Leave not a rack behind. We are such stuff
> As dreams are made on; and our little life
> Is rounded with a sleep.[40]

Within the boundaries of this utterance, Shakespeare accepts the philosophy of mortal existence against which the dark plays protest. Because once again he accepts the promise of the masque, the benediction of Juno and the rewards of Ceres, he can also accept the necessary condition that men and their works, as he knew them, are only visions and will dissolve like summer clouds. If the world that each man has made is a

[38] Theocritus, *Eidyllion* XVII.134; Vergil, *Aeneid* V.610.
[39] Hesiod, *op. cit.*, 266, 780.
[40] IV.i.146-57.

vision, then life as each man possesses it is a dream. To expound this idea, sturdy tradition aids us mortals, who like
Christopher Sly have only "an after-dinner's sleep" between
youth and age, to comprehend the topics that Prospero's aria
reveals.

First, it is interesting to scrutinize the dream metaphors
in *The Tempest*. Miranda, mindful of her childhood, says
that it was "rather like a dream than an assurance"; and Ferdinand, under the spell of both the girl and her father, finds his
"spirits" all bound up "as in a dream." The Boatswain, no
philosopher, thinks of dreams when he searches his mind for a
figure to express the rapid course of time: "On a trice, so please
you, / Even in a dream, were we divided from them." Even
Caliban, earth and filth that he is, brings dream and music together to describe the island:

> and then, in dreaming,
> The clouds methought would open, and show riches
> Ready to drop upon me, that when I waked
> I cried to dream again.[41]

Throughout Shakespeare's plays—and the custom is not pe-
culiar to him alone—*dream* is a metaphor of *life*, as if it were
difficult to separate the life of dreams from conscious existence.

The origin of this imagistic comparison begins, I suppose,
with human time. The Gentile hero, Job, whose poet almost
got him canonized, says of the lot of man: "He shall fly away
as a dream, and shall not be found: yea, he shall be chased
away as a vision of night." [42] Across the lines of Jehovah's ter-
ritory were less consecrated poets who would agree. For Pindar, "man is a shadow's dream." [43] and Sophocles describes
men in the *Ajax* as "dreams or shadows." [44] Aristophanes sum-

[41] III.ii.149–52.
[42] Job 20:8.
[43] *Pyth.*8.95–96.
[44] 126.

mons men, who "pass like dreams of sorrow," to listen to the singing of the *Birds*.[45] The Middle Ages improved on these images of the Greeks and the Romans to such an extent that its child and reformer, the optimistic Petrarch, could complain about the dreamlike quality of existence. He writes to Giacomo Colonna that life is a dream or shifting fancy. "Illa relegenti, totam mihi vitam meam, nihil videri aliud quam leve somnium, fugacissimumque phantasma." [46] It is interesting that this passage comes from a letter on the subject of the vanished glories of Rome, a city that had long been the subject of meditations on the transitoriness of mortal achievement.

Prospero's reverie about "cloud-capped towers," "gorgeous palaces," and "solemn temples" is a metropolitan intrusion into the primitive island realm. The former duke remembers the land across the waters, the cities of Carthage or of the Italian mainland. "The great globe itself" may be a playful allusion to the theater on the Bankside, and the whole speech may wave away the theatrical world of painted cloth and tinsel; but this is not a speech to father laughter or even smiles, for its conclusion is grave and its total import is serious. Man passes and so does what he makes. "My weakness . . . my old brain . . . my infirmity . . . my beating mind." The mind of the Renaissance reader is directed by Prospero's words not to the island or to England, but to Rome, the ruined imperial city, where man had pondered for many generations on the impermanence of life and art.[47]

---

[45] 686–87.

[46] *Opera* (Basel, 1554), p. 667.

[47] There was present in the imperial Romans, who looked on the ruins of Athens ("vacuae Athenae," says Horace in *Epistulae* II.2.81), a modest sense of personal unworthiness and the melting glory of man; nonetheless, they were equally possessed by a reassurance that man's material remainders contain and preserve him. An anonymous late Latin poet might write a poignant epitaph of the great city in which the autumnal music of the Middle Ages is audible (*Anthologia Latina,* ed. Riese [Leipzig, 1922], I, 267), yet the view of the mighty city stirred emotions far more deep.

The Middle Ages had two opinions about the fallen towers, palaces, and temples of Rome. One was that the material ruin that lay about the sojourner in the city was full evidence of its spiritual ruin.[48] Alcuin saw in the broken stones the great symbol of the foolishness of human glory. "Roma, caput mundi, mundi decus, aurea Roma / Hunc remanet tantum saeva ruina tibi." [49] To a second group, of which Hildebert of Lavardin [50] is a good representative, there are two Romes: the ruined center of paganism and the splendid capital city of the Christian world. For Dante the ruins are venerable; [51] and though Petrarch reads their lesson, he hopes to see splendor reborn from the debris that by itself filled him with adoration.[52] Some of the humanists agreed with the mediaeval sermons on the ruins, but most of them saw in the fallen arches and columns the fragility of all human effort. Poggio finds dignity and greatness in the

---

Propertius escapes from the obdurate Cynthia to *doctae Athenae* to purge himself of foul passions by seeing those places in which were stored recollections of noble emotions and of men healed of error (III.21.25–30). Cicero describes a walk among its ruins that, he says, made the persons of Sophocles, Plato, and Epicurus more vivid to him than their books (*De Finibus* V.1–6). Two centuries later, Dio Chrysostom pondered the ruined land, but he was certain that the ruins make manifest the greatness of Greece (*Orationes* VII.38–39) for the ruins are far more gracious than the living cities (XXXI.160).

[48] "Versus Romae," in *Poetae Latini Aevi Carolini*, ed. Traube (Berlin, 1896), III, 555–56. This poem is discussed by A. Graf, *Roma nella Memoria e nelle Immaginazioni del Medio Evo* (Turin, 1882), I, 46–47. This pioneer work has been somewhat superseded by Schneider, *Rom und Romedanke im Mittelalter* (Munich, 1926), but it is still the best for literary texts.

[49] *Opera*, ed. Dümmler (Berlin, 1891), I, 230.

[50] B. Haureau, *Notices et Extraits des Quelques Manuscrits Latins de la Bibliothèque Nationale* (Paris, 1890–1893), pp. 330–36. The theme appears in Sedulius Scottus, *Carmina*, ed. Traube, *PLAC* (Berlin, 1896) III, 170–76; in a tenth-century poem in Novati, *L'Influsso del Pensiero Latino* (Milan, 1899), pp. 172–74; and in Neckham, *De Laudibus Divinae Sapientiae*, ed. Wright (London, 1863), p. 445.

[51] There have been numerous studies of Dante's attitude; for the most recent, see Davis, *Dante and the Idea of Rome* (Oxford, 1957).

[52] *Opera* (Basel, 1554), pp. 731, 1169.

ruin—"sola ruina praeteritam dignitatem ac magnitudinem
ostentantem"—but he is also moved by them to speculate on
the power of Fortuna, a non-Christian lady.[53] Traversari reads
them as torn documents, to the same end,[54] and Urceus wanders through the decaying city to write an epigram on man's
fate.

> Roma fuit periere patres periere quirites
> Restat deserto sola ruina solo
> Quaeque tamen restat doctorum poena virorum
> Hic labor; hic non sunt praemia: nulla quies.[55]

The poets of the vernacular follow the same themes, and
the ruins, as symbols of man's tender hold on life and the
world, haunt such lyrics as Castiglione's "Superbi colli, e voi
sacre ruine," and Guidicconi's "Degna nutrice de le chiare
genti." The sixteenth-century Italian poet, Bernardino Baldi,
who wrote a sonnet sequence on Rome, likewise saw in the
wreckage about him the eternal lesson of the "insubstantial
pageant faded." A fragment of his poem on the Coliseum is
sample enough of the mode and mood.

> Da questo campo abbandonato ed ermo,
> Cui fanno alte ruine ampia corona,
> Prender può esempio ogni mortal persona
> Come contro l'eta perda ogni schermo.
> O fugaci bellezze, o mondo infermo,
> O nostra fama che sì breve suona,
> Ben sei nubilo ciel che splende e tuona
> Tutto in un punto, e nulla è 'n te di fermo.[56]

Although the Italian poets lamented the ruins of Rome, they
also lived on them. The distance was not great enough for real

---

[53] *De Fortunae . . . Romae et de Ruina Eiusdem*, in De Sallengre, *Novus
Thesaurus* (Hague, 1716), I, 502.

[54] Graf, *op. cit.*, I, 52.

[55] *Silvae* (Venice, 1506), Li verso.

[56] *Versi e Prose*, ed. Ugolini and Polidori (Florence, 1859), p. 258.

nostalgia. It was a French poet, Du Bellay, who built these broken stones into a giant European symbol of evanescence.

In the sonnets of *Les Antiquitez* and in the Latin "Romae Descriptio," Du Bellay proclaimed his love of the past and told his contemporaries what their future contained. These sonnets are separate and numbered, but they seem like stanzas in a long poem on the inconstant nature of life. In some the poet imitates Latin and Italian predecessors; in others he makes poetic excursions into history; but there is always the implication of decay, the sense of impermanence. Rome may seem to be renewing herself, but we may look at her broken body for the mortal lesson (XXVII). She resists time, but time will have her in the end (VII). Only the flowing Tiber is unchanged because only change endures in a world of change (III). Consolation is to be found, but it is the consolation of mutability.

> Ainsi quand du grand Tout le fuite retournée,
> Ou trentesix mil' ans ont sa course bornée,
> Rompra des elemens le naturel accord,
> Les semences qui sont meres de toutes choses,
> Retourneront encor' a leur premier discord,
> Au ventre du Chaos eternellement closes. (XXI)

When Prospero talks about ruined towers, temples, and palaces, he may be speaking in general terms, but a travelled Jacobean who listened to him would certainly think of the waste of Imperial Rome. No dream was ever greater than this imperial one; no dream ever passed more sadly and left grander evidence of its passing. The text for Prospero's speech was provided by *Lear:* "Oh ruined piece of nature; this great world / Shall so wear out to naught." But a world and a life that are dreams is a common enough theme for Shakespeare. The fate of the dreamer is a great topic in all the tragedies, whose heroes, dreams in themselves, awaken from dreams unable to endure the reality in which they find themselves. The island is where they were born, and when they cross to the mainland, they learn that they "are the stuff that dreams are made on." With *The Tempest* Shakespeare returns to his old belief in the continuity of man—the heroes of the tragedies, even Lear, die childless. The doctrine is a simple one. Life will go on; only the individual passes. This is the "brave new world."

CHAPTER SIX

George Herbert

"The Rose"

The poetry of George Herbert, like that of Henry Vaughan, is mainly supported by the metaphoric tradition of the Bible and the Liturgy. For this reason its images should not be difficult for the reader who has lived in a Christian community. But although the allusions are not necessarily clear, Herbert does not really intend to trap us. He simply assumes that as Christians we have Christian knowledge. When he put aside his vast classical learning (plain enough in his Latin and Greek verse), when he abandoned the "dark style" and burned his papers, he almost dismissed the searcher for hidden symbolism from his company:

> Must all be vail'd, while he that reades, divines,
> Catching the sense at two removes.

In spite of Herbert's conscious pursuit of plainness and lucidity, there are occasions when a knowledge of the traditions, known to him but now strange to us, brushes away difficulty, or, as in the case of "The Rose," expounds the classical and Christian symbols of the poem and enhances its meaning.

The most familiar rose poem of the seventeenth century is not that of Herbert, but Herrick's revision of Ausonius' "Collige rosas," which gathers into its four stanzas the full sadness of transitoriness as it is expressed by the fragility of flowers, the rising and setting of the suns, and the winged departure of youth. These definitions of the rose are traditional, and Herrick does little more than turn their classical past into an English present. The same topic returns with somewhat more suavity and a finer meaning in Waller's "Go, Lovely Rose"; but this poem, too, pleasant as it is, maintains the pagan and hence worldly transcription of the flower as a sign of human hopelessness and helplessness. It is Herbert's poem, conscious of the worldly tradition, that brings in the Christian meanings of the flower and permits the pagan rose to be contrasted with the spiritual one. The text of the poem should now lie before us.

> Presse me not to take more pleasure
>   In this world of sugred lies,
> And to use a larger measure
>   Then my strict, yet welcome size.
>
> First, there is no pleasure here:
>   Colour'd griefs indeed there are,
> Blushing woes, that look as cleare
>   As if they could beautie spare.
>
> Or if such deceits there be,
>   Such delights I meant to say;
> There are no such things to me
>   Who have pass'd my right away.
>
> But I will not much oppose
>   Unto what you now advise:

Onely take this gentle rose,
    And therein my answer lies.

What is fairer then a rose?
    What is sweeter? yet it purgeth.
Purgings enmitie disclose,
    Enmities forbearance urgeth.

If then all that worldlings prize
    Be contracted to a rose;
Sweetly there indeed it lies,
    But it biteth in the close.

So this flower doth judge and sentence
    Worldly joyes to be a scourge:
For they all produce repentance,
    And repentance is a purge.

But I health, not physick choose:
    Onely though I you oppose,
Say that fairly I refuse,
    For my answer is a rose.

It is possible that the meaning of this poem would be reasonably clear to someone who did not know the symbolic history of the rose. An uninformed reader would discover that the first four stanzas summarize the advice given the poet by a child of the world; whereas the latter four stanzas are the poet's replies based on the lesson of the rose. "Onely take this gentle rose,/ And therein my answer lies." The first four stanzas do not seem to be about the rose, but it is quite plain that the flower, symbolically unfolded petal by petal in the second part of the poem, is substantially present in the first. The opening lines, "Presse me not to take more pleasure/ In this world of sugred lies" has two literal meanings. The man of the world has urged Herbert to take more pleasure in material things, but the rose is also pressed to make an electuary called "sugar of roses." When we notice this second meaning,

we also see that the rose as well as the poet is a speaker in the
first stanzas, and we shall learn from tradition that the lecture
on the rose in the second part is delivered by a man and a rose.
The double nature of the rose is the subject of continuous
poetic comment. The flower is fair and sweet, but it purges.
The purge discloses the cause of the malady and indicates
where temperance is required. Or we can read this in another
fashion. Lying in the hand, the rose is sweet; close the fist on
it and discover its thorns. This is the life of the world, sweet
in the opening but bitter in the close, leading to final purgation
or repentance, to eventual judgment and sentence. Since the
poet does not wish to be made sick with worldliness, his
answer is "a rose." To see all of these meanings, we need only
read; but a knowledge of the metaphoric tradition of roses
makes these observations firmer and more elegant.

   The rose is a metaphor of worldliness in poems of antiquity,
and it is a worldliness that passes swiftly. The flower is bright
in the crown of Eros, as we discover when Anacreon puts it
into verse:

> Ῥόδον ὦ παῖς ὁ κυθήρης
> Στέφεται καλοὺς ἰούλους,
> Χαρίτεσσι συγχορεύων. . . . ,[1]

Yet the blossom that is here fresh will not last, for neither
roses nor love, says Philostratus, endure: "χρόνον δ' οὔτ Ἔρως
οὔτε ῥόδα οἶδεν."[2] The same theme of transient loveliness is
sorrowfully echoed by Horace, "Nimium breves/ Flores
amoenae ferre jube rosae";[3] and if we turn to Ovid, we are
reminded of the short existence of beauty in terms of the rose.

> Forma bonum fragile est; quantumque accedit ad annos
> Fit minor; et spatio carpitur ipsa suo.

[1] XLIV.9–11.
[2] *Epistolae* LV.34.
[3] *Carmina* II.3.13–14.

Nec violae semper, nec hiantia lilia florent;
Et riget amissa spina relicta rosa.[4]

The flower that stood for love, and youth, and the brevity of
both continued to bloom throughout the Middle Ages in gardens where Venus and her child conversed and lovers came
for their benediction. In such a garden grew the "grant Rosier"
of the *Romance of the Rose,* and the renowned lovers, Flor-
ance and Blanche Flor, support this symbolism when they
make rendezvous on a May morning in a place where "Roses i
ot entremellées/ Les lates i sont bien ovrées." [5]

During the Renaissance the rose poem of Anacreon was
rendered into French by Belleau,[6] and other members of the
Pléiade knew the flower in all of its symbolic transformations.
Ronsard begins one of his sonnets to Marie with the metaphor
of the rose, sacred to Venus but brief as a perfume.

Douce, belle, amoureuse et bien fleurente Rose,
Que tu es à bon droit a amours consacrée;
Ta delicate odeur hommes et Dieux recrée,
Et bref, Rose, tu es belle sur toute chose.[7]

The rose is consecrated to love and love's little moment, and
owing to a theme of Catullus [8] that Ariosto [9] enlarged, the
flower was used to celebrate a love of a virginal sort.

La vierge est semblable à la rose
Qui fleurist dans un beau jardin,
Sur l'espineux rosier declose:
Elle a la rosee au matin:
La terre, l'eau, l'air, le vent doux,
Qui leur faveur luy donnent tous.[10]

[4] *Ars* II.113–16.
[5] *Fablieux et Contes,* ed. Barbazon (Paris, 1807), IV, 360.
[6] *Œuvres* I.43.
[7] *Œuvres,* ed. Marty-Laveaux (Paris, 1924), II, 22.
[8] LXII.39–47.
[9] *Orlando Furioso* I.42–43.
[10] Baif, *Œuvres* I.295. See DuBellay, *L'Olive* XCVII.

Baif who wrote this can, in his elaborate "Les Roses," comment at length on the Ausonian theme; but it is the master, Ronsard, who condenses all the topics and sweeps the way for Herrick.

> Mignonne, allons voir si la rose
> Qui ce matin avoit declose
> Sa robe de pourpre au Soleil,
> A point perdu cette vesprée,
> Les plis de sa robe pourprée
> Et son teint au vostre pareil.
> Las! voyez comme en peu d'espace,
> Mignonne, elle a dessus la place
> Las, las, ses beautez laissé cheoir!
> O vrayment marastre Nature,
> Puis qu'une telle fleur ne dure
> Que du matin jusques au soir.
> Donc, si vous me croyez, mignonne,
> Tandis que votre âge fleuronne
> En sa plus verte nouveauté,
> Cueillez, cueillez vostre jeunesse:
> Comme à ceste fleur la vieillesse
> Fera ternir vostre beauté.[11]

So with this group of French poets, the rose retains its ancient values; it is the sign of love, of young virgins, of ephemerality, and even of death;[12] but the flower had other meanings than these.

Although the rose made the chaplet of Venus and wreathed the sickle of Chronos, the ancients also wove it into the crowns of the disciples of Bacchus. In its vinous connection the rose had a double sense, for it not only adorned the brows of the wine-god but reminded the rose-crowned revellers of the sick tribulations of the next morning. Philostratus, consequently,

[11] *Op. cit.,* III.75–76.
[12] See Ronsard, "Ode a Monsieur d'Orleans" III.163; "Sur la mort de Marie" II.22.

describes Comus with a disorderly crown of roses slipping
from his drunken head; [13] and Propertius [14] and Martial associate the flower with alcoholic relaxation. The latter poet,
sending some verses to Pliny, advises the Muse who will be
his messenger to seek out that learned and diligent man after
sundown, when roses reign with the wine-god.

> Seras tutior ibis ad lucernas:
> Haec hora est tua, cum furit Lyaeus,
> Cum regnat rosa, cum madent capilli:
> Tunc me vel rigidi legant Catones.[15]

To make all of this plainer, Ovid describes an evening when
Bacchus came with roses, with Flora and her daughters. Flora,
he tells us, is not one of those sour ones, "not one of those high
nosed ones"; "she advises us by a vision of age to use life while
it flowers; the thorn is despised after the rose falls." "Et monet
aetatis specie, dum floreat, uti;/ Contemni spinam, cecidere
rosae." [16] This is, of course, the rosy path, the world through
rose-colored glasses, "the colored griefs," "the blushing woes."
We stagger through a riot of antique roses to hear the Comus
of Milton sing "ad lucernas":

> Braid your Locks with rosy Twine
> Dropping odours, dropping Wine.
> Rigour now is gone to bed,
> And advice with scrupulous head
> Strict Age, and sour Severity,
> With their grave Saws in slumber lie.

In the sour dawn, let us hear "sour Severity."

"The Christian," Tertullian states, "will not wear a crown
of flowers." [17] This prohibition is strongly supported by

[13] *Imagines* I.2.4.
[14] III.5.21–22.
[15] X.19.19–21.
[16] *Fasti* V.335–54.
[17] *Opera*, ed. Kroymann (Vienna, 1942), II, 2, p. 156.

Clement of Alexandria when he writes about crowns: crowns of flowers and floral perfumes are not needed by Christians; the banqueting room and the scent-house are not for them. "To us, who are not only forbidden drunkenness but also the liberal use of wine, crowns of roses and violets are of no use." [18] Prudentius, master of Christian verse, places all of this before us when he commends the man who can sit to supper without a crown of flowers or perfumes.

> Hic mihi nulla rosae spolia,
> Nullus aromate fragrat odor,
> Sed liquor influit ambrosius,
> Nectareamque fidem redolet.[19]

This Christian is not unlike Prudentius' St. Eulalia, who scorned "the roses of the world" in order to win her "crown of life." [20] So after a few centuries of Christian striving, the rose as the sign of wine and riot, of Bacchus and Venus, has lost its fragrance and its beauty; it stands, as Herbert says, for the "deceits" of life. But as we notice this, we also remember the last great symbol of the *Divina Commedia*, the "candida rosa"; and we know, too, that the Mother of God is the rose without a thorn. The rose which stood for virgins and fleshly love has come to be the sign of the Virgin and heavenly love.

St. Ambrose was, I think, the first gardener to discover the rose, thornless indeed, in the landscape of an Eden through which the first human pair wandered.[21] Dracontius, who knew his classical poets well enough to describe in his "De Origine Rosarum," as Herrick does, how roses first "came red," notices the flower, too, as he follows Adam and Eve through the garden. "They walked through flowers and gardens all of roses."

---

[18] *Opera*, ed. Dindorff (Oxford, 1869), I, 267, 276.
[19] *Carmina*, ed. Dressel (Leipzig, 1860), pp. 14–15.
[20] "Spernere sucina, flare rosas, /Fulva monilia respuere," *ibid.*, pp. 332–33.
[21] *Opera*, ed. Schenkl (Vienna, 1897), I, 91.

"Ibant per flores et tota rosaria laeti." [22] St. Avitus, the first
Christian poet of France, looks at the Adamic plantation with
the eye of a flower lover.

> Lilia perlucent nullo flaccentia sole
> Nec tactus violat violas roseumque ruborem
> Servans perpetuo suffundit gratia vultu.[23]

Once the scene of man's fall is ablaze with roses, the flower,
denied to the temperate Christian as a crown, becomes a sign
of conjugal love. When Milton describes Adam and Eve em-
bracing and asleep while "the flow'ry roof/ Show'r'd Roses,
which the Morn repair'd," he is reminding us that the rose
had something to do with love on a sacramental level; [24] and
after proper consultation with St. Ambrose, the English poet
tells us that these roses are "without thorn." [25] We are thus
ready to understand why Eve, the thorn in man's flesh, is replaced by Mary, the rose on the thornless bush.

The roses that flourished in the good soil of the earthly
paradise were brought thither from Heaven, for Milton informs us that the bright floor of God's land was "Impurpl'd
with Celestial Roses." [26] Milton did not invent this fact because Prudentius, who denied crowns of earthly roses to
Christians, describes the roses of the celestial fields: "Illic
purpureis tecta rosariis/ Omnis fragrat humus." [27] A few generations later, Venantius Fortunatus wrote a poem about
Heaven and the spiritual virgins, as he calls them, wandering
through its meadows as they gather heavenly roses and violets.[28] These blessed ones wear triple crowns, feed their eyes

[22] *Carmina,* ed. Vollmer (Berlin, 1905), p. 46.
[23] *Opera,* ed. Peiper (Berlin, 1883), p. 209.
[24] *Paradise Lost* IV.772–73.
[25] *Ibid.,* 256.
[26] *Ibid.,* III.364.
[27] *Op. cit.,* p. 31.
[28] *Opera,* ed. Leo (Berlin, 1881), p. 182.

on roses and lilies, and breathe the divine perfumes. "Floribus aeternis oculos rosa lilia pascunt/ Et paradisiacus naribus intrat odor." [29] The crowns and perfumes denied to Christians on earth are eternally theirs in Heaven.

So the rose of love and virginity, covering the floor of Heaven and decorating the Garden, is also a part of the Christian botany. Dante finds it in his sky and makes it into a purer and higher sign—at its heart the bees of Christ drink nectar. The rose has spiritual grace; the rose has moral significance. The virgins of Fortunatus are not to be confused with those of that almost-persuaded pagan, Ausonius, and the spiritualized flower is to be understood as a sign of virginal modesty. In a letter to Rusticus, who should know the flower, St. Jerome describes it as a superior instructress in modesty.[30] Alexander Neckham, who probably listened to some of the secular rose songs of the *Carmina Burana*, writes a little poem about the virginity of roses and their medicinal uses, showing that the flower, like all important symbols, has many meanings simultaneously.

Et rosa, purpureo vestita rubore decenter
Vernans est horti gloria, laetus honos.
Flos est virginibus aptus, gratusque juventae,
Grataque virginei signa pudoris habet.
Virginis est speculum rosa vernans, sed cito marcens,
Et quod sit species res fugitiva docet.[31]

But blushes of virgins are no more red than the blood of martyrs, and the rose, fragile flower that it was, could accept that symbolic burden, too.

The legends of the martyrs, we remember, are garlanded with roses. St. Dorothea says to the proconsul, who gives her a choice of idolatry or death, "I am ready to suffer as you desire and I shall do it for Jesus Christ, my spouse, with whom

[29] *Ibid.*, p. 192.
[30] *Epistolae*, ed. Hilberg (Vienna, 1918), p. 120.
[31] *De Laudibus Divinae Sapientiae*, ed. Wright (London, 1863), p. 479.

I shall have eternal life. I have gathered roses, spices, and fruit in his delicious garden." [32] St. Rose of Lima, according to the *Acta Sanctorum*, gathered roses in the garden and threw them into the air as an offering to the "Great Gardener." The flowers hung in the sky, then formed themselves into a cross, the rosy-cross, symbol of their acceptability to Christ.[33] Besides the legends, the poetry of martyrology is adorned with rose metaphors. Sometimes the saints shine in their crowns of roses; [34] sometimes the rose itself awards a garland to a dying Christian.[35] The rose, pagan sign of worldly pleasure, is also the emblem of those who scorn the world and its fragile joys. The martyr, who seeks for everlasting life, becomes in this world the ephemeral rose.

The equation between roses and Christians can be further extended, for the rose represented any Christian who lived in the thorn patch of the flesh. St. Ambrose writes that the rose, once it has taken thorns, is the symbol of man surrounded by the briars of pricking care and sharp desire. St. Nilus, who esteemed this metaphor, points out that like the rose bred among thorns, the Christian virtues are born among the beguilements of life.[36] It is a short distance between this analogy and the comparison of the rose to the Virgin Mary, the rose of roses, the miraculous flower of the thorn. Adam of St. Victor intones the hymn.

> Flos de spinis spina carens,
> Flos spineta gloria,
> Nos spinetum, nos peccati
> Spina sumus cruentati
> Sed tu spina nescia.[37]

[32] *Golden Legend*, trans. Caxton (London, 1900), VII, 45.
[33] XXXVII.970.
[34] Aldhelm, *Opera*, ed. Ehwald (Berlin, 1919), p. 430.
[35] Scottus, *Opera*, ed. Traube, *PLAC* (Berlin, 1896), III, 230–31.
[36] *Capita Paraenetica* (PG, LXXIX, 1257).
[37] *Opera* (PL, CXCVI, 1502). The authority behind the figure of the thorny Eve and the central theme of these lines rest on the tradition. I cite

It stands to reason that the son of the Virgin, the flower of the tree of Jesse, is also the flower of the rose. The closed garden, says Dante, on which the light of Christ shone, brought forth the rose in which the Divine Word is made flesh. "Quivi è la rosa in che il Verbo Divino/ Carne si fece."[38] It is the crown of thorns, agent of Christ's suffering and wounds, that made firm the comparison between the greatest of the martyrs and the flower, for Christ was one who grew among the thorns of the world and knew their sharpness. To explain the relationship between blossom and God, Christian poets remade the old legend of how white roses became red. Bion had written that Venus, distracted by the death of Adonis, ran with her bare feet through the white roses and stained them with her blood.[39] Many centuries later, Walafridus Strabo wrote a poem about the "merito florum flos" and said that the white roses became red through the death of Christ, "Morte rosas tinguens."[40] From the tenth century onward, Christ is frequently described as the mystic rose. "Bloom on our vine, blessed Jesus, rose red and burning, red with the blood of passion, burning with the fire of love."[41] Thus the rose of fleeting worldly pleasure is also the Christian and his God, a God who is love, but who is also judge and sentencer. So there are two

two texts: "Eva ergo spina fuit, Maria rosa exstitit: Eva spina, vulnerando; Maria rosa, omnium affectus mulcendo. Eva spina, infigens omnibus mortem: Maria rosa redens salutiferam omnibus sortem" (Pseudo-Bernard, *De Beata Maria Virgine Sermo* [*PL*, CLXXXIV, 1020]); and "Et velut e spinis mollis rosa surgit acutis/ Nil quod laedat habens materemque obscurat honore:/ Sic Evae de stirpe sacra veniente Maria/ Virginis antiquae facinus nova Virgo piaret" (Sedulius, *Carmina*, ed. Huemer [Vienna, 1885], p. 46).

[38] *Paradiso* XXIII.70–75.

[39] I.19–22.

[40] *Carmina*, ed. Duemmler, PLAC (Berlin, 1884), II. 348–49.

[41] Pseudo- Bernard, *Vitis Mystica* (*PL*, CLXXXIV, 184, 708, 711, 715). The theme of Christ the rose is prominent in Neo-Latin verse; see Joannes Maior, "Rosa Imago Christi" and Frenzelius "Rosa Imago Christi," in C. Dornavius, *Ampitheatrum* (Hanover, 1619), I, 193–94.

flowers, an earthly one and a heavenly one; and on this doctrine of the rose, the poem of Herbert rests.

The first part of the poem is obviously about two roses: the
Christian rose and the pagan rose, Christian and Mr. Worldly.
The latter rose, the symbol of feasting, drunkenness, passionate
love, and the joys and honors of the world has, before the
poem begins, been singing a rose song to the Christian rose
that lives among the thorns. This rose has "pass'd" its "rights
away" to what the worldly rose represents because it has returned to the Garden and risen from there to adorn the floor
of Heaven. But Herbert, the Christian rose, does not care for
a furious discussion of the two states of rosehood. He will be
quiet in this counterargument and show his opponent another
rose filled with the light of Christ. The literal rose that he re-
moves from his bosom and displays is at once Christian and
Christ. This is the life of the rose. It is, indeed, a rose that contains purgation—even the ancients knew that—but it is also
in its symbolic likeness a judge and a sentencer. For Herbert,
who in imitation of the Rose has renounced the roses of the
world, all pagan meanings of the rose, though known to him,
are valueless. He will not need the purge; he knows what the
sentence will be. The sickness of the rose can never infect
him now, for he can rely on the words of St. Peter as reported
in Acts 3:16—"And his name, through faith in his name, hath
made this man strong, whom ye see and know: yea, the faith
which is in him hath given this perfect health in the presence
of you all."

CHAPTER SEVEN

John Milton

Elegy Five:
"In Adventum Veris"

The *Poemata* Joannis Miltoni Londinensis appeared as the second half of the Poems of 1645. In *The Reason of Church Government*, published four years earlier, these poems are described as trifles composed when their author was not yet twenty or while he was traveling on the Continent after his departure from the university. Although Milton's Italian friends praised them,[1] Latinists beginning with Salmasius[2] and ending with Bishop Charles Wordsworth[3] have had harsh things to say about their syntax and prosody. Modern classi-

[1] *Works* (New York, 1931–38), III, 235–36.

[2] *Responsio* (London, 1660), p. 5; see W. R. Parker, *Milton's Contemporary Reputation* (Columbus, Ohio, 1940), pp. 23, 39, 119.

[3] "Some Faults in Milton's Latin Poetry," *Classical Review*, I (1887), 46–48.

cists have been more generous,[4] but none of these poems
has been read for its literary merit or been assigned a place
in the poetic tradition. To this end I want principally to
consider the Fifth Elegy, "In Adventum Veris," written by
a boy of twenty, who probably knew Ovid's comparison of
the seasons of life to those of the year, and who will shortly
complain that his own "late spring no bud or blossom
show'th." [5]

The tradition behind this poem begins with Lucretius'
pomp when Ver comes forward with Venus while Zephyr
and Flora fill the world with color and fragrance.[6] These
figures are later joined on occasion by a shepherd poet, Bion's
Myrson or Vergil's Moeris, who rejoices that "rosy spring"
loiters by the rivers as earth dresses herself in flowers.[7] These
rivers flow swollen from the mountain snows when Vergil
gives us a glimpse of the Roman spring in the first *Georgic*.[8]
This is the land of "ver adsiduum," [9] of the two harvests,
and Vergil, to explain this double fecundity, uses the old
theology that we may hear Earth moaning for the "genitalia
semina" when Aether descends to cohabit with his broad-
breasted spouse. The union repeated in the world of creatures
reminds Vergil of the days of creation. "I could believe at
the world's first beginning/ the days that shown them
were not unlike these/ nor was the course of things." [10] The

---

[4] E. K. Rand, "Milton in Rustication," *Studies in Philology*, XIX (1922),
109-35; J. H. Hanford, "Youth of Milton," *Studies in Shakespeare, Milton, and Donne* (Ann Arbor, Mich., 1925); D. Bush, *Mythology and the
Renaissance Tradition* (New York, 1963), pp. 261-65; W. H. Semple, "The
Latin Poems of John Milton," *Bulletin of the John Rylands Library*, XLVI
(1963), 217-35; and the prefaces of Walter MacKellar whose *The Latin
Poems of John Milton* (New Haven, Conn., 1930), is the source of my text.
[5] V.737-40.
[6] *Idyls* VI.11-18.
[7] *Eclogues* IX.40-41.
[8] I.43.
[9] II.149-50.
[10] II.336-38.

younger Horace was somewhat sadder and looked through
spring's joys to man's mortality. His poems open on April
vistas, but they are really about the few, frail, happy hours
before winter destroys all life. In a familiar one, Death knocks
with his "impartial foot" to warn Sestius;[11] in another, Tor-
quatus is informed that the gods may add no tomorrow to
our day: "Pulvis et umbra sumus." [12]

Both moods are common to Ovid. The happy poet of the
Fasti asks Janus why the year does not begin in April, "time's
new season," when "suns are sweet and pilgrim swallows
come." [13] When the swallows really come, Ovid, like Horace,
remembers the tragedy of Philomela and Procne and fears
lest winter return and break the spell of spring.[14] Then on
the edge of April he raises the paean to "the mother of
Aeneas, joy of gods and men." "Formoso Venus formoso tempore digna est." [15] Venus and Ver are followed by Flora, who
tells her story. Once when she was wandering, Zephyr saw
her. "I retired; he pursued; I fled; but he was stronger." Now
she dwells in a noble garden which her husband fills with
flowers.[16] The violent union of Earth and Sky has become an
urbane arrangement in an imperial villa. But Ovid, who would
have surpassed both Homer and Vergil, according to Milton,
had he not been exiled, also suffered in the bitter springs of
frozen Tomis.

> Iam violam puerique legunt hilaresque puellae,
> Rustica quae nullo nata serente venit,
> Prataque pubescunt variorum flore colorum,
> Indocilique loquax gutture vernat avis,
> Utque malae matris crimen deponat, hirundo

[11] *Odes* I.4.
[12] *Odes* IV.7; see also IV.11.
[13] I.151–57; III.235–42.
[14] II.853–56.
[15] IV.85–132.
[16] V.183–220.

Sub trabibus cunas tectaque parva facit,
Herbaque, quae latuit Cerealibus obruta sulcis,
Exit et expandit molle cacumen humo,
Quoque loco est vitiis, de palmite gemma movetur:
Nam procul a Getico litore vitis abest,
Quoque loco est arbor, turgescit in arbore ramus:
Nam procul a Geticis finibus arbor est.

. . . .

O quater et quotiens non est numerare beatum,
Non interdicta cui licet Urbe frui,
At mihi sentitur nix verno sole soluta,
Quaeque lacu durae non fodiantur aquae,
Nec mare concrescit glacie nec, ut ante, per Histrum
Stridula Sauromates plaustra bubulcus agit.[17]

While these Augustan poets were shaping a tradition for
the English boy, Meleager of Gadara, writing in Greek, put
together a calendar on the coming of spring. The Εἰς τὸ ἔαρ,
which fathered poems by Peletier du Mans, de Baïf, Belleau,
and Sannazaro before Milton was born, relates the springtime experiences of men as a poet knows them.[18] Winter
retreats from the sky; fields laugh in crimson; earth puts on
her green crown; the trees are young in leaves; the roses bud
and blow. The shepherd's pipe is heard in the hills; sailors
make for the sea; and men, binding their heads with ivy, sing
the praises of Dionysus. In the air, birds fly, singing in colored
flocks: the halcyon on the sea, the swallow about the house,
the swan on the stream, the nightingale in the coppice.

Εἰ δὲ φυτῶν χαίρουσι κόμαι, καὶ γαῖα τέθηλεν,
Συρίζει δὲ νομεύς, καὶ τέρπεται εὔποκα μῆλα
Καὶ ναῦται πλώουσι, Διώνυσος δὲ χορεύει,
Καὶ μέλπει πετεηνά, καὶ ὠδίνουσι μέλισσαι,
Πῶς οὐ χρὴ καὶ ἀοιδὸν ἐν εἴαρι καλὸν ἀεῖσαι.[19]

[17] *Tristia* III.xii.
[18] *Arcadia*, ed. Scherillo (Turin, 1888), pp. 10–13.
[19] *Anthologia Palatina* IX.363.

All the traditional metaphors are here, but in addition there is the visible figure of the poet. When creation renews itself shall he alone be silent? It is the same question, inverted into statement, that the boy Milton will phrase in the Fifth Elegy. "Fallor? an et nobis redeunt in carmina vires, / ingeniumque mihi munere veris adest?" But Milton's assertion here may be an abrogation of the lament with which the famous "Pervigilium Veneris" closes.

Greek and Roman responses blend in the "Pervigilium Veneris," a hymn for the eve of St. Venus and rebirth of the world. "Vere natus orbis est." It is also the season of marriage and Dione, the pre-Olympian Venus, adorns her throne. Aided by Favonus and the distillation of stars, she calls the roses, "nude virgins of the morning," into flower while her boy Cupid, naked and unarmed, wanders among the nymphs. Artemis, of course, is exiled, but Ceres, Bacchus, and the God of Poets, "poetarum deus," attend the three-day ceremony where Dione, accompanied by the Graces and nymphs of forest, hill, and springs, sits in Hybla and gives laws. Those who wait about the goddess see, as if they were in a great theater, the marriage of Earth and Sky. "Tomorrow is the day," they are told, "when Aether first wed," and they watch as he flows into his mighty bride. The year is quickened by the clouds of spring and flame goes round the earth to kindle all creatures. But the poet, listening to Philomela and Procne, asks impatiently,

> Illa cantat; nos tacemus. Quando ver venit meum
> Quando faciam ut chelidon, ut tacere desinam?
> Perdidi Musam tacendo; nec me Phoebus respicit.[20]

This poem was written sometime between the first and the fourth centuries; by the fifth century the tone changes.

The "Ver erat" attributed by the seventeenth century to

[20] XXII.

the sometimes Christian Ausonius is different from the spring
poems of pure pagans and totally different from the "Ver
avibus voces aperit" of Paulinus of Nola. Walking in a garden
touched enough by May's warmth for Venus to be manifest
in her symbolic roses, Ausonius sees mortality in the flowers
and with "collige, virgo, rosas" intones the chant against virginity that was still heard in Milton's day.[21] St. Paulinus, his
devoutly Christian pupil, has, on the other hand, no objections
to virgins. When he watches the snows melt and the vari-
colored, multi-tongued birds return, he sings in honor of his
patron, St. Felix. The soul's winter ends with the God Incarnate, not with the arrival of Ver and Venus; and the poet,
liberated by Christian spring, waves his wings and sings.[22]
The pagan themes are assumed only to be reshaped, and the
tradition of Christian spring is now poetically stated. Writing
in the new ambience, Dracontius turns the gardens of Venus
and Flora into that of Eden;[23] Venantius Fortunatus, learned
in pagan topics,[24] celebrates spring as the Feast of Easter;[25]
and Walafrid Strabo makes the resurrection of God, not of
God's world, his central theme.[26]

The Latin poets of the Renaissance, jealous as they were of
ancient ways, had both thematic modes to choose from and
chose from both. Sometimes they do little more than rephrase
the songs of Rome. For many Horace is the gifted master.
The "De Calendis Aprilibus" of Calcagini begins with the
weaving of violet crowns and the heaping of flowers for the
bright day of Venus. "Haec dies nobis Veneris calendas/
candida profert." In time we arrive at the altar of the "ab-

---

[21] *Appendix* II.
[22] *Carmina*, ed. Hartel (Vienna, 1894), pp. 194–95.
[23] *Carmina*, ed. Vollmer (Berlin, 1905), pp. 31–32.
[24] *Opera Poetica*, ed. Leo (Berlin, 1881), pp. 124–26.
[25] Pp. 59–60.
[26] *Carmina*, ed. Dümmler (Berlin, 1885), pp. 336, 354, 370.

sentum numen." [27] Garlands are also woven and perfumes of India scattered in the first stanzas of Sannazaro's "Kalenda Maii"; then wine smokes in the crystal cup to remind the revelers that "grapes do not grow in Hell's acres" and that "black Death comes while a joke is being told." "Mediis mors venit atra jocis." [28] Marco Antonio Flaminio, best of neo-Latin poets, sees Flora and Zephyr look on as Amaryllis leads her flock to a secret grove, and then he sacrifices a garlanded lamb to Venus.[29] The offering is of no avail, because in two further poems he weighs the joys of spring against the sad absence of his mistress, Lygda.[30] His major poem, "Iam ver floricomum," is darkened with Horatian pessimism. Snows melt, the grass appears, birds sing among the flowers, Venetian sails fill the Adriatic, but the wintered poet sings in weeping and finds rest only in the thought of death. "Soles non aliquo tempore candidi/ sic me perpetua est hiems." [31] Flaminio's contemporary, Fracastorio, draws in his "Incidens" a series of spring scenes for a memorial pillar. He describes the marriage of Earth and Sky, the spring of the world itself, and the flawless Age of Saturn; he also portrays the spring pastimes and tasks of Italian country life.[32] Other Latin poets celebrated with lesser success the advent of spring,[33] but more pleasing to the boy Milton, perhaps, were the poems of

[27] *Antologia della Lirica Latina in Italia nei Secoli XV e XVI*, ed. Costa (Citta di Castello, 1888) pp. 85–86.

[28] *Opera Omnia* (Naples, 1732), p. iii.

[29] *Carmina* (Padua, 1743), p. 91.

[30] Pp. 97–98.

[31] Pp. 83–84.

[32] *Opera Omnia* (Venice, 1555), pp. 282v–283v.

[33] Erasmus wrote a long, unpoetic "Certamen . . . de Tempore Vernali," *Opera* (Leyden, 1706), VIII, 565–66; there are other poems on the topic in J. C. Scaliger, *Poemata* (s.l., 1600), p. 115; Andrea Dazzi, *Poemata* (Florence, 1549), pp. 112–13; P. Lotichius, *Opera* (Leipzig, 1586), p. 175; J. Cameno, *Libri duo* (Venice, 1570), p. xxxix.

George Buchanan, the "Buchananus noster" of the *Second Defence.*[34]

Buchanan wrote a poem in alcaics and one in elegiacs on spring. The first praises "Holy May Day" and spring as relics of the Golden Age, which will return when God has purified the world with fire. The elegy begins with a shout, "Festa!" Then Lascivia, Amor, and Indulgentia, celebrants all, are joined shortly by Joy, Cupid, Genius, Pleasure, and the Graces. Once these latter, blander personifications, pleasing to their counterparts in "L'Allegro" and "Il Penseroso," have assembled, the Lady of Cyprus enters. Her yellow hair is woven in a coronet; her fingers are starred with emeralds; her golden palla flows to her feet. She is adorned "as if to be pleasing to her Mars." "Marti seu placitura suo." Earth and its creatures testify, as tradition demands, to her fervent presence and men are urged to be cheerful so that the battle of love "in which many seek to die" may begin. Thus far the poem is a vernal chant in the ritual of Venus, but it is, nonetheless, annotated by the music of dismay. The calm measures swell suddenly as "hard husbands" are required to release their young wives and timid virgins are encouraged to escape their mothers and show their "breasts white as milk." But black death, shadow, and dust, the faces of winter, are thinly masked by May's splendors.

> Gather roses; they perish if you do not.
>   See in this the reflection of life.
> Harsh Boreas destroys the fields' beauty;
>   He fills them with his white frosts,
> Strips leaves from wood, flowers from the garden,
>   Puts reins of ice on the slow river.
> So Time, the deformer, will age you, too;
>   Dry wrinkles will wither your face;
>   Your skin will bag; your teeth will rot;

[34] *Works* VIII. 79.

> Your eyes will redden; and all sweet grace
> Will leave your once so fecund tongue.

Having heard this advice for many centuries, the young do not need the lesson; so the poet turns to old men, his contemporaries, and assumes the cheerful Horatian tone. "While the envious Fates spare us old boys, let us enjoy this season as in youth." [35] The experiences of Buchanan were also shared by the Cambridge undergraduate, who never scorned the wisdom of his great predecessors; yet what he gathered from others, he continually refreshed. By these precocious acts he justified the comment of a seventeenth-century German professor of poetry: "the man," writes Morhof of Kiel, "was apparent in the boy." [36]

The boy Milton wrote three poems on the spring: the Fifth and Seventh Elegies and "Song: On May Morning." The Fifth Elegy seems to stem directly from the poems of his predecessors; the Seventh Elegy, dated "anno aetatis undevigesimo" but thought to be later, appears more original at first reading than the Fifth Elegy, which begins with excruciatingly conventional phrases. The return of the perpetual circle of time is recorded; we hear of the fresh Zephyrs, "Zephyros novos," the warmth of spring, "vere tepente," the brief youth of Earth, "induiturque breven Tellus iuventam," and the softly greening fields, "dulce virescit humus." Within twenty lines Philomela, that dusty traveler, returns without Procne and begins to sing "dum silet omne nemus." A year later she will reappear in Milton's first sonnet helping the Hours lead in May by warbling "at eve when all the woods are still"; and in another year, the "mute Silence" of "Il Penseroso" will "hist along/ 'Less Philomel will deign a song."

---

[35] *Opera Omnia* (Leyden, 1725), II, 415, 304–8.
[36] D. Morhof, *Polyhistor Literarius* (Lübeck, 1732), I, 301–2.

After these commonplaces, Milton describes in more mythological detail the alterations of day and night, repeating
notions from his earlier prolusion, "Utrum Dies aut Nox
praestantior sit." Then, as a modest prelude to the passion of
Tellus and Phoebus, the traditional spring shepherd, who
matches his seven reeds against Phyllis' song later in the poem,
jollies the Sungod, implying that like the vigilant poet of the
"Pervigilium Veneris" he also has been loveless for the night.
The jest is so sharp that Phoebus turns it against Aurora made
frustrate by her flaccid spouse Tithonus. Desert the senile
couch, says the Sun, "the hunter, Aeolides, stays for you on
the green." The goddess is clearly on this occasion not "trickt
and frounc't as she was wont/ With the Attic Boy to hunt,"
her subsequent Miltonic good fortune. She is also unaware
that she will take on the role of Ovid's Flora in "L'Allegro"
and find herself, thanks to her bad judgment in rollicking
with Zephyr on a Maytime bank of violets, apocryphally
gravid with Euphrosyne. Carnal playfulness, not unknown to
the fallen hero of *Paradise Lost*, is the portion, too, of spring-
besotted Jupiter. "Jupiter ipse alto cum coniunge ludit
Olympo." Similarly, the Ovidian pursuit of the half-reluctant
Flora is rerun when Milton sends Faunus dashing after a slow-
footed and anonymous Oread.

But the theme of the Fifth Elegy is not the same as that of
Comus, and after the adolescent poet has urged Phoebus and
Earth to cohabit, he frees earthlings and half-earthlings that
they may imitate the example their mother hopes to set them.
His line "Matris in exemplum caetera turba ruunt" hints that
something like the marriage of Earth and Sky has occurred,
but the poem is not very explicit. On the other hand, Cupid,
who will have the leading part in Elegy Seven, appears with
a torch significantly kindled in Phoebus' fire, with new strings
to his bow and points to his arrows. Buchanan, who knew his
Horace, also saw him at this paragraph in spring's story, sharp-

ening his darts, retempered "in the Sicilian furnace," on a whetstone red as blood.[37] His luscious mother has hardly any part in Milton's poem, but the boys and girls who attend her church are here and so is Meleager's sailor, who sings a new song to the stars and like Arion calls up dolphins as if they were the hounds of spring. Lastly, the venerable gods of venery, who usually appear separately, arrive in a body to do the body's service. Sylvanus, a non-classical "semicaperque deus semideus caper," Maenalian Pan, and Faunus lead the troop through field and thicket to threaten the virtue of practiced fertility goddesses like Ceres and Cybele.

All these incidents are fragments of an honored tradition, and it is interesting to watch the boy Milton fit them together into a new poem. He describes Tellus, for instance, as his masters described Venus and acknowledges the identification with an easily recognized phrase, "cum Paphiis fundit amoma rosis." He remembers then the serious connection of the "diva Sicana" and the "deus Taenarius" with the mythology of spring, and so he opens the door just long enough to let the dank melancholy of Horace mist the lines. Again we see the thin visages of the monarchs in whose sterile garden grow no vines. This poetic experience is hardly ended before Zephyr, henchman of Ver, drops down and shakes his cinnamon-scented wings. This is a new perfume for the West Wind. Does it come from the "Arabum messes" of the superior lines or is it really the phoenix, bird of the sun, fragrant, according to Ausonius[38] and Claudian,[39] with cinnamon that hovers here and settles? If this is the case, the half view of the dead world is lightened by the symbolic creature of resurrection and eternity. But all of these bright fragments are merely ornaments to the wooing of Phoebus by Earth, the radiant myth at the center of the poem.

[37] *Works* II. 305; Horace, *Odes* II.viii.14–16.
[38] *Griphus* 17.
[39] XXII.421–22.

In the "Theogony," Hesiod traces the beginning of things to the great union: "Huge Sky came bringing night, and desiring love, embraced Earth and lay on her and stretched out." [40] To these forces Homer gave name and season when in the *Iliad* Zeus clasps his consort in his arms. "And beneath them the divine earth sends forth fresh new grass, and dewy lotus, and crocus, and hyacinth, thick and soft, that raised them aloft from the ground. Therein they lay and were clad with a fair golden cloud, whence fell drops of glittering dew." [41] To these accounts of the hierogamy, Venus, speaking in Aeschylus' "Danaides," adds her remembrances. "The pure Sky yearns passionately to pierce the Earth and love lays hold on Earth to join in wedlock. The rain falls from the steaming heavens and impregnates earth; and she brings forth the pasturage of sheep and Demeter's gift for mortals and the ripe season of trees." [42] From these Greek origins came the tradition that the Latins gave to Milton.

But Milton lived in a cold latitude where spring is sun rather than rain; hence, he proposes Phoebus, rather than Aether, as the spouse of Earth. In "On the Morning of Christ's Nativity," written a half year after "In Adventum Veris," Nature wears the drab gown of winter because it is "no season then for her / To wanton with the Sun, her lusty Paramour." But the sun of the elegy is more than sun; it is Phoebus Apollo, the sun-god patron of spring. This is the god whom we meet in the *Aeneid* as he leaves his winter home in Lycia and walks the Cynthian summits, shaping his hair with laurel and binding it with gold while the arrows, the rays of the sun, rattle on his shoulder.[43] Claudian, last of the Roman poets, also recounted the journey of the wandering god.

---

[40] Ll.176–78; see *Prolusion One, Works* XII.128.
[41] XIV.346–51.
[42] Athenaeus *Deipnosophists* XIII.600.
[43] IV.143–49. Macrobius, writing about A.D. 400, informs us that Phoebus

> Cum pulcher Apollo
> Lustrat Hyperboreas Delphis cessantibus aras,
> Nil tum Castaliae rivis communibus undae
> Dissimiles, vili nec discrepat arbore laurus,
> Antraque maesta silent inconsultique recessus.
> At si Phoebus adest et frenis grypha iugalem
> Riphaeo tripodas repetens detorsit ab axe,
> Tunc silvae, tunc antra loqui, tunc vivere fontes,
> Tunc sacer horror aquis adytisque effunditur Echo
> Clarior et doctae spirant praesagia rupes.
> Ecce Palatino crevit reverentia monti
> Exultatque habitante deo potioraque Delphis
> Supplicibus late populis oracula pandit
> Atque suas ad signa iubet revirescere laurus.[44]

It is this god, who like the "dea Sicana" spent half a year in cold darkness and took with him music, dancing, and prophecy when he departed; it is this god whom Milton would lure into the bed of Earth.

Because Phoebus Apollo turns the shepherd's jibe against blushing Aurora, Milton, a self-appointed "magister amoris" and warmer of cold beds, recommends to him an amatory exercise. "Earth," he informs the sun-god, "is throwing off her hated age," and fifty lines later he reports that Venus is rejuvenating her ancient flesh. The two ladies are thus made equal; hence, we are not perplexed when Tellus escapes the unflattering Vergilian "magne corpore" and is described as if she were the Cyprian. She bares her voluptuous breast; she is scented with Asian perfumes; she winds flowers in her hair. Her only physical defect is the grotesque "lucus sacer"

and Apollo were the same, *Saturnaliorum libri VII* I.vii.13–14; XVIII.5. His arrows are the sun's rays (I.xvii.60) and his moderation of the seven strings of the lyre is the equivalent of the sun's dominance of the planets (I.xix.15). When we visit the palace of Helios in *Metamorphoses* II.23–30, Phoebus is surrounded by the hours and seasons and spring is represented by a young man with a floral crown.

[44] "Sixth Consulship of Honorius," 25–38.

with which she crowns herself. Phoebus, however, is no Mars.
He learns that Earth is eager for his caresses; he is encouraged
by compliant *putti*, "faciles amores"; honeyed entreaties are
conveyed to him; but wanting the vigor of Aether, he holds
back. He even seems to have lost the amorous drive that a
lover of Daphne, Clymene, Rhodos, Circe, Clytie, and Leuco-
thoe should have. To improve the marital attractiveness of
Tellus, Milton remarks that she is not "sine dote," and has
already provided her hesitant lover with herbs that help him
in his healing. "Alma salutiferum medicos tibi gramen in usus/
praebet, et hinc titulos adiuvat ipsa tuos." It is clear that
Milton is addressing the father of Aesculapius, who taught
Iapyx, Aeneas' physician, "the power of herbs and the art of
healing." [45] We can hear him, Milton being absent, speak to
Daphne for himself:

> Per me quod eritque fuitque
> Estque patet; per me concordant carmina nervis.
> Certa quidem nostra est, nostra tamen una sagitta
> Certior, in vacuo quae vulnera pectore fecit.
> Inventum medicina meum est, opiferque per orbem
> Dicor, et herbarum subiecta potentia nobis:
> Ei mihi, quod nullis amor est sanabilis herbis,
> Nec prosunt domino, quae prosunt omnibus, artes! [46]

Not every poet has the audacity to counsel a god in matters
of the heart, but Milton was born in London, the city where
Venus, as he states in the First Elegy, now lived. Deserting
her southern shrines, she had come northward, attracted by
the beauty of English girls, a beauty which had even brought
about the regeneration of that weary womanizer Jupiter.
Milton does not inform Charles Diodati, the recipient of the
First Elegy, about any English girl in particular; in fact, find-

[45] XII 391-97.
[46] *Metamorphoses* I.517-25; see II.618 and *Tristia* III.iii.10.

ing the city uncongenial to a disciple of Phoebus Apollo, he plans to retreat while he has "the indulgence of the blind boy," "pueri indulgentia caeci," and before Amor, employing one of those goddesses with waving, blond hair, catches him in a golden snare. "Aurea quae fallax retiatendit Amor." The danger thus avoided overwhelms this counselor-at-hearts in Elegy Seven.

"L'Allegro" and its companion poem describe Milton's rambles about London and its suburbs. The solitary walker appears first in Elegy One in London and in a suburban grove of elms noble in shade, "suburbani nobilis umbra loci." It was in this grove that he encountered the dazzling but fearsome bands of British maidens. The perambulation of the First Elegy is continued into the Seventh, where, on the first of May, the boy once again saunters through the city and "the pleasing suburban villages." Once again crowds of radiant girls pass, and Milton asks, "Is this where Phoebus gets his rays?" Then, like the poet of the *Vita Nuova*, he sees one girl who far surpasses the others. Love consumes him; he is all flame. "Uror amans intus, flammaque totus eram." He never sees her again, and his plight is hopeless, because he can neither overcome nor obtain his desire. The poem ends; Cupid has had his revenge on Milton, adviser of gods.

The trouble began, Milton tells Venus Amathusia, because he did not learn her laws, was wanting in Paphian fire, and had mocked Cupid, saying to the little bowman,

> Tu puer imbelles dixi transfige columbas
> Conveniunt tenero mollia bella duci.
> Aut de passeribus tumidos age, parve, triumphos,
> Haec sunt militiae digna trophaea tuae:
> In genus humanum quid inania dirigis arma?

Now Love, as Ovid, and even George Herbert, knew, was a man of war, a veteran commander, who is justifiably angry

when a poet of nineteen proclaims himself among "fortes viri";
hence, when Milton, like the lover of Beatrice, awakens on
May Day morning, he finds Eros at his bedside. The god
rebukes the poet who is ignorant about his victories over gods
and heroes. Orion, Hercules, even thundering Jove, have
been victims of his fantastic marksmanship. At the top of the
casualty list is Phoebus Apollo. In fact, says Cupid, reciting
Ovid's "vince Cupidineas pariter Parthasque sagittas," [47] the
"Parthian horseman is no better shot than I." He informs
young Milton, who had already nominated himself in English
as the servant of "the Muse of Love," that neither the Muses
nor the healing arts of Apollo, the Musagetes, can save him.
Perhaps this experience with Cupid really qualified Milton to
advise Phoebus Apollo, but he was also simply reliving in
A.D. 1628 a love story that had taken place sometime before 50 B.C.

"Daphne, daughter of Peneus," Ovid says surely, "was
Phoebus' first love." The tale is familiar. The god, returning
from dragon killing, asks Cupid, "lascivus puer," what he is
doing with a man's armaments. The bow, he insists, is his personal weapon, and he orders Cupid to be content with his
torch and to leave shooting to the experts. But Cupid, who
Milton said was "prompter to wrath" because Ovid said he
was filled with "savage anger," notches his golden arrow,
as he does in the Seventh Elegy, and shoots Apollo. "Tanto
minor est tua gloria nostra." Milton had seen a girl who
"surpassed all others," and Apollo saw Daphne. Milton, we
remember, became all fire; Apollo burst into blaze. "Sic Deus
in flammas abiit; sic pectore toto/ uritur." Both loves are hopeless. Milton can only follow in his imagination the girl he will
never see again, but he is reconciled to Eros in the end and
sacrifices at his altar. The luck of Apollo is no better. Daphne
pursued is changed into the symbolic laurel and the poet of

[47] *Remedia Amoris* 157.

the gods writes a hymn to his tree. "When the healer was done," says Ovid, "the laurel inclined her newmade branches." [48] The stirring of Apollo's laurel helps us find the true meaning of Milton's Fifth Elegy.

In keeping with Meleager's spring resolve to sing and the complaint about Apollo's desertion voiced by the author of the *"Pervigilium Veneris,"* Milton expresses, after the opening conventional quatrain, the moving force of genius he feels within. Suddenly the "deus poetarum" is manifest. "Deus ipse venit—video Peneide lauro/ implicatos crines—Delius ipse venit." Once again Milton agrees with Ovid. "There is a god in us; we are warmed by his motion which sows seeds of inspiration. Whether I am a poet or sing of holy matters, it is especially fitting that I see the gods' faces." [49] Ovid writes in the age when, if we can believe the "Carmen Saeculare" of Horace, the god and his sister had special honors in the city of Augustus, but Milton's reverend outburst could also have been heard three centuries earlier. We could be at Cyrene listening as Callimachus raises the chorus, Callimachus whose "Magnifick Odes and Hymns," Milton wrote, are with those of Pindar "in most things worthy." [50] The bough of laurel trembles; the shrine shakes; "Phoebus knocks at the door with lovely foot." The celebrating poet sees the palm of Delos nod; he hears the swans singing; he sees the bolts and bars draw back of their own accord; and he warns the young men about him. "For Apollo does not appear to all, only to the good; and he who has seen him is truly great but who has not is, indeed, of poor estate." [51] We know the names of some of these "truly great": Hesiod, who knew the Muses; Demodocus, to whom Apollo gave song; the blindman guest at the

[48] *Metamorphoses* I.452–567.
[49] *Fasti* VI.5–8.
[50] *Works* III.238.
[51] II.1–8; one should compare this hymn to Apollo with the so-called Homeric Hymn.

divine feast in the first book of the *Iliad;* and Pindar, older
than Callimachus, but joined with him in Milton's mind. And
Pindar, like Milton, also was present when the god came.

Πρόφρων δὲ καὶ κείνοις ἄειδ' ἐν παλίῳ
Μοισᾶν ὁ κάλλιστος χόρος, ἐν δὲ μέσαις
Φόρμιγγ' Ἀπόλλων ἑπταγλωσσον χρυσέῳ πλάκτρῳ διώκων.[52]

It is not then beyond credence that when Apollo appears
the imagination of Milton soars into the liquid sky and passes,
free of body, through vagrant clouds. Like Adam, who will
see the history of man from the "Mount of the Visions of
God," or like Christ, who will reject the glory of the world
from Niphates' height, Milton, disregarding both time and
space, visits the haunts of the poets, the homes of the gods,
seeing all that is done on Olympus and all below. "Intuiturque
animus toto quid agatur Olympo/ nec fugiunt oculos Tartara
caeca meos." Shortly before he had this experience, Milton
proposed a similar ecstatic journey to his fellow students
in his Third Prolusion. He had urged them to fly into the sky,
to soar beyond terrestrial limits, to know "those holy minds
and intelligences with whom after this you will join in eternal
society." [53] Within months he will follow again the stages of
this "iter mentis" so attractive to him.

> Such where the deep transported mind may soar
> Above the wheeling poles, and at Heav'n's door
> Look in and see each blissful Deity
> How he before the thunderous throne doth lie,
> Listening to what unshorne Apollo sings
> To th' touch of golden wires, while Hebe bring
> Immortal Nectar to her Kingly Sire:
> Then passing through the Spheres of watchful fire,
> And misty Regions of wide air next under,

[52] *Nemean* V.22–24.
[53] *Works* XII.170.

And hills of Snow and lofts of piled Thunder,
May tell at length how green-ey'd *Neptune* raves,
In Heav'n's defiance mustering all his waves;
Then sing of secret things that come to pass
When Beldam Nature in her cradle was;
And last of Kings and Queens and Heroes old,
Such as the wise *Demodocus* once told
In solemn songs at King Alcinous' feast,
While sad Ulysses' soul and all the rest
Are held with his melodious harmony
In willing chains and sweet captivity.

By the time Milton wrote these lines many saints had made journeys into Christian space; but before they had, Er, son of Armenius, went the pagan course and heard the same sirens,[54] who will "lull the daughters of Necessity" in Milton's "Arcades." The pious Scipio, too, following the lead of his great ancestor's forefinger, looked down from the bourn of souls and saw a universe so vast it beggared the ambition of mortals.[55] For the young Milton, the verses about the Milky Way in the *Metamorphoses* undoubtedly were impressive also. On this bright boulevard, he read, live the important and distinguished gods, whereas the other celestial citizens live in the narrow streets of the stellar Trastevere. "Were I permitted to speak boldly," says Ovid carefully, "I would call this the Palatine district of high Heaven." [56] It is to residential areas of this nature that a poet can ascend when Phoebus Apollo comes down to allow the clear singer to look on his face. "Phoebus gave me," says Horace, who knew the Delian well, "the inspiration and the art of song and the name of poet." [57] The nature of this inspiration, Horace's "spiritus,"

---

[54] Plato, *Republic*, pp. 614–18.
[55] Cicero *De Republica* VI.9–26.
[56] *Metamorphoses* I.163–76.
[57] *Odes* IV.6.29–30.

and the praise of its bestower are the true topics of the "In Adventum Veris."

The theme that called forth this elegy is one that had engaged all poets beginning with Plato. In the *Phaedrus*, poets are said to be possessed by a Muse-given insanity,[58] and this assumption is confirmed in the *Apology* where it is observed that they can never explain their poems. "There is hardly a person present who would not have talked better about their poetry than poets do."[59] The whole doctrine of inspiration is voiced in the well-known conversation with the rhapsodist, *Ion*. The poet "does not sing by art but by divine power," Plato writes, comparing lyric poets to the Corybantian revellers or to bees, "light and winged and holy things," who feed in the gardens of the Muses. God speaks to men through poets, and it is evident "that these beautiful poems are not human, or the work of man but divine and the work of God; and that poets are the only interpreters of the gods by whom they are severally possessed."[60] Pindar, who lived almost a century before Plato, said all of this more tersely: "when the brightness comes and God gives it, there is a shining of light on men."[61]

Horace's "spiritus" was θεία δε δύναμις for Plato, but Pindar's αἴγλα διόσδοτος is perhaps closer to what Milton has in mind. To substantiate this decision we can read the plea of Tellus to Phoebus which follows that of the advising poet. She requests that Apollo rest in her cool shades and assures him that she does not fear the fate of Phaeton or Semele. It is clear, however, that, unlike her great classical ancestress, she does not yearn for his physical embrace. She asks only that he "lay his light on her breast." "Et gremio lumina pone meo."

[58] 245, 265.
[59] 22A–C.
[60] 533–35.
[61] *Pythian* VIII.96–97.

Within a few lines she repeats the same prayer: "Cum tu, Phoebe, tuo sapientius uteris igni,/ huc aedes, et gremio lumina pone meo." It is light she asks, not heat or fire. The poet also prays that the gods remain in the wood, that Jupiter return with the Golden Age, that Phoebus Apollo delay his northern journey. It is the poet's right, as Ovid insisted, to look on the faces of the gods; and it is his desire that cold sterility, the long dark of nights, the great polar shadows, be slow to come. Within a half year Milton will remember the winter, the night, the shades of Christian December, and the abdication of the pagan god of light. "*Apollo* from his shrine/ Can no more divine/ With hollow shriek the steep of Delphos leaving." But in the Fifth Elegy it is more than the god whom Milton addresses. It is the power that the god represents that both he and Tellus supplicate. It is Pindar's αἴγλα διοσδοτος or, to dress it in Latin, the "lumen divinum." An older Milton will make this plain when he invokes the Muse Urania as now he invokes Phoebus Apollo.

> The Meaning, not the name I call: for thou
> Nor of the Muses nine, nor on the top
> Of old *Olympus* dwell'st, but Heaven born.

When he wrote this, however, he had known the inward blaze of the heavenly light.

I have been implying that "In Adventum Veris" is a poem more on the ecstasy of poetic insight in its Apollonian manifestation than on the ancient topic of the annual renewal of earthly life. But the "advent of spring" is not to be read under, for the poem intends to remind us that the force of poetry is also renewed with each generation. Standing on the margin of promised poetic achievement, Milton recognized the eternal revival in himself. Filled with noble plans, he was not ready to settle for anything other than the difficulties of success.

He is different in this desire from Propertius, visited also by Apollo, who criticized his intention to succeed Ennius as a heroic poet. "The meadows are soft over which your little wheels must run," said the unshorn god, "that often your book may be read by some lonely girl waiting for her absent lover." [62] It is enough, says Propertius afterward, "if my writings set boys and girls on fire." [63] The Milton who attempts to reject love in the Seventh Elegy and who rejects both love and these elegies in the Platonically inspired recantation with which the *Poemata* ends, could not be happy with only the affection of Calliope. The brighter hopes of him who wrote the *Culex* at the age of sixteen were more like his. It is possible that he saw a strong similarity between his own plans and those expressed in the *Catalepton*[64] and the *Ciris*,[65] just as he may have found in his own guarded virginity a reflection of Vergil's reputed chastity. But they had other experiences in common, for both had seen Apollo. In the seventh bucolic Phoebus pulls Vergil's ear for prematurely thinking about "kings and battles"; in "Lycidas" the same god pulls the ear of Milton to remind him of the eternity of a poet's glory. By the time that this last pastoral was forced from Milton he had perhaps planned his own "marble temple beside the water" to a greater power than Vergil's Caesar.

These poetic plans, however, did not include further compositions in Latin. With the exception of the "Ode to John Rous" on the loss of the 1645 volume from the Bodleian Library, Milton attempted no Latin verse of consequence after 1646; in fact, with the exception of the "Epitaphium Damonis" of 1640,[66] all of the *Poemata* was done before he was thirty.

[62] III.3.
[63] III.9.45.
[64] XIV.ix.
[65] Ll.92–100.
[66] "Ad Patrem" is sometimes thought to be late, but see Douglas Bush, "The Date of Milton's Ad Patrem," *MP*, LXI (1964), 204–8.

Other distinguished English poets who had the skill—Abraham Cowley, George Herbert, Andrew Marvell, and Tom May —wrote with both pens for most of their lives. As a consequence, they were read in continental Europe, whereas Milton's great poems had to wait for Latin translation before they could be widely known abroad. Though Milton used the Latin tongue to defend his country and his faith, he turned to his native language when his "celestial patroness" spoke through his lips. He was prompted paradoxically both by a modest sense of his powers and by a proud conviction of his artistic mission. To understand this seeming contradiction, we may hear him speaking in *The Reason of Church Government*.

> That if I were certain to write as men buy Leases, for three lives and downward, there ought no regard be sooner had, then to Gods glory by the honour and instruction of my country. For which cause, and not only for that I knew it would be hard to arrive at the second rank among the Latines, I apply'd my selfe to that resolution which *Ariosto* follow'd against the perswasions of *Bembo*, to fix all the industry and art I could unite to the adorning of my native tongue; not to make verbal curiosities the end, that were a toylsom vanity, but to be an interpreter and relater of the best and sagest things among mine own Citizens throughout this Iland in the mother dialect. That what the greatest and choycest wits of *Athens*, *Rome*, or modern *Italy*, and those Hebrews of old did for their country, I in my proportion with this over and above of being a Christian, might doe for mine: not caring to be once named abroad, though perhaps I could attaine to that, but content with these British Ilands as my world.[67]

[67] *Works* III.236–37.

CHAPTER EIGHT

Robert Herrick

"Rex Tragicus"

The corpus of Robert Herrick's verse—almost 1,400 poems, many of them difficult to tell apart—is large enough to make him a "great" poet even though this bale of butterflies does not make him a good one. Swinburne, few of whose literary judgments have been sustained by the upper court of time, thought him the greatest of song-writers, capable in this corner of poetry of being favorably measured against Shakespeare in the drama. F. W. Moorman maintained that Herrick modified or quieted the impulses of the impulsive Elizabethans by seasoning them with a few dashes of his poetical "purity." An obviously religious man himself, he cannot be pleased with the childish religiosity of the poems in the "Noble Numbers," but in many other aesthetic details he finds Herrick better than better poets. F. R. Leavis, no easy bestower of literary laurels, writes in "The Line of Wit" that Herrick

138

illustrates the advantages enjoyed by poetry in an age which permitted the poet to be both classical and in touch with "a living popular culture." This is a most sensible statement if Leavis means that the modern reader who has lost all contact with classical literature, in fact, with any learning whatsoever, finds in Herrick only the remnants of a popular culture. Whatever has been said about the *Hesperides* or the "Noble Numbers," it is clear that the commentary on Herrick has not become much more discriminating than it was in the last century, when Gosse in his *Seventeenth Century Studies* anointed the poet with pleasant prolixity.

There is no question that Leavis is right; Herrick wrote in a strong classical tradition. If this condition is not immediately apparent, one can read about his debits to poets of Greece and Rome in the monographs of Mrs. McEuen and Miss Aiken. But simple verbal echoes, the phrases of the past remembered in the reeking boredom of a Devon parish house are only a small piece of the collected imagination that Herrick shared with other poets of his generation. There is more to a tradition than this, and it must be sought out. After all, it is the impelling recollection that lurks within the fabric of a work of art which is the true, but often obscured, tradition, demandingly pushing even the most simple utterance into being. Such an intense pressure no poet escapes, even though he may be unaware of it; and, if he does not escape, his good reader is in the same delightful predicament. A poem—if I may recall Donne's stanza—is a room in the imagination which is both closed and dark and also has lights and doors. The poet may think he has left this room when the poem is written, but he is still confined by bolts of metaphor and half-blinded by his single vision. The reader's duty, partly for the sake of the poem, but mostly for his own selfish ends, is to see where the hidden locks are, to touch them; and, though he may never emerge from the room, he may expand it to the size of the world. To effect this enlargement, the reader must sometimes rewrite a poem in terms of a wider context or more intense meaning than the poet was capable of or intended. Bruno did something of this sort with Tansillo's very conventional lines, and I, perhaps, am about to do the same thing with "Good Friday: Rex Tragicus, or Christ going to His Crosse," the text of which I draw from L. C. Martin's excellent edition.

Put off Thy Robe of *Purple*, then go on
To the sad place of execution:
Thine houre is come; and the Tormentor stands
Ready, to pierce Thy tender Feet, and Hands.
Long before this, the base, the dull, the rude,
Th' inconstant, and unpurged Multitude
Yawne for Thy coming; some e're this time crie,
How He deferres, how loath He is to die!
Amongst this scumme, the Souldier, with his speare,
And that sowre Fellow, with his *vineger*
His *spunge*, and *stick*, do ask why Thou dost stay?
So do the *Skurfe* and *Bran* too: Go Thy way,
Thy way, Thou guiltlesse man, and satisfie
By Thine approach, each their beholding eye.
Not as a thief, shalt Thou ascend the mount,
But like a Person of some high account:
The *Crosse* shall be Thy *Stage;* and Thou shalt there
The spacious field have for Thy *Theater.*
Thou art that Roscius, and that markt-out man,
That must this day act the Tragedian,
To wonder and affrightment: Thou art He,
Whom all the flux of Nations comes to see;
Not those poor Theeves that act their parts with Thee:
Those act without regard, when once a *King,*
And *God,* as Thou art, comes to suffering.
No, No, this *Scene* from Thee takes life and sense,
And soule and spirit, plot, and excellence.

Why then begin, great King! ascend Thy Throne,
And thence proceed, to act Thy Passion
To such an height, to such a period rais'd,
As Hell, and Earth, and Heav'n may stand amaz'd.
God, and good Angells guide Thee; and so blesse
Thee in Thy severall parts of bitternesse;
That those, who see Thee nail'd unto the Tree,
May (though they scorn Thee) praise and pitie Thee.
And we (Thy Lovers) while we see Thee keep
The Lawes of Action, will both sigh, and weep;
And bring our Spices, to embalm Thee dead;
That done, wee'l see Thee sweetly buried.

At first reading this poem, which appears to be a perfect paradigm of simplicity, produces an uncomplicated response. It requires, one would think, only an indifferent prose paraphrase of five thousand words to be a fine literary analysis. An experienced reader has known it with different emphases in other Renaissance poems on Good Friday; he recognizes that it belongs to the contemplative mode that selected memorial moments in Christian history for its subjects of discourse. It differs in method from the meditation, an ordinary and conventionally logical process of thinking. The meditation, if it follows a pious event, squeezes out its moral juices. The contemplation is an imaginary reconstruction of the event adorned with an orchestra of the emotions playing at top key. The difference between these two types of literary comment can be observed in St. Bernard's *Liber de passione Christi* and in his *Meditatio in passionem et resurrectionem Domini*. The contemplative method is followed by Milton in the "Ode on the Nativity"; the meditation is poetically remembered by Donne in "Good Friday." In both, however, the poets pretend that time is frozen in eternity and immediate place erased by universal space. These normal limits are removed because the great event is relived by the pious heart in each of its dilations. The contemplation is a beat-by-beat recording of the emotional reaction to the mental fantasy. In his Easter sermon of 1630, Donne quotes an expert: "I was crucified with Christ upon Friday, saies Chrysologus, *et hodie resurgo,* to day I rose with him again." [1] The event is spectacle and theater. Herrick not only sees the Crucifixion as the penultimate chapter in the life of Christ but also finds it a tragedy about a king's fall. We are, therefore, not only present with him at Golgotha but in a theater as well, a theater more real than reality. "The world is the Theater that represents God," Donne wrote, "and every where every man may, nay must see him. The whole frame of the world is the Theater, and every creature the stage, the medium, the glasse in which we may see God." [2] The theater in which we sit at this tragedy is without circumference, and its proscenium is everywhere.

The death of Christ was a tremendous scene in which an incarnate God acted out the tragedy of man. It was not an unnatural role for God, because earth and heaven were joined in simile, and God was often understood in human terms. The veil of the temple had been torn, and light was seen in the shadows. Long before Herrick's time, Adam of St. Victor had told it all in verse.

> Jam scisso velo patuit
> Quod vetus lex praecinuit;
> Figuram res exterminat,
> Et umbram lux illuminat.[3]

God was for the seventeenth century a great geometer who governed the Keplerian universe by a more exact mathematics

[1] *The Sermons,* ed. Potter and Simpson (Berkeley, Calif., 1953–62), IX, 203–4.

[2] *Ibid.,* VIII, 224.

[3] *The Liturgical Poetry of Adam of St. Victor,* ed. Wrangham (London, 1881), I, 60.

than Pythagorean number combinations. God was also a supreme musician who mixed the simple phrases of St. Francis' creatures on the polyphonic organ, the chords of which were heard by the inner heart of St. Cecelia. God was many other men: an architect, a physician, and a poet. The last divine vocation was likewise a divine avocation and had been assigned to God by pagans and Christians alike. For Plato, Horace, and Ovid, God spoke with the poet's mouth; for Caedmon, for Milton, for many other Englishmen, God gave the poet his lines. He who can do this must indeed be a poet.

Writers of obscene poetry, a neo-Latin poet of Renaissance Italy tells us, profane both the name of poet and the name of God, because, in the Greek Church, God was adored as a poet. In the western liturgy, says Piero Valeriano, "we say *Maker of Heaven and Earth*," whereas the Greeks pray to "the poet (ποιητης) of Heaven and Earth." [4] Following the same turn of thought, Scaliger finds in the poet's ability "to make other outcomes for men's acts" a quality that makes him "another God," who not only "relates what had happened" but, "as a God," created the happening.[5] Sir Philip Sidney gladly accepted this analogy and discerned the likeness of God in the poet, who "with the force of a divine breath" brought forth things above and beyond the power of Nature.[6] Tasso follows the same simile in comparing the harmonious variety of creation with the concord of discords so pleasing in the heroic poem. "Thus similarly, I say, the great poet is called 'divine' because he resembles in his works the Great Artifex and shares in his divinity." "Della sua Divinità viene a partecipare." [7]

God, of course, does not write sonnets or villanelles. His

---

[4] *Hieroglyphica* (Basel, 1556), p. 211v.
[5] *De Poetice* (s.l., n.d.), p. 3.
[6] *Apologie for Poetry*, ed. Collins (Oxford, 1907), p. 9.
[7] *Discorsi del Poema Heroica* (Naples, 1597), p. 78.

epic is the visible universe ornamented with sacramental symbols for man to enjoy as he reads the lines. It is, as Hugo of St. Victor puts it, a book written by the hand of God in which each creature is a letter established by the Divine Will. "If an illiterate looks on an open book, he sees the forms of the letters but he cannot read. The man who sees only the outsides of the creatures and does not realize what there is of God in them is as dull as an animal; he knows the outside but not the inner meaning. The spiritually gifted man, who understands all things, considers the beauty of the outward form, but also perceives in the inner nature the marvellous wisdom of God." [8] But, in addition to his vast heroic poem, God also writes a great drama in which there is a part for every man destined to come alive. That the divine poet should also be a playwright is not surprising; it is a talent that even unbelievers accorded to divine being. In the *Laws*, Plato states that man's best fate is that he is "a plaything in the hands of God." It is, therefore, the duty of men and women to accept their assigned roles and to play them to the height of their powers.[9] Epictetus, who played the role of a slave, urges the actor, who may think of himself as nothing beyond his mask and buskins, to open his mouth so that it will be known, when he comes on stage as God's witness, whether he is a tragedian or comedian.[10] A wider consideration of man as an actor in God's drama can be found in the *Enchiridion:* "Remember that you are an actor in a drama of the sort the playwright wishes. If short, of a short one; if long, of a long one. If he wishes you to assume the rôle of a poor man, see to it you act it well. Do the same if it is the part of a cripple, a magistrate, or a private person. For this is your task to act rightly the part given you; to select the part is the task of

---

[8] *Didascalicon, PL,* CLXXVI, 835.
[9] 803C, 5–6.
[10] *Diatribes* I.29.41–47.

another." [11] The idea that God wrote a play with innumerable personae for the tragedy of human time was turned into a firm philosophical topic by Plotinus.

The transmigration of souls, the great neo-Platonist explains, is like an actor's changing of his makeup and costume when he assumes a new part. To change bodies is only to change roles, for death is like the actor's exit when his turn is over. "He will return to act on another occasion." In a sense all our experience is spectacle, the various scenes of a play in which we are both audience and actors. We "act out the plot on the world stage which men have filled with stages of their own making." The plot may seem to be torn by conflict, but it ends in harmony when the struggling characters become one. Now the great poet who devises the play gives each man a part with suitable words, but he does not create a leading actor or one second or third to him. Each man assumes a part by nature, for "the actors bring to this play what they were before it was ever acted." "But these actors, souls, have a particular worthiness; they act in a larger place than any stage. The dramaturge has made them the masters of all the world. They have a large choice of places. They decide themselves the honor or dishonor with which they act because their place and part are determined by their nature. . . . Everything in the cosmos is just and good and every actor is put in his proper place." [12]

As any reader of Renaissance literature knows, the comparison of life to a dramatic role and of the world to a stage supplied a theme to poets, regardless of the language in which they rhymed. A poet of the *Greek Anthology* had said rather simply, "life (is) a stage" (σκηνή πᾱς ὁ βίος),[13] but later poets, Shakespeare for example, rolled out the metaphor to far

[11] XVII.
[12] *Enneads* III.2.15-17.
[13] X.72.

greater length.[14] If this is the case, we should not be bemused when Herrick's divine dramaturge descends from heaven and takes the part of man. For Herrick and for almost anyone else of the seventeenth century, it would be consonant with the theory of divine nature for God to act out the death, the final scene in the tragedy of Everyman. To understand how the undying can play a part about the dying, one can remember what Plotinus had said about the role of the blasphemer: "A dramatist has written a part in which he maligns himself and given it to an actor to play." When Herrick's Christ puts off his purple robes, the comic but symbolic costume with which his mockers had disgraced him, he was also putting off, in an ironic way, his universal majesty in order to play for man's benefit the tragic scene, which he had written for himself, about the death of God. In this moment, Christ becomes the greatest of actor-playwrights; and while he plays his "severall parts of bitternesse," the event is remembered by his "lovers," who see him "keep/ The Lawes of Action." They recall that the drama was written at the beginning of time. Now the time is right: "Thine houre is come." The καιρός is just; the cue has been heard. He who has just played a comic scene must play a tragic one. The place is one with the time: "The Crosse shall be Thy Stage." The action is supreme: "to act Thy Passion."

As the contemplative Herrick watched the "Rex Tragicus" in his highest role, he could remember only one actor with whom to compare him. This actor was no great Elizabethan or Jacobean master of fustian, but one whose skill and renown had been praised throughout the ages.

---

[14] Jean Jacquot, "Le Théâtre du Monde," *Revue de Littérature Comparée,* XXI (1957), 341–72; Mario Costanzo, "Il Gan Theatro del Mondo," in his *Dallo Scaligero al Quadrio* (Milan, 1961), pp. 239–78. The latter work has an enormous bibliography.

> Thou are that Roscius, and that markt-out man,
> That must this day act the Tragedian
> To wonder and affrightment.

The comparison of Roman Roscius to Christ seems strange at first reading, because any educated man of Herrick's generation knew that Roscius was no tragedian but rather the greatest comedian of the age of Cicero. Was Herrick, we ask ourselves, alone ignorant of this fact? Perhaps he had some other private reason for bringing the names of Christ and Roscius together. Perhaps he meant the master of comedy must for once be a tragedian.

The classical accounts of Roscius' life and reputation are slight; but, if Herrick had read the epistles of Horace, he would have found him linked with Aesopus, the comedian, and given the title of "doctus." This descriptive adjective required a note by Horace's early editor Porphyrio, whose commentary is found in most Renaissance editions of the genial Venusian. Roscius' acting, Porphyrio states, was of immense moral import because he portrayed the foolishness of men who were "without merit and virtue." [15] There are other scattered references to Roscius, but his best biographer was his pupil in oratory, Cicero. In the *De Oratore*, we are told that Roscius was famed for his bearing and elegance, "gestum et venustatem," [16] that anyone who excelled in anything was known as "a Roscius" in his craft.[17] When he defended this teacher of his in court, Cicero assured the judges that what Roscius knew "few understood; where he learned it, all sought to know." The great comedian had never done aught depraved or perverse, and, consequently, Panurge, whom he had trained, was like the good son of a

[15] *Epist.* II.1.82.
[16] I.251.
[17] I.130.

fine father. Because he had studied with Roscius, he seemed to
know more than he knew. To illustrate the kind nature of his
client, Cicero told the court the story of Eros, who took refuge
in the house of Roscius as if it were a sanctuary. "Sicut in
aram confugit in huius domum." [18] In the *Pro Quinctio*,
Cicero inserted a commendation of Roscius: an actor "who
alone seemed worthy to be on the stage when he was there
and such a man that he alone seemed worthy to come there." [19]
But the hyperboles of Cicero surpass these.

In the *De Divinatione* we are told of a miracle that occurred in the childhood of Roscius. The child's nurse, entering his sleeping quarters with a lamp, found a large serpent
coiled about the unwitting child. She summoned aid; the
serpent disappeared; and later Roscius' father, having consulted the oracle, learned "that no one would be more noble
or famous than his child." "Nihil illo puero clarius, nihil
nobilius fore." [20] This phenomenon which attended the birth
or childhood of other heroes and demigods was indicative not
only of Roscius' character and virtues but of the way in which
men described the actor. In the *De Natura Deorum*, we hear
of Cicero's colleague, Quintus Catullus, who arose one morning to greet the ascending sun and suddenly, in the midst of
his worship, saw Roscius standing at his left. He returned
home and wrote a poem, which Cicero preserves, about the
event. It concludes with a statement about the actor-god.
"Celestial powers grant me peace to say/ A mortal he seemed
more beautiful than a god." [21] We can almost understand
from these accounts why Rome mourned widely when
Roscius died. "Quis nostrum tam animo agresti ac duro fuit,

[18] *Pro. Q. Roscio Comoedo,* 30–31.
[19] 78.
[20] 78.
[21] I.79.

ut Roscii more nuper non commoveretur?"²² Although the
legends of most men of excellence have invariably a Christlike
coloration, we may imagine that Herrick heard in this praise
of the godlike actor, the praise of his actor-like God, his Rex
Tragicus. All of the statements about Roscius come from
pagan texts, and, though they may evoke or elucidate a possible connection, they can never properly explain how the Rex
Tragicus can be equated with the Deus Comoedicus. To
understand this seemingly insolent relationship, the Christian
must turn to his own venerable philosophers.

It is St. Paul, not Cicero, who supplies us and may have
shown Herrick those lines of thought which transformed
tragedy into comedy and made the Jewish buffoon, sneeringly
dressed in the regalia of kingship, the eternal king of mankind. Writing to the Corinthians, St. Paul inquired, "Has
not God made foolish the wisdom of this world?" In response
to his own question, he had stated that "the foolishness of
God is wiser than men, and the weakness of God is stronger
than men." As all men know, he expounded the point more
fully with "For God has chosen the foolish things of this
world to confound the wise, and God has chosen the weak
things of this world to confound the mighty things." From
this premise, St. Paul drew his final, immortal figure of the
Christian comedian: "We are fools for Christ's sake." The
circle once again comes round. If we are fools for Christ's
sake, Christ has been a fool for man's sake.

The notion that Christ was the first of "the fools in Christ"
is expressed in commentary after commentary on the texts
from the first and fourth chapters of the apostolic letter to
Corinth. No matter what commentaries one reads, be they by
communicants of either Church, the emphases are the same.
The salvation of the Cross, according to the *Glossa Ordinaria*,

²² *Pro Archia Poeta*, 8.

is the true foolishness of God and explains why He preferred foolish men to wise men, why Peter was called and Nathaniel not.[23] "The lecture of the crucifixion, this folly," Grotius writes, "has led more men to probity than the labors of philologians and philosophers."[24] "The Cross of Christ," says Zeger, "seems total folly when compared with Eternal Wisdom." In his notes on Corinthians, Jacob Tirinus, like his great Roman contemporary Cornelius à Lapide, reminds men how Ambrose, Augustine, Anselm, and others had talked about this foolishness, and concludes that Christ's folly was made manifest in the Incarnation, the Passion, and the Death. "This foolishness makes Christ now seem the wisest of all."

For the seventeenth century the great Old Testament type of Christ was Samson, and Milton had this whole texture of the comedian who assumes the role of the tragedian, the fool who is the hero, before him as he wrote his *Samson Agonistes*. In his first speech to us Samson proclaims himself a fool (77), and a little later he asks the Chorus whether he was not sung "and proverb'd for a Fool" (203). When Manoa comes, Samson reiterates the enormous scope of his folly (496), which has brought him into the power of God's enemies. Toward the end of the play, the admitted fool at first refuses the order of the Philistine officer to follow him to the great arena.

> Although thir drudge, to be thir fool or jester
> And in my midst of sorrow and heart-grief
> To show them feats, and play before thir god,
> The worst of all indignities, yet on me
> Join'd with extreme contempt? I will not come.
>   (1338–42)

---

[23] *PL*, CXIV.
[24] The source of these references is *Critici Sacri: Sive Annotata Doctissimorum Virorum in Vetus ac Novum Testamentum* (Amsterdam, 1698).

But this is not the proper choice of ways for the Christian Hercules, because it is only when he becomes a fool for God that Dagon and his Philistines are overthrown. In this single action, the type of the fool in Christ, or even of Christ the fool, becomes the Rex Tragicus.

Milton's tragedy ends in purgation; Herrick's concludes with the audience mounting the stage and bearing the hero to his tomb. The passion of Milton's witnesses is spent because Samson has behaved like Samson. The quiet tears and calm of Herrick's cast of playgoers are the manifestations of those who know that the play is not quite over. The comedian of the buffeting has become the tragic hero of the Cross; but with this happening, the tragedy of man has become a divine comedy. The point was clear to all Christians of Herrick's time, but an Italian writing at the beginning of the seventeenth century expounds the predicament and resolves it. "I have wondered for a long time," writes Gregorio Mastrilli, "whether one should call the holy and blessed life of Christ a Comedy or a Tragedy." After this opening observation, he continues with the hair-splitting technique of a true Jesuit to explain why and why not the whole story of Christ is a comedy or a tragedy. In the end he reaches the proper conclusion: "Let us call it then a tragicomedy." "Chiamarolla dunque Tragicomedia." [25] What Mastrilli reasoned about at some length, Herrick may have settled with the half line, "Thou art that Roscius." But that he intended what I have expressed will never be known.

[25] *Discorsi sopra la Passione e Morte di Christo* (Rome, 1607), pp. 50–51.

CHAPTER NINE

Richard Lovelace

''The Grasse-Hopper''

This poem was written and sent by Lovelace to his fellow poet and royalist, Charles Cotton, sometime after the collapse of the great cause and the execution of King Charles. It is not unlikely that it was written by Lovelace in a moment of dejection after his own imprisonment and impoverishment. The story of the summer grasshopper that makes no provision for winter, that plays its violin while the ants are busy at harvest, obviously supplies the pre-text of the poem. The cavaliers were grasshoppers, and when this poem was written they were learning the lesson of the insect. Any reader can find all of this in "The Grasse-Hopper," and it is not surprising that the poem has been usually described as a simple cavalier lyric, a powerful overflow of alcoholic feelings recollected in adversity. But the poem is richer than it seems on first reading, and an examination of the tradition, of the metaphoric his-

tory of the insect that is the subject, will suggest that the
theme has emotional possibilities that have not been understood.

> Oh thou that swing'st upon the waving haire
>   Of some well-filled Oaten Beard,
> Drunke ev'ry night with a Delicious teare
>   Dropt thee from Heav'n, where now th'art reard.
>
> The Joyes of Earth and Ayre are thine intire,
>   That with thy feet and wings dost hop and flye;
> And when thy Poppy workes thou dost retire
>   To thy Carv'd Acron-bed to lye.
>
> Up with the Day, the Sun thou welcomst then,
>   Sportst in the guilt-plats of his Beames,
> And all these merry dayes mak'st merry men,
>   Thy selfe, and Melancholy streames.
>
> But ah the Sickle! Golden Eares are Cropt;
>   *Ceres* and *Bacchus* bid good night;
> Sharpe frosty fingers all your Flowr's have topt,
>   And what sithes spar'd, Winds shave off quite.
>
> Poore verdant foole! and now green Ice! thy Joys
>   Large and as lasting, as thy Peirch of Grasse,
> Bid us lay in 'gainst Winter, Raine, and poize
>   Their flouds, with an o'reflowing glasse.
>
> Thou best of *Men* and *Friends!* we will create
>   A Genuine Summer in each others breast;
> And spite of this cold Time and frosen Fate
>   Thaw us a warme seate to our rest.
>
> Our sacred harthes shall burne eternally
>   As Vestall Flames, the North-Wind, he
> Shall strike his frost-stretch'd Winges, dissolve and flye
>   This *Aetna* in Epitome.
>
> Dropping *December* shall come weeping in,
>   Bewayle th' usurping of his Raigne;

But when in show'rs of old Greeke we beginne,
    Shall crie, he hath his Crowne againe!

Night as cleare *Hesper* shall our Tapers whip
    From the light Casements where we play,
And the darke Hagge from her black mantle strip,
    And sticke there everlasting Day.

Thus richer then untempted Kings are we,
    That asking nothing, nothing need:
Though Lord of all what Seas imbrace; yet he
    That wants himselfe, is poore indeed.

At first reading, the poem separates rather naturally into two parts. Stanzas I–V set a familiar measure by recalling in a submerged but personified fashion the literary ancestry of the insect that is the subject. We recognize the subtune at once; it is Anacreon, whose poem on the grasshopper had been earlier translated by Belleau and Cowley. But Lovelace's poem is no forthright rendering; it is a more complicated chorus of voices. With the sixth stanza the imaginative rhythm begins to alter, and not only is Horace heard, but there is also an immediate contrast between the past and the present, between the symbolic history of the grasshopper and the immediate history of the poet and his friends. The prudent morality of stanzas IV and V is rejected and, after a series of variations, replaced by a Horatian act of will. In this artistic voluntary there are both Christian and pagan tones. The remedy for the moment is provided by the doctrine of Horace, although the inner conviction of an infinite present, once satisfaction is procured, is totally Christian. This rough summation, however, must be annotated in terms of Lovelace's gift from his predecessors.

Almost at the beginning of the history of poetic transformations, Anacreon of Teos heard the grasshopper in the fields of summer and put him into song. He took delight in the insect because it could be as drunk as a happy king on dew, because it owned all that it saw about it and took tribute from the seasons. It is beloved of the Muses for its singing, he tells us, and blessed by Phoebus; and if this is not merit enough, the unsuffering song-lover is as ethereal as a god.

> Ἀπαθής δ', ἀναιμόσαρκος
> Σχεδὸν εἰ θεοῖς ὅμοιος.[1]

This in substance is what Anacreon wrote, and the first twelve lines of Lovelace's poem [2] reproduce these themes against a now universal landscape. But in these stanzas there is obviously more than a pleasant rewarming of Anacreon's poem, and we do well to turn the hands of the poetic clock backward for a better understanding.

Hesiod had also known the "blue-winged" grasshopper that perched on green boughs, singing in the heat of the dog days when the beard grew on the oats;[3] the grasshopper that made sonorous odes in the luxuriant months when goats were fattest, wine best, women amorous, and men languid.[4] It is, however, Homer who creates a symbolic prejudice, when he compares the song of the grasshopper to the "lily-like voices" of the old Trojan aristocrats, who chattered on the wall as Queen Helen walked through the wide-way to the Skaian Gate.[5] From poems of this nature, the champions of Charles might imagine that the grasshopper, the βασιλεύς of Anacreon, had

---

[1] XXXIV.17-18. The Greeks do not distinguish clearly between the various singing insects, and it is not always clear what they mean when they use τεττιξ, καλαμαια, μάντις, and ἀκρίς. The translators have done little better, for Anacreon's poem is probably about the cicada.

[2] I have used the text of C. H. Wilkinson (Oxford, 1930). The two last lines of the third stanza may be paraphrased as "days make men merry, yourself merry, and melancholy streams away" or "make melancholy streams (rivers) also merry."

[3] "Shield of Achilles," *Opera*, ed. Flach (Leipzig, 1878), pp. 393-400.

[4] *Theogony* 581-86.

[5] *Iliad* III.151-53.

aristocratic pretensions; if they did not heed the whisper of these texts, there were those that flatly stated the case. "It is only recently," Thucydides writes of the Athenians, "that their rich old men left off . . . fastening their hair with a tie of golden grasshoppers." [6] The so-called Suidas states that the grasshopper was the insignia of the Athenian nobles because not only was the insect a musician, but like Erechtheus, founder of the city, it was also born of the earth.[7] So the insect that sings throughout the rich and prosperous seasons of the year, the insect of warmth and light, is given the colors of wisdom possessed among the Greeks by the noblemen of Athens.

If for the Greeks the grasshopper is a symbol of the gay months and their magic, if he is also the representative in nature of the ἄριστοι, he is most triumphantly the analogue of the poet-singer, whose verses he so delicately graced throughout antiquity.[8] For this reason Meleager is securely in the tradition when he invokes the grasshopper as the "Muse of the cornlands" (ἀρουραίη Μοῦσα), the song writer of the dryads, the challenger in voice and verse of the great Pan.[9] In one ancient myth, a singing grasshopper, by alighting on the peg from which the lyre string had broken, helped Eunomos of Locris win the prize at the Pythian games by supplying the wanting notes.[10] Another legend, probably invented by Plato, may be used to fortify this one.

Once, when Socrates and Phaedrus were talking, the old philosopher heard the grasshoppers singing and said that they

[6] *History* I.6.

[7] *Historica* (Basel, 1564), col. 959.

[8] It is everywhere part of rural decoration; see Theocritus XVI.94–96; Vergil *Eclogues* II.12–13; *Georgics* III.328; "Culex" 151; *Copa* 27–28. The *Greek Anthology* is filled with poems to the grasshopper; see VII.189–94, 197–98, 201; IX.92.

[9] *Greek Anthology*, VII, 195–96.

[10] Strabo *Geography* VI.1, 9. Paulus Silentiarius (*G.A.*, VI, 54) puts this myth into elegant verse.

had received gifts from the gods which, in turn, they imparted to men. When the exquisite Phaedrus inquired about the nature of these gifts, Socrates related the following story:

> A lover of the Muses should surely not be ignorant of this. It is said that once these grasshoppers were a race of men that lived before the Muses existed. When the Muses were born and song appeared, they were so moved by pleasure that as they sang, they forgot to eat and death caught them unawares. They live now in the grasshoppers, having that boon from their birth until their death. When they die, they inform the Muses in Heaven who worships them here below. Terpsichore, they tell of those who have honored her in the dance, and thus make them dearer to her; Erato, they tell of her lovers and to each sister they report according to her honorers. But to Calliope, the eldest, and to Urania, the second of the nine, they bear tidings of those who pass their lives in philosophic study and the observance of their special music; for these are the Muses, who having Heaven for their particular sphere and words both human and divine, speak most gladly.[11]

So with Plato, whose own musical voice was likened by Timon [12] to the "lily-songs" of the Hecademian grasshoppers, the insects become the apotheoses of human singers who have lost their lives through their love of art. "Dropt thee from Heav'n, where now th'art reard." The insect—Plato's myth and Anacreon's poem intermarry—is now a poet, and the evidence of its transformation, with a further qualification, is found in the writings of Flavius Philostratus.

Among the letters of the author of *Apollonius* and the *Imagines*, books popular with men of the Renaissance, is one commending the poet Celsus to a wealthy patron. This poet, Philostratus writes, has, "as do the good grasshoppers [οἱ

---

[11] *Phaedrus* 259. I cannot find this legend in any text prior to Plato's; Photius mentions it as if it were common knowledge (*Bibliotheca* [PG, CIII, 1354]).

[12] Diogenes Laertius *Lives* III.7.

χρηστοὶ τέττιγες], devoted his life to song; you will see to it
that he is fed on more substantial food than dew." [13] At the
touch of metaphor the poet is made a grasshopper; but in the
Apollonius, Philostratus associates the grasshopper with the
plight of men who have lost out. The philosopher Demetrius,
exiled to Dicaearchia by the Roman despot, cries out in envy
of the singing insects and says to Apollonius that they, at least,
are never in danger of persecution and are above human
calumny, for they have been set aloft by the Muses so that they
"might be the blissful poets of that felicity which is theirs." [14]
This comparison of Demetrius is close to the central tone of
"The Grasse-Hopper."

By following the tradition through antiquity, we come on
imaginative identifications that help us read this seventeenth-
century poem. We know that the grasshopper was beloved of
the Muses; that it had once been a human artist and continued
to accompany and instruct human artists; that it was a king,
an aristocrat, a badge of royalty, a poet; and that it was identified with men in political disfavor. This multiple suggestive-
ness may explain why Cowley translated Anacreon's poem
and why Lovelace sought to remake it into something at once
familiar yet novel. When we read the first three stanzas of
Lovelace's poem, all that we have learned from the Greeks is
born again. The grasshopper is drunk on dew, now a "Delicious teare"; he swings from the oaten beard on which Hesiod
had placed him; but like the song-obsessed Platonic grasshoppers, he has been "reard" to Heaven. We see at once behind the literal front, for we know that the grasshopper is an
aristocrat, a King. We have been reading a poem about a King
and a cause that are dead on earth but living in Heaven. The
poem has nothing to do with grasshoppers.

Choosing what in many respects was an optimistic symbol,

[13] *Opera,* ed. Kayser (Leipzig, 1870), p. 364.
[14] *Ibid.,* p. 261.

Lovelace annotated it with melancholia. According to the bright Attic tradition, as represented by the poem of Meleager, the grasshopper's music was the anodyne of sorrow, and Lovelace remembers this in the latter lines of the third stanza. But the living grasshopper of the Greek solar months is made a poetic prelude to the inexperienced innocent, "poore verdant foole," who is in Heaven. In this interplay of life and death, tersely suggested by stanzas IV and V, we pass from what is light and warm into the cold darkness of inescapable defeat and death.

> But ah the Sickle! Golden Eares are Cropt;
>   *Ceres* and *Bacchus* bid good night;
> Sharpe frosty fingers all your Flowr's have topt,
>   And what sithes spar'd, Winds shave off quite.
>
> Poore verdant foole! and now green Ice! thy Joys
>   Large and as lasting, as thy Peirch of Grasse,
> Bid us lay in 'gainst Winter, Raine, and poize
>   Their flouds, with an o'reflowing glasse.

The quiet warning of the first stanza, which had been further muted by the bright Anacreontic quatrains, is now made into a torrent of trumpets. Behind the allegory of nature and the classical figments, the emotional current of the decade in which the poem was written comes plain. The grasshopper King, who symbolically loved the sun, has been harvested with the harvest. The flowers of his realm are topped by the "sithes" or, spared by these, shaved by the cruel winds. The merry men, faced by winter, look to the lesson of the summer singer. At this point, too, the poet makes his own self-identifications, for all that antiquity had attributed to the grasshopper—the sign of the aristocrat, the symbol of the poet singer, and the man in political ill favor—suit him. The emphasis is solemn enough and with it Lovelace remembers many things. He recalls, perhaps, the legend of the impotent Ti-

thonus, but he expresses the tragedy of the summer-happy insect with that prudent variant of the Aesopica.[15] He leaves
the myrtles and laurels of the Greek sea islands to inhabit for
a while the north of cold and sunlessness.

In the gathering shadows of the world of death we hear for
a moment an ancient funeral chant. The crops are harvested.
Ceres and Bacchus have departed to a deeper sleep than that
enjoyed by the sunlight grasshopper when its "Poppy
workes." Winter has frozen even Fate. The North Wind
strikes with "his frost-stretch'd Winges." December comes in
tears far different from those that "Dropt thee from Heav'n."
Sullenly, the "darke Hagge" hangs about "light Casements."
Anacreon's season is over. Nature is now sternly present,
thinly veiling with her realities the parallel actualities of the
poet's life. We leave the dark external world to enter the
poet's heart. In this black moment of cold, the Christian tone
begins, for Lovelace remembers the once bright celebration
of the wintered year.

> Dropping *December* shall come weeping in,
>   Bewayle th' usurping of his Raigne;
> But when in show'rs of old Greeke we beginne,
>   Shall crie, he hath his Crowne againe!

Pathos and hope, together with December memories of the
Roman Saturnalia, are joined in this somberly happy stanza,
but to increase its emotion we must remember the Christmas
prince, who wore his crown during the festivities of the Christ-

[15] The fable of the industrious ant and the careless grasshopper was
popularized in the Middle Ages by Alexander Neckham (*Novus Aesopus*
XXIX). It also appears in various French redactions; see J. Bastin, *Recueil
General des Isopets* (Paris, 1929), and Marie de France, *Poesies*, ed. De
Roquefort (Paris, 1832), II, 123–25. Seneca suggests the legend in *Epistolae
Morales* LXXXVII.19–20. The early Fathers think of the insect in the
metaphoric manner of the poets (Ambrose, *Hexameron* [PL, XIV, 251–52]),
or commend it for some Christian quality (Gregory, *Oratio* [PG, XXXVI,
59]; and Jerome, *Epistulae* XXII.18).

mas week as proudly as Charles had worn his.[16] But the royalty
of Christmas, shared by all who kept the feast, had been despoiled, as the royalists were despoiled, by the new masters of
the state. For a number of years John Evelyn recorded the
dismal fall of the Christmas king. One of his entries reads:
"Christmasday, no sermon any where, no church being permitted to be open, so observed it at home." [17]

Lovelace's solution, like Evelyn's, is based on privacy and
withdrawal. The aristocratic poets may be the victims of a
frosty fortune, but they can "create/ A Genuine Summer in
each others breast," a summer that inwardly is more real than
the winters of Nature and Fate. So when December comes
lamenting the usurping of "his Raigne," the "his" means both
the King of England and the King of Christmas. To emend
this tragic state, Lovelace and Cotton can make bowers in
each other's breasts where the two rejected kings may dwell
with them. By this act of the imagination, Christian in its import (for "the Kingdom of Heaven is within you"), they will
privately establish a reality greater than the facts allow. To
the winter rains, which are December's tears as opposed to
those that banished Ceres wept for the crops, the poets will
offer a counterblast, "show'rs of old Greeke," wine and, perhaps, the Greek point of view. Both they and the mourning
month can then say of the two dead kings, "he hath his Crowne
againe."

It could be said that "The Grasse-Hopper," in spite of these
more subtle undertones, is simply a cavalier drinking song,

[16] The career of such a prince, who had in his titles the distinction of
"high Regent of the Hall" (probably Gloucester Hall, Lovelace's college)
has come down to us in an eyewitness account; see G. Higgs, *An Account
of the Christmas Prince, as it was exhibited in the University of Oxford
in the year 1607* (London, 1816).
[17] See the *Diary* (De Beer edition) for December 25 in 1652, 1654, 1655.
The parliamentary order of December 19, 1644, abolished the observance
of Christmas.

not unlike Cotton's "Chanson à Boire" or "Clepsydra." Alcohol had always been a cavalier cure, and Alexander Brome can advise his friends to seek refuge in wine, "in big-bellied bowls," "true philosophy lies in the bottle." Some of this drunken logic certainly seeps into Lovelace's poem; in fact, it is the ostensible mode. We must not forget that the poem, though it began in death, passed into warmth and light, that though we are now in the night and the cold, we shall emerge into an eternal beatitude that will cancel temporal despair. A consciousness of eternity is present in this poem even when the metaphors of death and despair are paraded in stanzas IV and V; it comes resolutely forward in "Our sacred harthes shall burne eternally/ As Vestall Flames." Opposed to the North Wind, the savage symbol of death and evil, are the virginal fires of the ever burning hearth within the human heart. This is the kingdom of the heart—this "Aetna in Epitome"; but it is also something that cannot be lost because it is something "we will create." The general state has perished and Lovelace proposes to replace it with another state, one that is inner, private.

The kingdom of the heart that Lovelace would restore is not one of retreat and withdrawal, the resolution in isolation that charmed so many of his fellow sufferers; [18] it is rather a revision of his own cosmogony. The hovering emblem of the winged North Wind, against which Lovelace directs the symbolic fires of the "sacred harthes," makes firm this revision; for Lovelace must have seen in Aquilo, as Milton did, the bony face of death. The wind that the ancients called "horrisonus," "saevus," "ferus," "horrifer," and "crudelis" was a bitter symbol for this generation. Evil was North, from

[18] On the cavaliers' praise of solitude as an escape from the evils of the Commonwealth, see H. G. Wright, "The Theme of Solitude and Retirement in Seventeenth Century Literature," *Études Anglaises*, VII (1954), 22–35.

whence streamed the gonfalon of death, a banner that men said blew significantly "ab sinistro." [19] The vestal fires that blast with their heart heat the North and the cold, the "show'rs of old Greeke" that dry up tears and rain, are augmented in their symbolic services by the display of lights that whip the "darke Hagge" of Night from "the light Casements." Within themselves, the frozen poets will remake the lost summer of the grasshopper. It is more than a lost summer; it is a shore of light as Vaughan would have understood it. This will be done, Lovelace informs Cotton, by means of candles as potent as the planet Venus, the "cleare *Hesper*." They are candles in the way that the fire is a fire; in one sense they are wax, in another, they are an inward light. By them Night is stripped forever of her dark cloak, for they will "sticke there everlasting Day." The warmth and brightness of the grasshopper's year, realized literally and, consequently, finitely in the early part of the poem are thus made eternal. The poet puts down Gothic horror; the grasshopper is made immortal; antique fearlessness is restored.

With the last stanza, the king, who has until now been hidden from us by a series of artistic translucencies, is revealed in his clear title. He is more than king of the summer fields or of Britain, for in governing the world of his creative imagination, he is untempted by the world. The poet and his friend, who may also be the "himselfe" of the last line, have created a kingdom privately. This kingdom cannot go down because it is invincible to outward attack. With this last stanza, the Horatian music that we have heard steadily since the dreary center of stanza V seems to achieve symphonic fullness. We have the impression of the Horatian tone because we know it has to be here. Horace, who fought on the wrong side

[19] For some associations, see St. Augustine, *In Iobam,* ed. Zycha (Vienna, 1895), p. 608 and his *Epistulae,* ed. Goldbacher (Vienna, 1904), p. 201; see also Eucherius, *Liber Formularum* (PL, L, 740–41).

at Philippi, must have appeared to Lovelace and Cotton as a
Roman cavalier who, when all was lost, found the good way.
His metaphors repeat themselves once more. The tempest
comes with the rain and the North Wind, but one forgets them
before a heaped fire and a full cup.

> Horrida tempestas caelum contraxit, et imbres
>   Nivesque deducunt Iovem; nunc mare, nunc silvae
> Threicio Aquilone sonant. Rapiamus, amici,
>   Occasionem de die, dumque virent genua
> Et decet, obducta solvatur fronte senectus.
>   Tu vina Torquato move consule pressa meo.
> Cetera mitte loqui: deus haec fortasse benigna
>   Reducet in sedem vice.[20]

In Horace's poetic promises there is little eternity; this illusion
is shunned. The fire on the Sabine hearth is as real as the wind
and the rain. It is Lovelace who creates the illusion for which
he lives. In another sense "himselfe" may not be Cotton at all,
but the private world of the poet's heart, where all is warm and
light and the grasshopper lives in a kingdom made eternal by
his song.

[20] *Epodes* XIII.1–8; *Carmina* I.9.5–8, 13–14; 17; 18; II.7, 11.

CHAPTER TEN

Andrew Marvell

"The Nymph Complaining
for the Death of Her Faun"

The poem that Marvell shows us is about a "nymph," and unless he uses this word with indecorous irony, she is a young virgin, who lives in a world of pastoral innocence different from the world of "cruel men." Into this "little Wilderness," which is not a wilderness at all, has come a man with the significant name of Sylvio (no wonder "he grew wild"), who has won the girl's love. The fawn, which Sylvio gives the girl as a token of love becomes, when he abandons her, a *surrogatus amoris;* in fact, it becomes something like the child that might have been hers had Sylvio not proved "counterfeit." The poem is not, as critics have said, about kindness to animals, or the death of Christ, or the British Church; on the contrary, it is a sensitive treatment of the loss of first love, a loss augmented by a virginal sense of deprivation and unfulfillment.

The nymph has brooded so much over losing her lover that she has enlarged the token of love into a life symbol.

The mode of the poem is as honest as its literal reading. It is a pastoral epicedium recited while the creature that it celebrates dies. This is a new notion—to preach the funeral sermon before the heart stops and the breath is gone. To assure us about the nature of the poem, Marvell calls it a "complaint," putting it in a recognized poetic tradition. The topics that govern the formal complaint are altered because its subject is an animal. Even then, the physical and moral qualities of the fawn are mentioned; its death is described, and its immortality is promised. The fawn has "virgin Limbs"; it is white and loving; it is light-footed and fleet. It lies among lilies and devours roses. It is promised a tomb and an eternity, "in fair Elizium to endure." All of these expressions are adaptations of the normal themes previously applied to men, and they had been used before when the death of a beloved creature was lamented.

Complaints on the deaths of favorite animals fill the seventh book of the *Greek Anthology*,[1] but Marvell's readers would be more likely to remember Catullus' lament on the death of Lesbia's sparrow, a bird similar in some of its ways to the fawn but different in its fate.

> Nam mellitus erat suamque norat
> Ipsam tam bene quam puella matrem;
> Nec sese a gremio illius movebat,
> Sed circumsiliens modo huc modo illuc
> Ad solam dominam usque pipiabat.[2]

---

[1] VII, 189–92, 194–203, 207–16; see the *Supplement,* ed. Dübner (Paris, 1890), II, 387. For imitations of Catullus' poem in English, see J. A. S. McPeek, *Catullus in Strange and Distant Britain* (Cambridge, Mass., 1939), pp. 61–72; the author of this monograph was the first to notice the connection between Marvell and Catullus.

[2] III.6–10.

The fawn, too, would "stay, and run again, and stay"; it, too, nursed at the nymph's finger and kissed her mouth. The echoes of Catullus' poem combine also with Ovid's lament over Corinna's popinjay, a bird famous for his color and voice, and in its way a symbol of mortal existence. "Plena fuit vobis omni concordia vita,/ Et stetit ad finem longa tenaxque fides." For the tomb of this pet, so closely associated with the love and life of his mistress, Ovid wrote an epitaphic couplet in which he assured his readers that it was not excluded from Elizium, "whither Swans and Turtles go."

> Colle sub Elysio nigra nemus ilice frondens,
> Udaque perpetuo gramine terra, viret.
> Si qua fides dubiis; volucrum locus ille piarum
> Dicitur, obscoenae quo prohibentur aves.
> Illic innocui late pascuntur olores;
> Et vivax phoenix, unica semper avis.
> Explicat ipsa suas ales Junonia pennas:
> Oscula dat cupido blanda columba mari.
> Psittacus has inter, nemorali sede receptus,
> Convertit volucres in sua verba pias.[3]

A classically trained reader might remember these obvious texts and incorporate them as silent stanzas in this poem; but he might also ask himself why, with all of this tradition behind him, Marvell selected a fawn instead of a more ordinary creature for the immediate center of the nymph's complaint.

The literary antecedents once again supply us with a reading of Marvell's literal statement. The first of them, as Muir [4] pointed out, is from the seventh book of the *Aeneid*,[5] where the death of Silvia's pet deer at the hands of Ascanius is re-

---

[3] *Amores* II.6; for other earlier texts, see Herrlinger, *Totenklage um Tiere in der Antiken Dichtung* (Stuttgart, 1930).
[4] *Notes and Queries*, CXCVI (1951), 115.
[5] VII.475-504.

lated. It is also a tamed wild thing that has wandered into the
human world and been wantonly slain. The penalty for this
rash killing was the war between the Teucrians and the men
of Latium. In the second book[6] of the epic, there are some
oblique lines that remind us of Agamemnon's destruction of
Artemis' deer, a thoughtless act that brought death to Iphigenia in the depressing version of her myth. Sophocles'
Electra also informs us that the giant king, "once disporting
himself in the grove of the goddess," startled the dappled animal and boastingly shot it. For this impiety, he paid with his
daughter's blood.[7] In neither case is the deer made the subject
of a formal lamentation; nevertheless, the menace is made clear
and the nymph's "They cannot thrive" is illuminated by these
poetic predecessors.

  In both of the older legends, the slaughtered deer is more
a thing of the woods than the nymph's fawn, "Ty'd in this
silver chain and Bell"; hence, it is pleasant to come on the
ancestor of Marvell's fawn in the eclogues of Calpurnius,
where the pastor Astilius, who wagers the animal in a singing
contest, calls attention to its excellence.

> en aspicis illum,
> Candida qui medius cubat inter lilia cervum?
> Quamvis hunc Petale mea diligat, accipe victor.
> Scit frenos et ferre iugum, sequiturque vocantem
> Credulus, et mensae non improba porrigit ora.
> Aspicis, ut fruticat late caput, utque sub ipsis
> Cornibus et tereti pendent redimicula collo?
> Aspicis, ut niveo frons irretita capistro
> Lucet, et a dorso, quae totam circuit alvum,
> Alternat vitreas lateralis cingula bullas?

---

[6] II.116–17.
[7] VII.565–72; see Hyginus 98; Arnobius V.34; Servius, *ad loc*. Dictys says
that the animal was a "capra," (*De Historia Belli Troiana* [Venice, 1499],
B2v); Antonius Liberalis, 27, states that Artemis supplied a deer in the
place of Iphigenia.

Cornua subtiles ramosque tempora molles
Implicuere rosae, rutiloque monilia torque
Extrema cervice natant, ubi pendulus apri
Dens sedet, et nivea distinguit pectora luna.[8]

Marvell's nymph would know this deer—a lounger among lilies; his horns are wrapped in roses; and he has his collar and ornaments. He is, however, a wanderer, for he has strayed from the deer park of the *Metamorphoses*.

Marvell must have remembered the deer beloved by Cyparissus, the handsome friend of Apollo. The Ovidian deer has golden horns ("cornua fulgebant auro"), and a collar of gems and a silver bell. "Bulla super frontem parvis argentea loris/ Vincta movebatur." Its ears are hung with pearls, and it is exceedingly tame. It frequents houses ("celebrare domos"), allows strangers to stroke it, and is the possessive joy of its master, who leads it to brooks in fair pastures, adorns it with flowers ("texebas varios per cornua flores"), and rides on its back. This deer is inadvertently killed, not by wanton hunters, but by Cyparissus, who is so overwhelmed by grief that he resolves to die. His patron-god, in pity, changes him, not into a memorial statue, but into the tree that is the symbol of grief.

Ingemuit, tristisque Deus, "Lugebere nobis,
Lugebisque alios, aderisque dolentibus," inquit.[9]

[8] VI.32–45.
[9] X.106–42. The association between the Artemis of the Agamemnon legend and the Apollo of the Ovidian account is made in the myth of Hercules' fifth labor, the capture of the deer of Ceryneia. This animal, with horns of gold and hoofs of bronze, was formerly dedicated to Artemis by the nymph Tagete, and Hercules, having captured it, was halted by the goddess and her brother and forced into an excuse (Apollodorus II.5.3; Euripides *Her. Fur.* ll. 378 ff.). The deer had earlier escaped from Artemis, when she captured its four fellows for her team (Callimachus III.97–109), and, according to Pindar (*Olymp.* III.50–52) wore a collar on which the nymph had inscribed the goddess' name. In the pseudo-Aristotelian περι Θαυμασιον Ακουσματον (110), we are informed that Agathocles of Sicily

Marvell's fawn is, perhaps, the offspring of these poetic recollections which seem to dominate and pervade the whole
poem, and we, as informed readers, will probably use some
of them. The first twenty-four lines of the poem make a
hymn, an opening liturgical phrase, and here the fawn has
special meaning; for we are led, as the song mounts in our
minds, into a numinous world where the wild things of the
wood are associated with the wild things of the solitary human
heart. The archaic word "deodand" establishes a ritualistic
emphasis for these lines, even though the betrayed nymph
reverses the usual definition of the word. The act of killing is
an act of impiety. Fawns are never slain; deer are killed in
season with ritual; and the butchery of the dead animal, in the
course of which the hands of the hunt master are washed in
blood, is a matter of extreme ceremony.[10] The "wanton
troopers" are unworthy of the hunt, which is made plain by
their ignorance of ceremony; hence they are both "ungentle
men" and "ungentlemen." Through their foul act, a quasi-
religious ritual has been debased and reduced to horrid slaughter. "Beasts must be with justice slain"; so a penalty must be

captured a deer wearing a collar marked with the name of Artemis. There
are other legends of deer with collars. Solinus (XIX.18) reports the capture
of a deer wearing the collar of Alexander, and collared deer appear in
the sonnets of Romanello and Petrarch. Mezeray, *Histoire de France*
(Paris, 1643), I, 930, contains an account of a deer captured in 1381 by
Charles VI with a collar on which was written "Hoc me Caesar donavit."
The allegorical deer of Fida in Brown's *Eclogues* mentioned by Bradbrook
and Lloyd Thomas in *Andrew Marvell* (Cambridge, 1940), and accepted by
Margoliouth in his notes to the *Poems* (1952) has, I think, very little to
do with this poem. One would do better to recall the Capuan deer of
Silius Italicus (XIII. 115-37), "quae candore nivem, candore anteiret olores."
It came readily to be stroked, combed, and bathed; it was thought to be
a familiar of Diana and the divine spirit of the city. It was killed by the
Roman general without serious consequences.
[10] *Le Livre de Chasse du Roy Modus*, ed. Tilander (Paris, 1931), pp. 7-43;
G. Turbervil, *The Noble Arte of Venerie or Hunting* (Oxford, 1907)
pp. 39-143.

paid and the nymph knows this well. The Capuan deer of Silius Italicus was killed for a just sacrifice, and Artemis could substitute a deer to save the person of Iphigenia, but the death of the nymph's fawn cannot "do them any good." It repeats the woodland crimes of Ascanius and Agamemnon.

The subject of the hymn has further meaning, because deer are blessed creatures. In classical texts they are sometimes revealed as spirits in animal form. Livy tells a legend of divine deer,[11] and Pausanius repeats two stories in which deer are workers of miracles.[12] During the Middle Ages, the sacred nature of deer was recorded in literary texts. It was a sacred deer, according to Benôit de Sainte-More,[13] who brought Paris to be judge in the contest between the three goddesses. Raimbert de Paris tells us that a deer, "blans come nois," showed Charlemagne the St. Bernard Pass, and that the great king considered the animal as God's messenger. "Ves le message que Dex a envoie." [14] In *Les Saisnes*, a fellow of this deer leads the great King to the only passage in the dangerous Rune.

> Qant ce voit l'empereres, n' i ot point de deshait;
> "Or quide il qe Dex por mostrance, l'ait fait,
> La ou cers ala, soit merchie et portrait." [15]

The more ordinary champions of the mediaeval romances were also associated in supernatural fashion with the holy deer. In the *Geste de Nanteuil*, the child Tristan is rescued from cruel fisherfolk by a deer that carried him into the forest and there looked to his nurture.[16] The knight Tyolet, who was brought up by his fearful mother in ignorant seclusion, learns

---

[11] X.27.8–10.
[12] II.30.7 and VIII.22.9.
[13] *Roman de Troie*, ed. Constans (Paris, 1904), ll. 3860–68.
[14] *Le Chevalerie Ogier de Danemarche*, ed. Barrois (Paris, 1842), pp. 11–12.
[15] Eds. Menzel and Stengel (Marburg, 1906), pp. 190–91. Similar legends are told about Clovis (Mezeray I.35).
[16] Paul Meyer, "Notice sur le roman de Tristan de Nanteuil," *Jahresbuch für Rom. u. Engl. Literatur*, IX (1868), 4–42.

about chivalry from a magic deer that "se transfigura. . . . / Et unchevalier resembloit." [17] But the most noteworthy experience with strange deer is that of Guigemar, who wounded a white doe and was retributively wounded himself when the arrow rebounded. The dying animal begins to speak French and tells the hunter that he will not be cured of his wound until he suffers much for a woman who has endured more than any other of her sex.[18] The mysteriousness of white deer is further enhanced by an episode in *Godefroid de Bouillon*, which narrates the rescue of Harpin by his friend Carbaran, who was led to the place of danger by three deer—not deer exactly, but "Seignor, c'estoit Saint Joires, Saint Barles, Saint Domis." [19] Some of these poetical precedents help us to understand the lines: "O help O help: I see it faint:/ And dye as calmely as a Saint." We also begin to realize why the nymph proposes placing a golden vial of the deer's tears as a reliquary in the shrine of Diana, patron saint of deer.

The association of deer with holy men does much to explain the under-chorus of the first hymn sung by the nymph, an under-chorus so vibrant that some critics have mistaken it for the whole poem. Probably the oldest legend that brings deer and sainthood together is that of St. Eustace or St. Placidas. It is found in prose in the *Acta Graeca* [20] and other calendars, but it was given poetic reality by an unknown poet of the Carolingian age.

> Dum esset magnus venator et saggittarius,
> Die quadam exivit more venancium;
> Aspexit grandem a longe cervorum numerum

[17] G. Paris, "Lais Inédits," *Romania*, VIII (1879), 43. In similar fashion, Richard of Normandy, hastening to deliver a message to Charlemagne, is shown the ford of the River Flagot by a white deer (*Fierabras*, eds. Kroeber and Servois [Paris, 1860], p. 132).

[18] Marie de France, *Lais*, ed. Warnke (Halle, 1925), pp. 9–10.

[19] *La Chanson du Chevalier au Cygne et de Godefroid de Bouillon*, ed. Hippeau (Paris, 1877), p. 264.

[20] *Analecta Bollandiana*, III (1884), 68–70.

Et unum candidum nimis stantem in medio:
Cepit persequi illum relictis omnibus.

Dum per spacia multa post eum curreret,
Ascendit cervus in summum saxorum verticem.
Placidas dum perpensaret, quid illi faceret,
Vidit in cornibus eius crucis imaginem
Et inter cornua pulcram Christi effigiem.

Placidas dum stupendo istud aspiceret,
Vocem sibi dicentem audivit taliter:
"Placidas, O Placidas, quid me persequeris?
Iesus ego, nescis quem fide credere,
Sed in operibus bonis visus es colere." [21]

The experience of Saint Placidas puts that of St. Giles or St. Godric,[22] who are more commonly associated with deer, in the shadow; and the conversion of this man, who became a martyr, is paralleled in literature by that of the father of the mediaeval French hero, Doon of Maience. In the *Romance of Doon*, we read that his father, hunting in the forest, slew with the same arrow a deer and its hermit master. In penitence for this deed, the hunter gave up chivalry and devoted his full service to God.[23] All of these accounts make it clear that salvation can come to a thoughtless hunter through the intermediation of the white deer, Jesus Christ.

The deer as the symbol of Christ was known to the Fathers and Doctors of the Church,[24] and the literary manifestations

[21] *Rythmi aevi Merovingici et Carolini,* ed. Winterfeld, PLAC (Berlin, 1899), IV, 593–94. See the English version in J. L. Weston, *Chief Middle English Poets* (Boston, 1914), pp. 78–79.

[22] For St. Giles and his deer, see *Analect. Boll.,* VIII (1889), 111–12, and the poetic "La Vie de Saint Giles" of Guillaume de Berneville, eds. Paris and Bos (Paris, 1881), pp. 46–52. For St. Godric, see Reginald of Coldingham, *Libellus de vita et miraculis S. Godrici* (London, 1847), p. 96.

[23] Ed. Pey (Paris, 1859), pp. 3–4.

[24] The deer is Christ: "imo cervi cervorum, id est Christi," writes Bede in *Psalmorum Librum Exegesis* (PL, XCIII, 702–703). There are many patristic references of this nature and the bestiaries also support it.

of the symbol were often brilliantly stated. According to one pious legend, a deer similar to the one that reproached St. Placidas appeared to two other saints in the forest of Brie, and subsequently reappeared in the presence of the whole congregation when these two holy men were assisting the Pope at mass in the Lateran.[25] The most charming literary account of the deer-Christ is that of Malory. Galahad, Percival, Bors, and Percival's sister are in a forest and see a white hart led by four lions entering a chapel, where a good hermit sings the mass of the Holy Ghost.

> And at the secrets of the mass, they saw the hart become a man, the which marvelled them, and set him upon the altar in a rich siege, and saw the four lions were changed, the one to the form of a man, the other to the form of a lion, and the third to an eagle, and the fourth was changed unto an ox. Then took they their siege where the hart sat, and went out through a glass window, and there was nothing perished nor broken, and they heard a voice say, In such a manner entered the son of God into the womb of a maid Mary.

The astonished watchers seek the full meaning of the moving symbols from a hermit, who informs them:

> And well ought our Lord be signified to an hart; for the hart when he is old he waxeth young again in his white skin: right so cometh again our Lord from death to life, for he lost earthly flesh, that was the deadly flesh which he had taken in the womb of the blessed virgin Mary; and for that cause appeared our Lord as a white hart without spot. . . . For wit ye well never erst might no knight know the truth, for, ofttimes ere this, our Lord shewed him unto good men and unto good knights in the likeness of an hart.[26]

[25] Pierre Hélyot, *Histoire des Ordres Monastiques* (Paris, 1714–1719), II, 127–29.

[26] *Le Morte Darthur*, ed. Strachey (London, 1912), p. 399. For previous interpretations of this poem, see the bibliography cited by E. S. LeComte, "Marvell's 'The Nymph Complaining for the Death of Her Faun,'" *MP*,

The assurances of the "good man in a religious weed, and in the armour of our Lord" have already been supported by symbolic examples in the metrical romances.

There is no doubt that the opening hymn of the nymph's epicedium contains a clear allusion to the "hinnulus cervorum," the name that St. Gregory gave to Christ. The innocence of the white fawn, the wantonness and injustice of the death, the washing of the hands, the reference to "Heaven's King," the sense of sacrifice and atonement, the concluding, "There is not such another in/ This World to offer for their Sin," point dramatically at this symbolic equivalent. But we should be aware that this subsurface suggestion is metaphoric rather than symbolic. The poem is not to be read as a mediaeval text, but as one in the baroque manner. The nymph who cries that even her own blood, which flows from her broken heart, is also not enough, "Yet could they not be clean," is not given to sacrilege. The poem is not about Christ. The deer is *like* Christ; it is not Christ. The poetic process that Marvell is here employing can be illustrated in reverse by two passages from the *Christiados* of Vives, who uses the metaphor of the hunted deer to explain the suffering of tormented holy ones. In the first, we witness the accusal of Susanna:

> Stabat conspectu in medio tremebunda puella,
> Iam suffusa oculos mortis nigrore propinquae,
> Et positis terram genibus submissa petebat:
> Non minus exanimata metu, quam in retia cerva
> Acta canum latratu, et longo exercita cursu,
> Cum iam consumptae vires, cum se undique cinctam
> Hoste videt, mortemque instantem certa moratur.[27]

L (1952), 97–101 and K. Williamson, "A Reply," *MP*, LI (1954), 268–71. For more recent proposals, see E. H. Emerson's article and Pierre Legouis' response in *Études Anglaises*, VIII (1955), 107–12 and "Marvell's 'Nymph Complaining for the Death of Her Faun': Sources versus Meaning," by Leo Spitzer in *MLQ*, XIX (1958), 231–43.

[27] *Opera* (Venice, 1538), p. 28.

The second passage shows us Christ before the Jews:

> veluti aspexit si forte Magistri
> Assuetum imperiis cervum media urbe Molossus,
> Sylvestrem ratus insequitur, vix voce coercet
> Venator rabido instantem cervicibus ore.[28]

In both of these instances, the figure is part of the lyrical flow and shares only obliquely in the full meaning; the martyrs are "like deer" and not deer.

The use of the Christ or saint metaphor is restricted to the complaining nymph, who is one person removed from the poet; the poet, on the other hand, employs the fawn in another metaphoric situation which the reader must understand to grasp the complexity of the poem. The implied metaphor supports the earlier decision that the animal is a *surrogatus amoris* and establishes a second point in the belief that the verse itself alternates between the secular and the divine, the classical and the Christian, in its literary allusiveness.

The poets of antiquity, it is well known, associated the deer with metaphors of love. Oppian finds them as emblematic of passion as birds;[29] and Theocritus' lovesick Cyclops feeds eleven fawns for the beloved but disdainful Galathea.[30] Horace compares his evasive Chloe to a frightened fawn ("Vitas inuleo me similis, Chloe"); assures her that he will not crush her as a lion or tiger would; and urges her to leave her mother and submit to him.[31] We find the two parts of the classical simile brought together in the fifteenth century *Gloria d'Amor* of Fra Rocaberti, who associates lovers with the hunting of the deer.

[28] *Ibid.*, p. 61.
[29] *Cynegetica* II.186–205. The metaphor is also used by Callimachus (*Epig.* 33), and by Agathias (*G.A.* V.292) whose girl-fawn is surrounded by roses and doves.
[30] *Eclogae* XI.40–41.
[31] *Carmina* I.23.

Com per lo giny del exercit de cassa
Los servos braus passen per via certa,
E qui. ls vol mort per lo fill los acassa
Axi viu jo per una selv' escura
Gran gent venir, arreglats a parella,
Vencuts d'amor; conegui lur figura,
Ab cants e lays de piedosa planta
Mostrant amor esser lur amat temple.[32]

In French literature of the sixteenth and seventeenth centuries, the game of love as a deer hunt, the beloved as a deer, and the lover as a wounded deer are common metaphoric equations. Marot makes one of these comparisons in his epigrams: "Les cerfz en rut pour les les bisches se battent,/ Les amoureux pour les dames combattent." [33] A little later, Ronsard frames his "Amours d'Eurymedon et Callirée" against the background of a deer hunt. The early seventeenth century saw the appearance of an anonymous "La Chasse et l'Amour"; [34] and Jean Passerat wrote a symbolic poem, "Le Cerf d'Amour," [35] and followed the analogy in "Sur la Comparaison des Cerfs et de Amoureaux."

Le Cerf et l'amoureaux, d'une diverse flame
Qu'allume un mesme Dieu, sont egaux en malheur:
L'un souffre maint travail, l'autre mainte douleur:
L'un court apres sa biche, et l'autre apres sa Dame. . . .
O Cerfs a quatre pieds, nous sommes vos parens,
Nous les Cerfs a deux pies qu'Amour a rendu bestes.[36]

---

[32] Ed. Heaton (New York, 1916), pp. 75-76.
[33] *Œuvres*, ed. Janet (Paris, 1873), III, 54.
[34] *Variétés Historiques et Littéraires*, ed. Fournier (Paris, 1855), I, 65-73.
[35] *Les Poesies Françaises*, ed. Blanchemain (Paris, 1880), I, 16-20.
[36] *Ibid.*, I, 20-21. The love theme of Poliziano's "La Giostra" is partly based on the love hunt. The hero Julio is overcome by Love while hunting the deer. "E con sue [Amore] man di leve aer compose/ La imagin d'una cervia altera e bella,/ Con alta fronte, con corna ramose,/ Candida tutta, leggiadretta e snella./ E come tra le fere paventose/ Al giovan cacciator si offerse quella,/ Lieto spronò il destrier per lei seguire,/

The metaphor came into English poetry through Wyatt and
Shakespeare, and certainly explains the punning passage that
supplies a kind of comic relief at the end of the initial hymn.
"Said He, look how your Huntsman here/ Hath taught a
Faun to hunt his *Dear*."

But the deer that is celebrated as it dies before our eyes,
the deer that the nymph associates not only with her own lost
love but also with her own death, is to be more closely defined than a plain, yet sometimes amusing, symbol of love. It
is a wounded deer, and as such it has a firm poetic ancestry,
because the theme which stems from the passage in the fourth
book of the *Aeneid* is introduced by Petrarch in sonnet CCIX.

> E qual cervo ferito di saetta,
> Col ferro avelenato dentr'al fianco,
> Fugge, e più duolsi quanto più s'affretta,
> Tal io con quello stral dal lato manco
> Che mi consuma e parte mi diletta,
> Di duol me struggo, e di fuggir me stanco.

The theme of the lover as a wounded deer was more particu-
larly worked out by Bembo in "Si come suol, poiche 'l verno
aspro e rio" [37] and given full voice by Ronsard in a sonnet that
makes Marvell's figure richer.

> Ainsi j'alloy sans espoir de dommage,
> Le jour qu'un oeil sur l'Avril de mon aage
> Tira d'un coup mille traits en mon flanc.[38]

This first hymnlike section of "The Nymph" with its multi-
plicities of literary suggestion is succeeded by an expository
passage (25–70) wherein the φύσις (as the classical epicedists
would call it) of the fawn is delicately announced. The fawn

Pensando in brieve darle agro martíre" (*Le Stanze*, ed. Carducci [Bologna,
1912], p. 274).

[37] *Gli Asolani e le Rime*, ed. Dionisotto-Casalone (Turin, 1932), p. 164.

[38] *Œuvres*, ed. Vaganay (Paris, 1924), I, 73.

is affectionate; it is swift, deserving its normal ancient epithet *alipes;* and it is whiter than a lady's hand. The almost heraldic blending and contrasting of red and white that dye a large portion of the remaining poem begin with, "I blusht to see its foot more soft,/ And white." The nymph shares the colors of the fawn, but the fawn is mainly important in that it is identified with the nymph, abandoned by her lover and condemned to idleness and solitariness. Time is also stated for us; it is the time that it takes to die, brief as the life of roses and lilies, of weanling fawns, or of young girls betrayed in their innocence.

> But I am sure, for ought that I
> Could in so short a time espie,
> Thy Love was far more better then
> The love of false and cruel men.

The emphasis in the capital letter is not without value because the fawn has become Love itself.

There is, however, a second hymn (71–91) that follows this expository passage, and, by enlarging the memory of the past, brings the poem to a peak of emotion. "I have a Garden of my own" is a statement that doubles the sense of possession, of loneliness, of inwardness. On the literal surface, the nymph is the mistress of a real garden of roses and lilies where she and the fawn joyed to be. But the garden is also a secret one, the mind and the heart of the girl, where, in one sense, the fawn played in the true spring. In another sense, while the fawn lived "it was all, the Spring time of the years." A number of critics have seen in Marvell's "The Garden" the symbol of the human mind, and this garden has undoubtedly the same intent. The garden of roses and lilies expresses the mind and the nature of the weeping maid, and she communes in it and through it with the fawn. Once again the tradition comes to support this identification and interpretation.

To Plato the imaginative mind is like a garden, for the

Phaedrus informs us that it is in such a propitious plot that men of letters plant flowers for their pleasure.[39] In the *Ion*, poets are described as bringing songs culled in the gardens and glades of the Muses, "Μουσῶν κήπων," [40] a metaphor that Pindar also uses to describe his literary occupation: "χαρίτων νέμομαι κῆπον." [41] The *figura mentis* of the mind as a garden was staunchly supported by the fact that Epicurus taught in a garden and that his cult could be called "κηπολογος." The garden of Epicurus, says Cicero figuratively, was watered by the fountains of Democritus: "cuius Democriti fontibus Epicurus hortos suos inrigavit"; [42] and the hostile Seneca defined the Epicureans as "alienus hortulus." [43] The author of the *Ciris* begins with the same sort of poetic turn:

> Etsi me, vario iactatum laudis amore,
> Irritaque expertum fallacis praemia vulgi,
> Cecropius suavis exspirans hortulus auras
> Florentis viridi Sophiae complectitur umbra:
> Ut mens curet eo dignum sibi quaerere carmen. . . .

The garden is a classical equivalent of the mind; and it is not unfitting to find in this garden of roses and lilies the history of the nymph's inner life. We notice, too, that the fawn, the amorous substitute, becomes part of the girl's self and blends into the flowers with a sort of invisibility. It loses itself, a bank of lilies in "the flaxen Lillies shade"; a white thought in a white shade. It fills itself with roses, and laps its "virgin limbs" in "Whitest sheets of Lillies cold." Had it lived longer —the poet insists—it would have become an intrinsic part of the nymph's inward life.

[39] 276D.
[40] 534A.
[41] *Olymp.* IX.27.
[42] *De Nat. Deorum* I.120.
[43] *Epist.* IV.10.

> Had it liv'd long, it would have been
> Lillies without, Roses within.[44]

The *hortus mentis* is, then, the inner life of the girl, but it has other meanings, too, that make it congenial with the topic of the "cerf d'Amour."

According to Athenaeus,[45] the second Hieron of Syracuse had a garden in which he talked to men and which he called (if transliteration may be substituted for translation), "the Myth." The myth of the garden leads us toward another literary equivalent that helps to enrich the meaning of the metaphors in the nymph's place of retirement. It was in such a place of flowers, the *Symposium*[46] states, that Penia conceived Cupid by Poros; and the "Jardin d'Amour" tenanted by Eros and his mother during most of the Middle Ages comes immediately to mind. This "vergier clos" is not one of the wicked bowers of the enchantresses of the Italian romances; it is not Acrasia's garden. If we must find one like it, we could look at the symbolic garden of Alcinous, the sheltered orchard where spring reigns forever. In such a place, a nameless guliard who was Silvio's ancestor hunted girls when spring had allayed the cruelties of winter.

> Dulcius est carpere
> Iam lilium cum rosa
> Dulcissimum est ludere
> Cum virgine formosa.[47]

[44] Though it is outside the limits of poetic expression, it is interesting to notice that the early Fathers found reason in the Bible to regard the heart or the mind as a garden: see Tertullian, *Adversus Marcion*, ed. Kroymann (Vienna, 1906), pp. 524–25; Ambrose, *Opera*, ed. Schenkle (Vienna, 1902), III.362; St. Augustine, *In Joannes* (PL, XXXV, 1957).

[45] XII.542.

[46] 203B.

[47] *Carmina Burana* (Stuttgart, 1847), p. 181.

In a similar garden the disconsolate lover of *De Venus la Deesse d'Amour* is consoled and instructed in love.[48] After this time, the garden of loving delights spreads over a wide area and is filled with blossoms. It becomes in Italy the "Giardino d'Amore" where Poliziano's Julio wandered: "Veste la campagna/ Di rose, gigli, violette e fiori."[49] In France, it is known as the garden of love, which is painstakingly described by Jean Passerat.[50] It was also familiar to the English, for it is found in that wintered land in "Twicknam Garden" where the lover John Donne cries out in frozen desolation. The garden of the mind can be transformed by poetic music into the garden of love.

It is also plain that this garden was sown with two flowers, the lily and the rose, because the poets of Eros cannot speak of love without them.

> Rosa rubicundior
> Lilio candidior
> Omnibus formosior
> Semper in te glorior![51]

The colors white and red suggest modesty and innocence, but both flowers possess the common implication of brevity, of the short lives of the nymph and her fawn. Valerius Flaccus supports this understanding when he compares the days of the lily to the flashing by of human life.

> Lilia per vernos lucent velut alba colores
> Praecipue, quis vita brevis totus que parumper
> Floret honor fuscis et iam Notus imminet alis.[52]

[48] Ed. Foerster (Bonn, 1880), p. 2.
[49] *La Giostra*, in *Le Stanze l'Orfeo e le Rime*, ed. Carducci (Bologna, 1912), pp. 299–316.
[50] *Œuvres*, ed. Blanchemain (Paris, 1880), I, 25–29.
[51] *Carmina Burana*, p. 208.
[52] VI.492–94.

In keeping with these verses, Horace, drinking in the company of friends, ponders the fate of the "breve lilium" and the tender rose.[53]

For the Latins and their cultural inheritors, the rose and the lily were symbols of youth, and of love and death in youth. The modest and anxious love of Lavinia is characterized by both flowers: "aut mixta rubent ubi lilia multa/ Alba rosa: talia virgo dabat ore colores";[54] and to this we may join all of the sad commentary on the worldly rose that helped to annotate Herbert's rose poem. The flowers often appear in mediaeval poetry as kindred emblems. In the "De Rosae et Liliique Certamine" of Sedulius Scottus, we follow a debate between the rose and the lily that Spring, the arbiter, brings to a close when she urges the sister flowers to remember that they are signs of innocence, youth, death, virginity, and martyrdom.

> O rosa pulchra, tace; tua gloria claret in orbe;
> Regia sed nitidis dominentur lilia sceptris.
> Hinc decus et species vestrum vos laudat in aevum:
> Forma pudicitiae nostris rosa gliscat in hortis,
> Splendida Phebeo vos, lilia, crescite vultu;
> Tu, rosa, martyribus rutilam das stemmate palmam,
> Lilia, virgineas turbas decorate stolatas.[55]

As a consequence of this tradition, the Renaissance knew the history of the rose and lily and adorned its poetry with it.

The two flowers are wisely employed by Marvell in both their priestly and secular meanings. With their aid, he maintains the tones of innocence, youth, love, and death that make the partial chorus of the complaint. The sacred meaning of the garden, which Bradbrook, Lloyd Thomas, and William-

[53] I.36.16.
[54] *Aeneid* XII.68–69.
[55] *Opera*, ed. Traube, *PLAC* (Berlin, 1896), III, 230–31.

son have felt, is also present; yet it stays in a symbolic memory that surpasses the nearer echoes of the Psalms and the Canticle. The nymph, who is a member of Diana's court and also a young girl bewailing the loss of love, is something like the weeping mother of Christ [56] just as she is, according to Spitzer, something like Niobe. She is a mother of a dying creature that is at one and the same time her love (and since she has created this passion, it is also herself) and the external token of this love. All of this is a complicated literary truth on phenomenal and numenal levels; but, essentially, she is not a mother and the thing in which she believed has "proved wild." For this reason, she is never quite certain of the token itself: "his Gifts might be/ Perhaps as false or more than he." The Virgin and Niobe are present in the same way that Christ is present in the first hymn. They are associative metaphors; they are not the poem.

The full union of Christian and pagan metaphors is found in the final section of the poem. The fawn, while it dies as an animal, becomes the "Saint" with whom its ancestors consorted. Its medicinal tears, famous in the Renaissance pharmacopoeia, are converted into relics for the shrine of the Virgin-Diana. They are described in terms of the Biblical "holy

[56] The likeness of Diana to the Virgin is as obvious as the impious-pious comparisons of Orpheus to Christ; moreover, thanks to Seznec (*La Survivance* [London, 1939], p. 233), we know that the comparison was made. The Virgin, we also know, is the closed garden, the "hortus conclusus" of Alanus de Insulis (*Anticlaudianus* [PL, CCX, 538]), or "le vergier clos" of Guillaume of Normandy (R. Reinsch, "Les Joies Nostre Dame de Guillaume," *Zeitsch. für Roman. Phil.*, III [1879], 222). Her association with the rose and the lily is everywhere in the Middle Ages and in the Roman poetry of the Renaissance. "Tu es li lis où Diex repose;/ Tu es rosier qui porte rose/ Blanche et vermeille," writes Rutebeuf (*Œuvres* [Paris, 1874], II, 146); and John of Garland follows the same theme through part of the *Stella Maris* (ed. Wilson [Cambridge, Mass., 1946], pp. 91, 121, 149). For an unknown poet of the Merovingian age, the Virgin is "Lilium inter spinas acutissimas" and "Rosa fulgentem castitatis robore" (*PLAC*, ed. Winterfeld [Berlin, 1899], IV, 516–17).

frankincense," and at the same time they are associated with the pagan "electrum." The Heliades, whose brother was killed in his youth, are brought into the garden to weep with the nymph who has lost her fawn. The proper passage which levels the imaginative path to the completely static and sculptural finale is found in the place indicated by Marvell.

> nomenque in marmore lectum
> Perfudit lacrymis, et aperto pectore fovit.
> Nec minus Heliades fletus, et, inania morti
> Munera, dant lacrymas.[57]

We are close to cepotaphic verse in these latter lines,[58] for the monument of the nymph and her fawn will mark their garden grave. The traditional statue of the fawn-loving Diana is similar to the Pietà, but it is not the same. The nymph realizes a satisfaction that she denied herself in life when she accepted a token and retreated to the garden. The fawn's affection, which might have passed, is now assured by its death. Love, which she found to be false in her one encounter with it in the real world; love, which was even uncertain in the garden, in the *hortis mentis*, is safe, unchanging, and everlasting only in the world of art. In this new world the nymph and the fawn are united eternally:

> but there
> Th' Engraver sure his Art may spare;

[57] Ovid *Metamorphoses* II.338–41. See also Hyginus 154; Claudian VII.125; XXVIII.165; Statius V.3.85–86; Martial IV.59.

[58] The ancient custom of garden burial is described by Tacitus (*Hist.* I.49.1) and Suetonius (*Galba* XX.2); for poetic records, see Ausonius CCXXXVIII; and Martial I.114. Since the previous critics of this poem have tried to assume that there is symbolism in the ermine, I can assure them that there is, although I do not think it is required. The ermine is associated with the lily as a symbol of purity and innocence in French literature from Marot's "De la Royne Claude," *Œuvres*, ed. Grenier (Paris, n.d.), II, 509 to St. Amant, *Œuvres*, ed. Livet (Paris, 1885), I, 300. One German minnesinger equated the ermine with Christ: see *Minnesinger*, ed. von der Hagen (Leipzig, 1838), II, 311.

> For I so truly thee bemoane,
> That I shall weep though I be Stone:
> Until my Tears, still dropping, wear
> My breast, themselves engraving there.

The flight from the realities of love to an ideal of love, Marvell seems to be saying, may be the course of caution, but even here the idea can be permanently fixed only by the hand of the artist. And yet the colors tell the story: whiteness alone remains; the red of sentient life is gone.

CHAPTER ELEVEN

Andrew Marvell

"Upon Appleton House"

"Upon Appleton House" was written after Marvell had gone to Nunappleton as tutor to Mary, the only child of the great Lord Fairfax. It was a moment of retirement for both the poet and his patron. Fairfax, who had led the armies against the King, was appalled by the actions of the victorious Parliamentarians. When the captive King was held for questioning, he refused to sit with the committee of inquiry at Westminster. Lady Fairfax, the "starry Vere," was present in the gallery and spoke her mind in praise of her husband's absence and in condemnation of Cromwell. To her, the Captain of the Saints was a traitor. General Fairfax was probably more controlled than his wife; he remained with the army, assisting the government in keeping the peace, until June, 1650. The occasion of his retirement is noteworthy. The generals met to consider the invasion of Scotland where rebellious troops were mustering;

Cromwell insisted that a preventive expedition was impera-
tive. The consultation, as Whitelocke records it, is solemn.
Fairfax saw no reason for the continuation of bloodshed; he
spoke out against it and resigned his command. "Every man
must stand or fall by his own conscience." [1] Marvell's stanza
XLV makes this honest conclusion into poetry.

> For he did, with his utmost Skill,
> *Ambition* weed, but *Conscience* till.
> *Conscience,* that Heaven-nursed Plant,
> Which most our Earthly Gardens want.
> A prickling leaf it bears, and such
> As that which shrinks at ev'ry touch;
> But Flowrs eternal, and divine,
> That in the Crowns of Saints do shine.

So Fairfax retired with his family to what his laureate called
in another poem "the happy Garden-state," leaving to those
of less conscience the "unweeded garden" of public life.

By seventeenth-century aristocratic standards, the place
to which they retreated was relatively modest.

> It was a picturesque brick mansion with stone copings and
> a high steep roof, and consisted of a centre and two wings at
> right angles, forming three sides of a square, facing to the north.
> The great hall or gallery occupied the centre between the two
> wings. It was fifty yards long, and was adorned with thirty
> shields of wood, painted with the arms of the family. In the
> three rooms there were chimney-pieces of delicate marble of
> various colours, and many fine portraits on the walls. The
> central part of the house was surrounded by a cupola, and
> clustering chimneys rose in the two wings. A noble park with
> splendid oak-trees, and containing 300 head of deer, stretched
> away to the north, while on the south side were ruins of the
> old Nunnery, the flower-garden, and the low meadows called
> *ings* extending to the banks of the Wharfe. In this flower-garden

[1] *Memorials* (Oxford, 1853), III, 207.

the General took especial delight. The flowers were planted in masses, tulips, pinks, and roses, each in separate beds, which were cut into the shape of forts with five bastions. General Lambert, whom Fairfax had reared as a soldier, also loved his flowers, and excelled both in cultivating them and in planting them from Nature. Lord Fairfax only went to Denton, the favorite seat of his grandfather, when the floods were out over the *ings* at Nunappleton, and he also occasionally resorted to his house at Bishop Hill in York.[2]

The prose account, written by Markham, who owned a lithograph no longer extant, supplies the poem with as many comments as the poem itself gives to the prose. In its way, it tells us no more than the poem, but the poem is really not about the house.

"Upon Appleton House" is a sequence of dramatic poems, skillfully divided, that celebrates the "house" in several ways. It is about the actual house, the actual gardens, fields, meadows, streams, and wood. It is about the house of Fairfax in past, present, and future. It is also about the house of flesh, the body and mind of man. The poem can be read as an ode in the manner of Pindar, for it not only praises Fairfax but also relates the necessary family myth, records the illustrious deeds, brings out the character of its subject, and phrases prophecies. The first ten stanzas are about the physical aspects of the house. It is architecturally British. No foreign architect vaulted (with Macbeth's notion of sprawling on the other side) "his brain" to produce it. As a consequence of this simplicity, the observer need not "arch the Brows" both in astonishment and in an optical effort to view it. "Vault" and "arch" are emphasized because the house contains, if Markham's print is correct, neither structural feature. The master builder abided, the poet then explains, by Nature's simple plan; he learned by the householding of bird, beast, and reptile

<hr>

[2] *Life of the Great Lord Fairfax* (London, 1870), p. 365.

that one needs a house only slightly grander than oneself.

The third stanza of the description of the house proper is based on the comparison, that had passed through many poetical fingers, of man's house of life to his tomb. Then, thinking of the entrances to Norman keeps and seeing in them stony symbols of the "needle's eye" of Matthew and Luke, Marvell, like Gascoigne or some other Tudor conservative, recalls the other England of Fairfax's great-grandfather.

> But all things are composed here
> Like Nature, orderly and near:
> In which we the Dimensions find
> Of that more sober Age and Mind,
> When larger sized Men did stoop
> To enter at a narrow loop;
> As practising, in doors so strait,
> To strain themselves through *Heavens Gate.*

The doctrine that true greatness is humbly expressed is illuminated by the examples of Romulus' "Bee-like Cell," the humble "short but admirable lines" of Appleton House, and the celebrated "homo perfectissimus" (the squared circle) of Renaissance painting. In the ninth stanza we arrive before an allegorical house not unlike Spenser's House of Holiness or Alma's House; and at the end of this stanza, Marvell offers a good poetical rendering of Fairfax's own bad lines, "Upon the New-built House att Apleton."

> Thinke not o Man that dwells herein
> This House's a Stay but as an Inne
> Wch for Convenience fittly stands
> In way to one nott made with hands
> But if a time here thou take Rest
> Yett thinke Eternity's the Best.[3]

The tenth stanza adds this total description to the remainder of the poem and provides us with a résumé of the topics that

[3] *The Poems,* ed. Reed (New Haven, Conn., 1909), p. 279.

will be poetically discussed: "fragrant Gardens, shaddy Woods,/ Deep Meadows, and transparent Floods."

The topics thus stated, topics that really weave the whole poem together and make a theme for the ultimate section on Mary Fairfax, are suppressed for twenty-five paragraphs while Marvell, directing our eyes toward the ruins of the nunnery, recites the legend of the family, satirizes the conventual life, provides his retired patron with an example of action in difficult times and circumstances, and sweeps the way for his eventual celebration of his charge, Mary Fairfax. We then leave the past and pass into the present garden, which is both the prelapsarian state and ante-bellum England. The garden's security enables us to view from afar the fields and water meadows in which is enacted an allegorical masque of the recent civil disorders. With stanza LXI, Marvell's personal *Apologia pro Vita Sua* begins as he forsakes history and biography for autobiography. The last poem is written in praise of the house in the person of its twelve-year-old heiress. Here we sense something similar to Donne's *Anniversaries*. The poem is, then, a group of poems on a central subject like those that Marvell wrote about the Mower. It has a place, as most Renaissance poems do, in a long poetic history.

Poems about great men and their houses begin with Homer's description of the palace and gardens of King Alcinous. It is to this house that Athena leads Odysseus when he is stranded on the Phaeacian shores. Bronze, the metal of the house—the hardest known to men of Hesiod's Third Age— symbolizes the qualities of both the king and his realm. But strength and solidity alone do not make a kingdom, so Odysseus has hardly reached the threshold before splendor assails his eyes. The blaze that almost confounds him and that fills the long hall is that of the sun and moon: "ὥστε γὰρ ἠελίου αἴγλη πέλεν ἠὲ σελήνης."[4] Opposites, as the Greeks understood them, embrace in this metaphor and time and space are

[4] VII.84.

Homerically cancelled. It is, however, only fiction that insists on the presence of the sun and moon in the hall; for it is their mundane representatives, gold and silver, that produce the illusion in the fire-shine. The two metals are everywhere. The doorposts and lintel are silver; the doorhook is gold. Pairs of silver and gold dogs, fashioned by the skill of Hephaestus, guard the house of the "great-hearted one" from death and keep it forever ageless.[5] The fact that time, even seasonal change, avoids the house is symbolically suggested by youths of gold who light the hall with torches.

Without are the gardens, the first and fairest in the history of man. Here nature lives and prospers under the true light of the sun and moon, but now the light and heat are divinely ordained. No dogs of precious metal protect the gardens; no figures of youthful firmness hold torches there. "Such are also the splendid gifts of the gods" that the gardens are beyond the rage of earthly time. Age and Death are divinely fended off. "Of these never does the fruit decay or fail, winter or summer, lasting through the year." [6] Solidity, endurance, timelessness, and eternity—qualities uncharacteristic of Odysseus' experiences before Troy and on the weary homeward voyage—are summarized in King Alcinous and expressed poetically by his house and gardens. It is small wonder then that he is named "Ἀλκι + νoos" (strength of mind) and that he is wisely married to Arete or "excellence."

The house and gardens of Alcinous are both real and ideal. They represent the habitation of a great magnate of a Greek kingdom; on the other hand, they stand for high qualities of character, for mental force. In these respects they are not unlike the "castellum mentis," the Acropolis of Plato,[7] and the "Arx" of Cicero; [8] the single strongholds in a failing world.

[5] VII.94.
[6] VII.117–18.
[7] *Republic* 560B.
[8] *De Natura Deorum* II.140.

Though the Greeks do not want for descriptive poetry about public buildings, there is, I think, no other poetical description of a royal abode like that of Alcinous, which supplies us with both a literal and a moral reading. The Middle Ages followed the moral sense when it erected the poetical structures, palaces and gardens, that housed and entertained its massive personifications; and from the mediaeval blueprints, the poets of the *romanzi* drew the details for the residences of their thinly clad creatures of vice and virtue. This is the tradition that eventuates in the allegorical houses of the *Faerie Queene*. I shall not pretend that Homer had anything to do with the fabrication of the tradition that the Middle Ages and Renaissance followed. The bridge between the house of Alcinous and that of Lord Fairfax is anchored on an Italian pier, because it was the Romans, rather than the Greeks who emphasized the private house as the expression of the character and biography of the great man. For them the villa was autobiography; whereas the tomb, scarred over with flattery, was the work of a hired biographer.

With his descriptions of the houses of Dido and Latinus, Vergil follows the direction of Homer, but the most allegorical house erected by an early Latin poet is the Palace of Pelops which appears in Seneca's *Thyestes*. This house is the moral antithesis of the palace of Alcinous. It stands on a high place and faces south; its halls gleam with many colors; but it is environed with desperation and death. Planted to yew and cypress, its garden is without sun, and through it flows a dismal stream, which gathers in black pools and is filled with the voices of the dead. There is fire but it provokes no metaphors of light; it blazes in a savage wood and reveals horror.

> Quidquid audire est metus
> Illic videtur; errat antiquis vetus
> Emissa bustis turba et insultant loco
> Maiora notis monstra; quin tota solet
> Micare silva flamma, et excelsae trabes

Ardent sine igne. Saepe latratu nemus
Trino remugit, saepe simulacris domus
Attonita magnis. Nec dies sedat metum;
Nox propria luco est et superstitio inferum
In luce media regnat.[9]

The House of Pelops knocks at the gate of allegory, but it
is also as real as its fate. Homer in his description of the palace
of Alcinous feathered over the moral with the literal reading;
in Seneca it is the second meaning that makes the surface
sheen. By placing the two texts together, we have the cross and
pile, the two faces of the coin of symbolism. Yet it is Statius,
rather than Homer or Seneca, who truly makes the die of the
mode that later poets followed when they praised a man by
describing his house.

In the epithalamium that he wrote for the marriage of Ar-
runtius Stella and Violantilla, Statius describes the bride's
house in Rome.[10] The description is full but not independent,
for it is part of the marriage hymn, a piece of scenic enamel
in the plaque of celebration. In two other poems of the *Silvae*,
one on the Tiberine villa of Manilius Vopiscus and another on
the villa of Pollus Felix at Sorrento, the poet makes house and
gardens describe their master. The first villa stands on both
banks of the Anio and is surrounded by forest; it is the emblem, consequently, of coolness and quiet. It is richly adorned;
but in contrast to things fashioned by men, Nature supplies
her final elaborations, sending a stream through every room
and a great tree through the roof. Calm, shade, temperateness
rule in the house and its yards, proclaiming that its master is
both a philosopher and a poet.[11] In contrast, the verses on the
villa at Sorrento exalt the qualities of beauty and self-content.
Like Lord and Lady Fairfax, Pollius and his wife have retired

[9] 670–79.
[10] *Silvae* I.2.140–60.
[11] I.3.

from the city with its hordes of ambitious people. Important once in the affairs of state, the master has withdrawn from public life in order to devote himself to permanent things. He is worthy, says Statius, of the peace and beauty that surround him. "Ite per annos/ Saeculaque et priscae titulos praecedite famae." [12]

Martial, the contemporary of Statius, takes over the mode in his comparison of Faustinus' villa near Baiae with Bassus' house at Rome,[13] setting, so literary historians have said, the pattern for English poems on country houses. His poem actually is somewhat outside of the tradition, for it is essentially a satire on the great villas in the imperial city. It certainly gave Browning the idea for "Up at a Villa"; but for the poets of the seventeenth century, the descriptions of Statius are far more suggestive. I think that this conjecture is reasonable because Statius stands behind the descriptive poems of the fourth century Bishop Sidonius, whose verses on the house of Pontius Leontius are the most fitting precursor of "Upon Appleton House."

The "Burgus Pontii Leontii" begins with a description of the natural location of the house; then a myth, similar to Marvell's nunnery legend, is told. Dionysus and Apollo meet and lament the desecration of their rites in Greece. Apollo proposes that they join powers and found a common shrine at the confluence of the Dordogne and Garonne. Gifted with foresight, the god describes the house that Paulinus Pontius, the founder of the line, will raise on this place and the illustrious race that there will be bred. Situated on a summit, the house will display two towers, signifying "splendor and aid." Its doorstone will be a memorial of celebrated names; its walls will shine with painting and sculpture. The eyes of Apollo-Sidonius, like those of Marvell, leave the house and wander

[12] II.2.145–46.
[13] III.58

over its cool colonnades, granaries, baths, gardens, fields, streams, and waterfall. The house speaks for the characters of its founders, but chiefly proclaims the greatness of Pontius and his wife, "than whom no other lady of the Pontian house ever rejoiced more in her husband's illustrious career." [14] In this house, the poet Sidonius was received and his poem about the retired Leontius, "easily the first of the men of Aquitaine," is very much like Marvell's poem on the house of the General who had left the service of the state.

The great house as the mirror of its owner is the subject of various continental poems [15] prior to those written by Jonson, Carew, and Marvell; but these English poems surpass their continental predecessors in skill and merit. There is no question that Marvell's poem is superior in its generation because of its hidden complications and its blending of traditions. But this can only be shown by explanation, and so I shall leave Nunappleton and follow Marvell into the garden.

The garden of Appleton House is not the garden of "The Garden" or the garden in which the Nymph, withdrawn from life, sported with her white fawn. This is a new garden, the work of a poet-gardener, who sees to it that we understand its meaning. In stanza XLI, Marvell tells us flatly that the place through which we saunter with Lord and Lady Fairfax is England. It is not the England of 1650, but the England of earlier years, not unlike the "hortus amoenissimus" of Adam and Eve. There is, however, a difference; the garden has not been corrupted by sin. It is the outside world that has fallen.

[14] *Carmina* XXII.

[15] See Lorenzo Gambara's "Arcis Caprarolae Descriptio," in *Poemata* (Antwerp, 1579), pp. 3–37; Marcantonio Flaminio's "Ad Villam Mariam," in *Carmina Quinque Illustrium Poetarum* (Florence, 1552), pp. 136–37; Francisco Berni's "In Descrizione della sua Casa," *Le Rime*, ed. Palazzi (Genoa, 1915), pp. 150–52; Théophile's "La Maison de Sylvie," *Œuvres*, ed. Alleaume (Paris, 1855), II, 193–230; Tristran l'Hermite's "La Maison d'Astrée," in *Les Amours*, ed. Camo (Paris, 1925), pp. 244–55. Jonson's "Penshurst" and Carew's "Saxham House" make up the English count.

The theme seems to be an elaboration of the notion that, had our first parents stood, they would have remained in the garden; but even then Cain, the founder of cities, would have brought sin to mankind. We do not need Marvell to tell us that the English state is a garden, for Shakespeare anticipated him in *II Henry VI, Richard II,* and *Henry V.* Old Gaunt knew that England was another Eden; but who told him?

There is, first, a Hebraic answer to the question asked by this metaphor. Besides the Garden of Eden, there was Solomon's maze of roses, lilies, and palms that fixed the Queen of Sheba in admiration and supplied the *mise en scène* for the Canticle. St. John tells us that Mary Magdalene mistook her risen Lord for the "hortulanus" of the garden; and if Christ-Pastor can become the shepherd-king, the king can be a gardener. To these figures can be added those supplied by the pagans. Semiramis, Cyrus, and Epicurus were garden-makers; Caesar willed his gardens to the Romans; and Scipio, Lucullus, Augustus, and Diocletian retired to cultivate their flowers. But the poetic connection between statecraft and gardening is made by associations beyond those of the Bible, history, and mythology.

For the ordinary Roman, the gardens that covered Italy had symbolic meaning; they represented the status of their masters and were microcosms of the Roman Empire. Vitruvius makes it clear that a garden was an aristocratic requirement, "suitable to their consummate majesty," "ad decorum maiestatis perfectae." [16] The significance of the garden as something beyond the hopes of an ordinary citizen is tacitly expressed by Cato and Varro in their books on agriculture. To make this point openly, Columella puts his book on gardening into verse. Even Vergil, who uses hexameters for his four books on agriculture, admits that gardening is beyond the limits of his poem and leaves it as a special subject for others. "Verum haec ipse

[16] VI.7.10.

equidem spatiis exclusus iniquis/ Praetereo atque aliis post me memoranda relinquo."

If the texts may be credited, the Roman aristocrat attempted to recreate the Roman world within the walls of urban gardens. Chrysippus, according to Plutarch, complained about the nobles who made their gardens into representations of the great world,[17] and Seneca the Rhetorician reports the speech of the lawyer Fabianus Papirius against this practice.[18] To these "Stoics Against the Gardens" one can add Pliny's account of the attempt to show the real world in the yard of a villa through the services of a "topiarius"[19]—a word made from *topia*, a "landscape painting." He describes the "picturae" and "imagines rerum"[20] that filled these open places and, then, the more specific Vitruvius tells us about "the ports, promontories, shores, rivers, fountains, temples, mountains, herds, and even shepherds" fashioned by the "topiarius."[21] So all of Nature and the Roman world were brought within these narrow limits and irrigated by streams to which one gave names like "Nile"[22] or "Euripus."[23] The little Syrian of the "Copa," a poem we can hope is Vergil's, gives us a charming verse description of a garden.

> Sunt topia et kalybae, cyathi, rosa, tibia, chordae,
>   Et triclia umbrosis frigida harundinibus.
> En et Maenalio quae garrit dulce sub antro
>   Rustica pastoris fistula in ore sonat.
> Est et vappa, cado nuper defusa picato,
>   Et strepitans rauco murmure rivus aquae.
> Sunt et cum croceo violae de flore corollae

[17] *De Stoicorum Repugnantibus* 21.
[18] *Controversariae* II.1.10.
[19] *Naturalis Historia* IV.29; XII.22; XVI.76, 140; XVIII.242.
[20] XVI.140.
[21] VII.5.
[22] Cicero *Ad Quintum* III.9.
[23] Statius, I.3.31.

> Sertaque purpurea lutea mixta rosa
> Et quae virgineo libata Achelois ab amne
> Lilia vimineis attulit in calathis.[24]

The garden, as Marvell certainly knew, was associated with kings and brightened with Christian meaning. Whether he understood its representational qualities as the Romans saw them I do not know; he had lately been in Rome and he cannot have missed its floral splendors. At any rate it is clear from explicit statement that the garden at Nunappleton is also a symbol of the state. It is, however, more than this, for Marvell plainly tells us that it is a garrison. Its planter was a man of warlike exploits, and the first baron was also a man to make flowery jests.

> Who, when retired here to Peace,
> His warlike Studies could not cease;
> But laid these Gardens out in sport
> In the just Figure of a Fort;
> And with five Bastions it did fence,
> As aiming one for ev'ry Sense.

When we follow Lord Fairfax through the garden, we are really attending a review. The flowers let "fragrant Vollyes" fly, and like regiments on parade "Under their *Colours* stand displaid." But the garden which is the state and the citadel of state is more specifically defined.

This is one of the least particularized of all gardens; it pales before those of the late Greek romances; [25] Perdita's garden is a Luxembourg compared to it; "The Garden" could give instruction to its planter. It contains only three kinds of flowers; it has no birds, for they and the butterflies have fled to the wood where Marvell will write his life story. The

---

[24] 7–16.
[25] See Achilles Tatius *De Clitophontis et Leucippes Amoribus* I.15; and Longus *De Daphnide et Chloe* II.3.

only living creature in the garden besides the poet, the
Fairfax family, and us is the bee. The bee hums through "these
known Allies"; he sounds reveille, "Beating the *Dian* with its
Drumms," to awaken the flowers; he stands watch at night.

> Then in some Flow'rs beloved Hut
> Each Bee as Sentinel is shut;
> And sleeps so too: but, if once stir'd,
> She runs you through, or askes *the Word*.

The bee is governor of the garden; the rose, the tulip, the
dianthus are the garrison troops.

It is not hard to understand why the bee dominates a garden
which represents an ideal state. The fourth book of the
Georgics, the Book of the Bee, is a poem on beekeeping
and an account of an ideal commonwealth. Bees, Vergil tells
us, live under the majesty of the law. They divide the labors
of state by covenant. The older bees have charge of the
towns, of hive-building, of making the well-wrought house.
The young work in the fields and bring the harvest home.
They are devoted to their king. While he is secure, they are
of one mind; when he is lost, they destroy everything. The
king is the guardian of their toils and they do him reverence.
They stand round him in crowds, attend him in throngs,
carry him on their shoulders. "For him they expose their
bodies to battle and seek death through glorious wounds."
They do all this because they have a share of the divine
intelligence.

> His quidam signis atque haec exempla secuti
> Esse apibus partem divinae mentis et haustus
> Atherios dixere.[26]

Vergil saw in the government of bees what the Greeks had
seen and what others were to see again and again. The hive

---

is an ideal state of ordered ranks governed by a king. The
bee alone inhabits Marvell's garden because it is the ideal
England, the fortress Eden shut off from the rest of the world
by the "watry . . . Sword" of the first of the "four Seas."
This passage probably records the disordered realm. The great
Lord was too tender in mind to endure any government except the best. His poetic companion, the old Corycian who
had a garden near Tarentum, the city of Pythagoras, also
appears in Vergil's fourth *Georgic*. Here in a land unfit for
the plough and the flock, unkind to the vine, the old gardener
grew the white lily, vervain, roses, apples, pears, plums,
hyacinths, and limes. His garden, too, rang with the hum of
bees and so, says Vergil, he equalled in contentment the
wealth of kings. "Regum aequabat opes animis." [27] The episode in the Latin poem symbolizes a higher existence, a turning away from the harshness of the world to make a park of
flowers near the city of the philosophers. In his concluding
stanza, Marvell almost says the same.

> And yet their walks one on the Sod
> Who, had it pleased him and *God*,
> Might once have made our Gardens spring
> Fresh as his own and flourishing.
> But he preferr'd to the *Cinque Ports*
> These five imaginary Forts:
> And, in those half-dry Trenches, spann'd
> Pow'r which the Ocean might command.

We now leave the ideal state of the garden to visit the fields
and the water meadows, where we shall see "how Chance's
better Wit/ Could with a Mask my studies hit." The masque
that we shall watch will be one of war and social chaos.

The sequence of stanzas (XLVII–LXI) that describes the
harvest and the flood, when "*Denton* sets ope its *Cataracts*,"

must be first read as a literal record. These things Marvell saw
and transmuted into poetical allegories. He saw men dive
into the long corn and bring up flowers that grew between
the furrows, and he thought of those who dived for pearl and
sponge. Then the waving grain became a great green sea, and
the reapers who fought its currents became Jews fleeing from
the hosts of Pharoah. This story touched off the memories of
quail and manna, of the time when the rails died under
the scythemen's strokes. The harvest dances, the flood in the
meadow, the stranded cattle were all literal pictures stored in
the gallery of his mind. They hung there, like those of Clora,
ready to be transferred to canvas or plaster by Lely or the
Davenant artist; and Marvell mentions these painters so that
we can know these scenes are first to be understood as real.

Marvell's main purpose is not to construct a panorama.
There is more to see in this landscape than fifty acres of
country life, and Marvell forces us to see it by a series of
blunt suggestions. The grass is massacred; the low-nesting rail
is slain; the field is transformed into "A Camp of Battail
newly fought"; the mowers change into "Victors" and,
covered with "*Alexanders sweat*," they dance "Triumphs."
The flood in the water meadow is, of course, also the Flood
that destroyed the antediluvian giants, the one from which
"the first Carpenter" escaped in his Ark. The "Toril" at
Madrid is "rase and pure" "ere the Bulls enter," but it is
shortly disarrayed and bloodied. The reference to the "Levellers" in stanza LVII is direct, and the concluding stanza (LX)
is so in the tradition of a Merlin or Nostradamus that we cannot avoid the political implications of the whole section.

The opening scene in the fields is traditionally pastoral,
but like its pattern, the *Eclogues* of Vergil, it means more
than it says. War, as Marvell and we know, is a harvest and
the soldier is a reaper under the master mower, Death. The
metaphor of the soldier-reaper first appeared in the *Argo-*

nautica of Apollonius of Rhodes when Jason, "hastening to make harvest of the sons of earth," is compared to a farmer who rushes out to gather his unripe grain at the approach of an army." [28] The metaphor is extended to all forms of hand-to-hand combat. Aeneas mows down lines of men as he seeks out Turnus: "Proxima quaeque metit gladio latumque per agmen/ Ardens limitem agit ferro, te, Turne, superbum/ Caede nova quaerens." [29] The *Punica* of Silius Italicus makes the same comparison over and over: "metit agmina" (IV. 462), "ense metit rapido" (X. 146), "est oblatum metit insatiabilis agmen" (XIII. 218), "gregem metite imbellem" (XIV. 134), "hanc segetem mete" (XVI. 615). The war-harvesting metaphor is widespread but one of the most striking classical references—the great hero, reaping soldiers as a mower cuts the grain—appears in a fourth-century epic, the *Johannidos*.

> Armipotens, hostes cernens obstare, Johannes
> Irruit in densas acies, turmasque rebelles
> Letifero mucrone secat, ceu messor acuta
> Falce metit segetes maturo tempore sollers;
> Et modo cum teneris culmos compressat aristis
> Laeva manus, nunc dextra secat, nunc fune tenaci
> Colligat innumeros gaudens per rura maniplos. [30]

To the metaphors of classical antiquity we must add those of Christian provenance, the reaping angel of The Revelation [31] and the scriptural comparison of man to grass. [32] The figure is now a cliché, but it was fresh enough for Marvell when he made it into allegory.

The metaphor of war as harvest is linked in the poetry of Horace with the companion metaphor of civil war as flood.

---

[28] III.1386–90.
[29] X.513–15.
[30] Ed. Partsch (Berlin, 1878), VIII, 534–40.
[31] 14:14–19.
[32] Isaiah 40:6; Psalms 90:6, 102:12; Job 5:26, 14:2; I Peter 1:24.

In the fourteenth ode of Book IV, inundation, reaping, and
the bull, though not at Madrid, are garnered in a series of
verses.

> Sic tauriformis volvitur Aufidus,
> Qui regna Dauni praefluit Apuli,
>   Cum saevit horrendamque cultis
>   Diluviem meditatur agris,
>
> Ut barbarorum Claudius agmina
> Ferrata vasto diruit impetu,
>   Primosque et extremos metendo
>   Stravit humum. . . . .

The flood metaphor of this poem really begins with the fifth
book of the *Iliad* where Tydeides is described as storming
"across the field like a winter stream in flood, scattering the
barriers; the long lines of dikes cannot hold it in, nor the
fences of fruitful orchards stop its sudden rush when the
rains drive it; and the works of the sons of men perish in
multitudes before it." [33] Sophocles [34] and Aeschylus [35] use
the same image for war, and in due course the Latins have it
too. Aeneas rages across the fields like a torrent of black
water; [36] the heroic Fabian gens marches down into the valley
like a river over its banks.[37] Sempronius, a hero of the *Punica*,
rides into the foe like a torrent falling from Pindus and racing
across the fields; [38] and elsewhere in the same poem, the
Romans sweep all before them like a flood while Hannibal,
forlorn in hope, observes the destruction.[39]

In Latin poetry the metaphor of the flood becomes special-

[33] V.87–91.
[34] *Antigone* 129.
[35] *Persians* 87–89, 412; *Seven* 1067–70.
[36] X.602.
[37] Ovid *Fasti* II.219–23.
[38] IV.520–23; XVII.121–24.
[39] XII.184–90.

ized as a symbol of internecine conflict. It was an inundation of the Eridanus, says Vergil, that preceded the Battle of Philippi:

> Proluit insano contorquens vertice silvas
> Fluviorum rex Eridanus camposque per omnis
> Cum stabulis armenta tulit.[40]

Horace, urging the Romans to accept Augustus and avoid civil war, uses the same topic in his second ode. Shall we, he asks, let the awful age of Proteus return when fish flounder in tree-top nests, when deer swim panic-stricken "through plain heaped on plain."

> Vidimus flavom Tiberim retortis
> Litore Etrusco violenter undis
> Ire deiectum monimenta regis
> > Templaque Vestae,
>
> Iliae dum se nimium querenti
> Iactat ultorem, vagus et sinistra
> Labitur ripa Iove non probante u-
> > xorius amnis.

To assure us that floods and civil wars are the same, Lucan prefaces his epic of the great internal struggle for power with the same trope: "Tethys maioribus undis/ Hesperiam Calpen summumque implevit Atlanta." [41]

The metaphors of harvest and flood make it plain that this portion of "Upon Appleton House" is concerned with war and civil disturbance. History has torn up the garden in which the royal bee presided and where the flowers marched in orderly regiments. The "sweet Militia" of rose and tulip, reminding us of Dante's "In forma dunque di candida rosa/ Mi si mostrava la milizia santa," [42] is dispersed and only the

[40] *Georgics* I.481–83.
[41] *Pharsalia* I.554–55.
[42] *Paradiso* XXXI.1–2.

sensitive flower of conscience that adorns the heavenly crown
of Fairfax is left. There are flowers among the corn, but
man must dive for them as for sunken treasure. Shortly these
flowers, wild and unvalued by the gardener, will be reaped
with the grain or strangled in the flood.

Poetry about mowers and harvest is usually in the pastoral
vein; but what a bitter pastoralism this is. Under a rural
disguise the war against the King is fought in rime. The
first word to be capitalized is "Abyss," the "barathrum" of
increate nature, of unspeakable depth. The grass of man's
flesh makes the substance of the chaos, but men "like Grasshoppers appear,/ But Grasshoppers are Gyants there." At
first sight, the image is excitingly natural, for the insects on
the "green spir's" are taller than the grass-men wading in the
sea-green vortex. The grasshoppers of this battle piece have
been identified [43] with the grasshopper metaphor in Numbers: [44] "And there we saw the giants, the sons of Anak,
which come of the giants: and we were in our own sight
as grasshoppers, and so we were in their sight"; but the Biblical
quotation that explains this more clearly is in Nahum: "Thy
crowned are as the locusts, and thy captains as the great grasshoppers, which camp in the hedges in the cold day, but when
the sun ariseth they flee away, and their place is not known
where they are." [45] The English insect has a Hebrew history.

Perhaps we must think of these grasshoppers, as Lovelace
does,[46] as soldiers and as kingly ones. It is not by chance that
the mowers follow them, destroying their food and refuge,
and laying the fields more bare than ever. Nicander, one of
the earliest of Greek poets, describes the grasshopper army,

[43] Joan Grundy, "Marvell's Grasshoppers," *N & Q* (N.S. IV, 1957), p. 142;
see Pierre Legouis' reply and announcement of his earlier notice in *N & Q*
(N.S. V, 1958), pp. 108–109.
[44] 13:33.
[45] 3:17.
[46] See Chapter Five.

its troops with wing-sedged backs, flying over the crops, eating the grain, and wasting the fields as with fire.[47] What seem first to have been allied in analogy by this poet become in time commonplace, and Alciati makes the insects symbolic for the Renaissance in his emblem, "Nil Reliqui," through which the grasshopper and the armies of Atilla and Xerxes are made figuratively the same.

> Scilicet hoc deerat post tota mala, denique nostris
> Locustae ut raperent quicquid inesset agris.
> Vidimus innumeras Euro duce tendere turmas,
> Qualia non Atylae, castrave Xerxes erant.[48]

The reign of the royal grasshoppers is short as the day, for their human counterparts, the parliamentary mowers, dramatically "enter next" and take their place in the masque. They are the "Israelites," God's chosen wasters who, after the plagues of frogs, lice, flies, and grasshoppers were ended, spoiled their Egyptian masters. One member of their party, the shepherdess Thestylis, now a cruel *vivandière*, is pointed out for our careful contemplation.

> But bloody *Thestylis*, that waites
> To bring the mowing Camp their Cates,
> Greedy as Kites has thrust it up,
> And forthwith means on it to sup:
> When on another quick She lights,
> And cryes, he call'd us *Israelites*;
> But now, to make his saying true,
> Rails rain for Quails, for Manna Dew.

The Hebraic allusions in these lines are explained by Genesis 32:28, where we read how the name of Jacob was changed to Israel, and by the sixteenth chapter of Exodus with its account of the miracles of quails and manna. Be-

[47] *Theriaca* 801–803.
[48] *Emblemata* (Paris, 1580), p. 469.

hind the Bible is Bible-quoting Cromwell, who, like a true
Puritan, regularly referred to his adherents in speech and
letter as "the People of God," an English translation of
"Israelites." After the victory at Marston Moor, the Captain
of the Saints anticipated Marvell's mowers when he wrote to
a friend: "God made them as stubble to our swords." So
Thestylis, queen of "The Women that with forks it fling"
who "represent the Pillaging," has both God and God's vice-
roy, the commander of "the Godly Party," in mind. Though
there is some slight connection between this shepherdess
and Deborah or Jael, she really comes from pagan antiquity
to make Marvell's bloody point.

Thestylis is not a very close relative of the girl who helps
Theocritus' Simaetha brew a love philter; she is better related
to Vergil's Thestylis, who grinds garlic and thyme for the
field laborers and who covets Corydon's roes, but she belongs
to the left side of the family. This girl is really more of a man
than the mowers, because as one of them recoils from his
inadvertent murder of the rail, she "thrusts up" the slain bird
and takes a live one (wringing its neck I suppose) from a nest.
The epithet that is attached to her is "bloody," and this adjective enables us to recognize her as the sister or wife of
Mars, "sanguinea Bellona." [49]

In Thestylis, the warlike amazon of antiquity is given
pastoral dress and placed at the exact center of the masque
of war; so her past is concealed while it is simultaneously
revealed. Vergil knew her as she wandered, bloody scourge
in hand, through the fields of war: "Quam cum sanguineo
sequitur Bellona flagello." [50] Silius Italicus discovers her with
gore-drenched hair among the fighting men; [51] and as Lucan
points out, she is always eager for more slaughter. In her

[49] Statius *Thebiados* IX.297.
[50] *Aeneid* VIII.703.
[51] V.220–21.

honor, the flamens slice their limbs and drink goblets of blood: "Tum quos sectis, Bellona lacertis/ Saeva movet, cecinere deos, crinemque rotantes/ Sanguinem." [52] She moves through the centuries, maddening soldiers with blood-lust and swinging her reddened lash. Most war poems mention her, and Shakespeare, we remember, calls Macbeth that "man of blood," "Bellona's bridegroom." For Marvell she represents the excesses that a long war brings, even when it is a war fought for principles and conducted by Christians. The history of Fairfax's horror at the King's execution (the slaughtered rail?) and his refusal to attack Scotland (the quick rail?) is possibly given a share in this poetic masque.

It is clear that the rails have political meaning, and that they also contain a lesson for both Fairfax and Marvell. As far as I know, the bird appears in these verses for the first time in a poetic context; but Marvell certainly knew that the "rallus crex" was known to the Italians as "re di quaglie" and to the French as "roi des cailles." The bird is the king of quail, though not a quail itself; hence God, who sent the quails to the hungry Israelites, now rains kings into the laps of the British Jews. The bird is also neutral. It is sometimes a wading bird and sometimes it comes to the fields and lives with the quails. It is difficult to classify.[53]

With the emphatic "Unhappy Birds!" of stanza LII, Marvell ponders the question of neutrality (his personal problem), and the question of retirement (Fairfax's problem). A question often posed by disturbed men through scores of centuries is also phrased implicitly: "Is there any place in which man is safe from disaster?" The general question provides a kind of text for the sermon to the rails: "To build below the Grasses Root;/ When Lowness is unsafe as Hight,/ And Chance o'retakes what scapeth spight." One must build

[52] I.565–67.
[53] U. Aldrovandus, *Ornithologia* (Bologna, 1637), III, 455–56.

so high, says Marvell ironically, that one is out of danger, or
one must be born early enough to be safely dead when
disaster occurs. "Or sooner hatch or higher build." Both
courses are clearly impossible. Marvell has heard the "Orphan
Parents" of many a dead man on each side of the conflict
lament the necessity of taking sides; but there is no salvation
in neutrality as the fate of the water and land rails proves.
"Neuters," said the Roundhead committees, "deserve neither
respect nor protection from Church or Commonwealth"; and
their decision was seconded by the clergy, preaching on a
text from the victory song of Deborah: "Curse ye Meroz,
said the angel of the Lord, curse ye bitterly the inhabitants
thereof; because they came not to the help of the Lord, to
the help of the Lord against the mighty." [54] The King's men
joined their opponents in their scorn and persecution of the
lukewarm attitude.

With stanza LIII the allegory of the Civil Wars ends.
The harvest is stacked, the reapers dance for the death of
the corn and for their victory. The green sea goes, leaving a
shoal of dangerous rocks or a desert as bare as the Sahara.
Death is present in the pyramids of Memphis or the Roman
funeral mounds. True enough, these are only hayricks, but
the poet's eye sees them as tombs. They are memorials of
"Soldiers Obsequies," but the trouble is not over, a few more
men must die. The flood spreads over the meadows, conflict
begins within the Parliamentary ranks.

The last forty lines of the war section of the poem may
have something to do with the Leveller Movement, and
especially with the political events of the spring of 1649.
The "Scene," which we are asked to observe, because, of
course, we are still at the masque, is "A levell'd space." It
is a flat canvas, the Toril, the world before the Flood, a

<hr />

[54] Judges 5:23; see G. M. Trevelyan, *England under the Stuarts* (London,
1926), pp. 226–27.

"naked equal Flat/ Which *Levellers* take Pattern at." This
is all in the open, but there are allusions that are hidden from
us. In stanza LVI, Marvell writes "The World when first
created sure/ Was such a Table rase and pure," and we hear
the Diggers singing, "And then we shall see/ Brave Community,/ When Vallies lye levell with Mountaines." [55] If we
have missed the point, Marvell refers us to Davenant's *Gondibert* and almost gives us a page reference.

> The strait an universal Herd appears;
> First gazing on each other in the shade;
> Wondring with *levell'd* Eies, and lifted Ears,
> Then play, whilst yet their Tyrant is unmade.[56]

The history of the Leveller Movement and of its splinter
party, the Diggers, is well known.[57] Marvell, however, was
so close to the whole eruption that he probably did not
distinguish between the aims of the two groups. Fairfax was
deeply involved in the attempt to suppress both parties, and
the spring of 1649, when the winter's thaw enabled Denton
to set "ope its *Cataracts*," the flood of rebellion occurred. By
decisive action Fairfax smashed the mutiny at Burford. The
tone of rebellion is supplied too by the last stanza (LX),
which looks toward "Nostradamus Prophecy" and repeats in
different form the tropes of Horace's poem on the Roman
revolution: eels in oxen, leeches on horses, boats over bridges,
fish in stables. It is all another way of saying, valleys as high
as mountains. Fairfax's service to the state has now been
poetically glossed, and Marvell has suggested to him that

[55] G. Winstanley, *The Works*, ed. Sabine (Ithaca, N. Y., 1941), p. 659.

[56] *Gondibert* (London, 1651), p. 192; the allusion helps to date "Upon
Appleton House" as posterior to this date. I have supplied the italics.

[57] See in addition to Sabine's work, A. S. P. Woodhouse, *Puritanism and
Liberty* (London, 1938); W. Haller, *Rise of Puritanism* (New York, 1938);
and T. C. Pease, *The Leveller Movement* (New York, 1916). Whitelocke's
Memorials and the *Clarke Papers* can also be consulted for this moment of
civil excitement.

retirement is not safety. No man is entirely secure, and for a soldier, action may be the fit solution. With his patron advised, Marvell will now talk about himself, and his own bosom-searching occupies the next twenty-two stanzas. It is a poetic chapter from his intellectual and spiritual auto-biography.

Twenty years after he wrote "Upon Appleton House," the poet repeated the sense of these stanzas in the prose of *The Rehearsal Transprosed*.

> Whether it be a war of religion or of liberty it is not worth the labour to inquire. Whichsoever was at the top, the other was at the bottom; but upon considering all, I think the cause was too good to have been fought for. Men ought to have trusted God—they ought to have trusted the King with that whole matter. The arms of the Church are prayers and tears, the arms of the subject are patience and petitions. The King himself being of so accurate and piercing a judgment would soon have felt it where it stuck. *For men may spare their pains when Nature is at work, and the world will not go faster for our driving.*[58]

The prose, written by Milton's colleague and the Member for Hull, expresses a mature conclusion; the stanzas before us pose the propositions and the inner debate. All of this hap-pens in Fairfax's forest, but it is also the woodland of the poet's mind. The Hebraic background that was expressed in the garden and the mowing scenes is now explicit when Marvell-Noah escapes from "the Flood" and takes "Sanctuary" in the "green, yet growing Ark" of the holy wood. We are also in the wilderness where Christ contemplated his mission for forty days, an event foreshadowed when Noah spent the forty days and nights of the Deluge in understanding the ways of God with men. When it is all over, when "the Waves are fal'n and dry'd,/ And now the Meadows fresher

[58] *Works*, ed. Grosart (London, 1872–1875), III, 175.

dy'd," the poet, like the patriarch, will come out of sanctuary into another world.

To understand this section, we must read "Upon the Hill and Grove at Bill-Borow," because both forests speak with us in the same language. They are both "ancient" and, hence, holy; in both, the union of the houses of Fairfax and Vere is commemorated. The grove, a preface to the wood, talks of mutual love and the genius of both houses. They are also both trees and *a* tree, the heraldic tree of pedigree. Man, says Marvell, repeating the old image, is an inverted tree, and so in both poems men are likewise trees. In "Upon Appleton House" (LXII), we hear about the growing trees and those that were cut for military use; and we know that the poet is talking, as the trees are, about the sons of the illustrious line. "Of whom though many fell in War,/ Yet more to Heaven shooting are." This is the wood. In the grove, the trees are also soldiers: "Groves of Pikes he thundered then." The pikes are both men and trees, and the trees also provide the military and civil crowns that the house has merited. The grove, however, gives Marvell a chance for recording a domestic event in the history of the family. "*Vera* the Nymph that him inspir'd,/ To whom he often here retir'd,/ And on these Okes ingrav'd her Name." The word "retirement" is here, and "Vere" becomes "*Vera*." But there is more than this in the scene in the grove, for the passage carries us back to a happy moment in the early history of Rome.

Instructed by the Camena Egeria, who had married him and led him into the assemblies of her sisters in the sacred groves, Numa, second king of the Romans, refined and revised the religion of the state. He reformed the college of pontiffs; he instructed the augurs, who knew the will of the gods; he purified the flamens, who conducted divine worship; he reformed the Vestals and the Salii. He prescribed the rites of worship and the form of prayer; he even forced Jupiter to reveal his purposes through thunder and bird flight. He, then, secured from the gods release from the necessity of human sacrifice. So Italy, say the chroniclers [59] of his fame, was filled with a peace like that of the Golden Age until Numa, ripe with years, fell quietly asleep and the bereft nymph melted into a fountain of tears. Marvell returns to the myth again in the second poem: "And as they Natures Cradle deckt,/ Will in green Age her Hearse expect." True enough, the grove is not Aricia, "sylva antiqua"—that is the wood at Nunappleton—and the nymph, visible enough, is not "Egeria" or "Belief" but "Vera" or "Truth." When Marvell enters the wood, he will be tutored by both women.

"The double Wood of ancient Stocks" to which the poet retires is, of course, the security of the house of Fairfax and Vere, but it is probably more than this. In a sense, by writing "Upon Appleton House" and other poems that come from the same years, he has composed his own "silva" or "ὕλη," [60] titles by which collections of verse had been known in ancient times. Statius had named his poetic works of a lesser nature *Silvae*, and Ben Jonson called his *The Forest*. But the wood is also a place of worship and contemplation, synonymous with the mind and heart of man,[61] and Marvell is hardly in this wood before he knows he is on holy ground.

> The arching Boughs unite between
> The Columnes of the Temple green;
> And underneath the winged Quires
> Echo about their tuned Fires.

[59] Besides Plutarch's account, see Livy I.18–21; Cicero *De Republica* II.13–15; and Dionysius of Halicarnassus II.58–66.

[60] Suetonius *De Viris Inlustribus: De grammaticis* 25; Quintilian *De Institutione* X.3.17; Cicero *De Oratore* III.26.103; Aulus Gellius *Noctes Atticae* Praef. 4–7; Longinus X.1; XIII.4.

[61] The fullest account of the symbolism of the wood can be found in John Evelyn, *A Discourse of Forest Trees* (London, 1679), pp. 252–76.

To live in a holy place is to become holy:

> The Oak-Leaves me embroyder all,
> Between which Caterpillars crawl:
> And Ivy, with familiar trails,
> Me licks, and clasps, and curles, and hales.
> Under this *antick Cope* I move
> Like some great *Prelate of the Grove.*

The retired poet, who enters the inner wood to contemplate, ends as a Gomerite, a Druid priest.

The wood at Nunappleton by artistic land-change becomes a *sylva mentis*, not unlike the *hortus mentis* of "The Nymph." [62] It is a place, dark without but "within/ It opens passable and thin." Encamped behind its growing ramparts, the poet, sheltered from those emotions that rise from within as a result of the stimulation of the senses, will, reason being king, contemplate the history of man in terms of the processes of Nature, for "Nature is at work."

> How safe, methinks, and strong, behind
> These Trees have I incamp'd my Mind;
> Where Beauty, aiming at the Heart,
> Bends in some Tree its useless Dart;
> And where the World no certain Shot
> Can make, or me it toucheth not.
> But I on it securely play,
> And gaul its Horsemen all the Day.

Unwed Marvell, safe behind bole and branch, can laugh at Love's archery; and, moving from pathless place to pathless place, he can have sport with the apocalyptic cavalrymen of the World. The passions of love and ambition cooled in the forest, the mind is enabled to reach a conclusion.

We hardly require the Miltonic echoes in stanza LXXVII to perceive that the experiences of "L'Allegro" and "Il

[62] On the garden as mind, see Chapter Six.

Penseroso" are being repeated in Nunappleton's forest. The choir is not the "full voiced Choir below" but "the winged Quires" above. In Milton's poem, the voices are human; here it is Nature speaking through the birds. Adam could speak the language of birds; Marvell can only whistle while they listen. But the birds, feathered symbols that they are, instruct the "Churl" by the more eloquent language of their actions. Before they teach him the doctrine of the state, good Aristotelians that they are, they give him domestic instruction. First, he is shown the lovelorn nightingale, then the married doves, then the "thrastles" begetting a family, and, finally, the heron sending its mature offspring into the world. The nightingale answers his questions about the profession of poetry; she sits low, but her singing is harkened to by noble oaks and venerable elders. The *"Stock-doves,"* age-old symbols of wedded bliss, may also instruct the hesitant bachelor.

> Yet always, for some Cause unknown,
> Sad pair unto the Elms they moan.
> O why should such a Couple mourn,
> That in so equal Flames do burn!

All the birds are, I expect, inferior in significance to the "hewel," for whose lectures they merely supply the prolegomenon.

The green woodpecker is of the utmost importance; and in order to understand this, we must once again turn to the *Aeneid.* In the seventh book we find Aeneas' companions, who having raised a mound for Misenus, "aggere composito tumuli," a deed that inspired Marvell's conclusion to the mowing scene, depart by sea for a new land. They skirt the Circean shores, and, looking across the flood, see the great forest filled with birds. "Variae circumque supraque/ Adsuetae ripis volucres." [63] Meanwhile in Latium, King Latinus wor-

[63] 32–33.

ships in the grove near high Albunea and hears the oracle speak from the depth of the wood. Latinus, we remember, is the son of Faunus, who was the son of "Laurentian Picus." Vergil, like Marvell, describes the palace of the King, where he finds the effigy of the augur Picus, holding the regalia of office. According to the Roman, this great King, son of Saturn, was changed by his jealous bride Circe into "picus," the woodpecker. "Fecit avem Circe sparsitque coloribus alas." [64] The myth of the transformation of Picus into picus is told with slight variations by Ovid, Silius Italicus, and many other poets and mythographers,[65] enabling the legend to hallow the bird and make it a quasi-religious symbol.

But the woodpecker is more than a priest, for the Latins associated the bird with the God of War, and usually speak of it as "picus Martius." It is the bird that companions the fiery God as the eagle consorts with Jupiter and the dove with Venus. Picus, however, was a son of Saturn, and so it is not illogical that he is also identified with Jupiter.[66] This makes the "hewel" a symbol of justice as well as of war and religion. I cannot assume that Marvell intends any of these meanings, but when he watches the bird cleaning the Royal Oak of wood moths, when he sees it make its hollow in the tree, rotten because of the "Traitor-worm," he is, I think, learning from nature that the Royal Oak, having fallen by the "*feeble Strok'*" of the bird, is also preserved, because the worms that hollowed it are dead. As Nature restores herself through death, so the state is revivified by the forces of war,

---

[64] 191.

[65] *Metamorphoses* XIV.390–96; Silius Italicus *Punica* VIII.440–44; Augustine *De Civitate* XVIII.15; Antonius Liberalis *Metamorphoseos* CXIX; *Scriptores Rerum Mythicarum*, ed. Bode (Cellis, 1834), I ,182; II, 213. The account in Boccaccio is interestingly moralized; see *Della Genealogia* (Venice, 1585), p. 140. For its association with Mars, see Plutarch *Quaest. Rom.* XXI; Pliny *Nat. Hist.* X.40.

[66] See Suidas *ad loc.;* and for the Renaissance summary, Aldrovandus, *Ornithologia* (Bologna, 1641), I, 835.

that are also those of religion and justice. The conclusion of stanza LXX may point to something specific. The oak may be Charles; the worm may be Strafford or Laud, or someone else. Howell, the author of *Dodona's Grove*, would probably know.

Having been tutored by the woodpecker in the natural processes that bring, without much human intervention, alterations in the affairs of men, Marvell reads further in the *"Sibyls* Leaves" of *"Natures mystick Book."* In these leaves, which are now history, he notices the same natural changes affecting the alterations in the political life of Greece, Rome, and Palestine. He finds in each history stories of the overthrow of kings and internal political ferment. He seems to say that in the natural progression of history, the prelate of the grove should observe, as he does in the glosses on the Book of Creatures, the writing of the divine hand. He says this by what seems to me to be an elaborate pun. All of the history of the past, through which I can make predictions of the future, says Marvell, "I in this light *Mosaick* read." The word underscored by the poet has two possible meanings. First, it may mean the sunlight that filters through the mosaic of the leaves overhead; second, and more mystically, it may mean the Light that Moses, also brooding in the wilderness, saw in the blazing bush. Marvell is like Moses in the wilderness but he is also an Aeneas who has gone into the forest, seen the Sybil, and seen the doves (but not those of Venus). The Golden Bough has become for him "The Bird upon the Bough," and Avernus is the memory of the human past. He must now emerge to read the future, not of the Roman, but of "the Fairfacian Oak."

When Marvell leaves the wood to sing the future of his patron's race, he has, I think, solved his own problem to his immediate satisfaction. He will be the nightingale singing among the lowly thorns. This is the place he hopes "he may never leave." He has advised his patron against retirement as best he can, holding up to him his magisterial duties, the excellence of his qualifications, the urgent necessities of the state of England, and the spiritual impotence and danger of withdrawal from the active life. He knew in his heart of hearts that Fairfax would remain aloof; so he makes his last effort—by praising Mary, he makes a Vergilian comparison. Augustus' line ended with Julia; the fortunes of the House of Fairfax depend on Mary.

The last section of "Upon Appleton House" is in some ways a playful continuation of the founder-myth, the second section of the poem which I have scanted in my analysis. The earlier stanzas (XI–XXXV) are a satire of conventual life and suit the pen of the author of the pamphlets against L'Estrange. The house, built from the nunnery's ruin, was also built when the great ancestor ruined the nuns by carrying off his bride. Fairfax is supposed to read the section as an exhortation to action. Sir William opposed convention and his religious conscience to gain his wife; the current family owes its actual existence to this act. We must now, says Marvell, bring the past to meet the present, "find a *Fairfax* for our *Thwaites*." The "great *Prelate of the Grove*" comes forward to cut the *"sprig of Misleto."* So these parts are brought together as history and prophecy, as "scatter'd *Sibyls* Leaves" and the "light *Mosaick*."

The tradition that controls this final section is not unknown to us; it descends from Vergil through Ariosto, Trissino, and Tasso to Spenser and Marvell. It is the conventional epic vision of the patron's noble line; but Marvell, as is his custom, gives tradition an individual turn. He has been fishing poetically by the stream, just as a fisherman, like Walton, might try for strikes in Aganippe's Well; then he puts aside his hooks, angles, and quills because

> The *young Maria* walks to night:
> Hide trifling Youth thy Pleasures slight.
> 'Twere shame that such judicious Eyes

> Should with such Toyes a Man surprize;
> *She* that already is the *Law*
> Of all her *Sex*, her *Ages Aw.*

Granting the excesses of seventeenth-century poetical compliment, this (and we can assume that Jonson would agree)
is pushing the praise of a twelve-year-old (the precocity of
yesterday's children and the affectionate humor of the poet
admitted) beyond the fence of decorum. Without question,
high compliment is being expended on both Mary and her
parents, but just as the "She" of Donne's *Anniversaries* is
sometimes Elizabeth and sometimes a *persona symbolica*, so
Mary Fairfax is possibly sometimes herself and sometimes
another person. The facts are undoubtedly accurate. The girl
was "Pure, Sweet, Streight, and Fair"; she showed a talent for
languages; she was about to be sought in marriage by many
young aristocrats; she had been born into "a Domestic
Heaven" and knew the lures of foolish vanity; and, a male
heir wanting, she would get the Fairfax "*Goodness*" in entail.
She is, however, more than this, and Marvell, as is his custom,
supplies the key to her mystery.

One of the hints about Mary's true nature is granted by
Milton, whose "Ode on the Morning of Christ's Nativity"
stands behind this section of "Upon Appleton House" in the
way that "L'Allegro" and "Il Penseroso" stand behind the
woodland stanzas. One should first notice that in both poems
the appearance of a special person in the realm of Nature
results in a calm and quiet that is almost static. In Marvell's
poem, Nature puts forth "its *Bonne Mine*"; in Milton's she
"doffs her gaudy trim." In Milton it is the "Winds with
wonder whist"; in Marvell "every thing" is "whisht and fine."
In both poems the sun's bedroom is described; though Marvell's sun, unlike Milton's, is a modest bachelor. The halcyon
flies in both poems to insure calm. In the "Nativity Ode" the
oracles "are dum"; in "Upon Appleton House" "*Admiring*

Nature" is benumbed by "an horror calm and dumb." In the poem of 1629, the shepherds are taken by a "blissful rapture" comparable to Marvell's: "And men the silent *Scene* assist,/ Charm'd with the *Saphir-winged Mist*." And there is possibly a memory of Milton's "The Stars with deep amaze/ Stand fixt in steadfast gaze,/ Bending one way their precious influence" in Marvell's "No new-born *Comet* such a Train/ Draws through the Skie, nor Star new-slain." In both poems, we are in the presence of wonder. To understand the identity of Marvell's wonder we must return to "*She* that already is the *Law*."

The appearance of Mary in the twilight hour produces tranquillity. She is accompanied, almost as if she were a goddess, by the halcyon; in fact, it is almost as if she had become the mythical Alcyone herself. The bird, famous as a symbol of peace and calm, appears, as Vergil informs us, in the hush between the setting of the sun and the first rays of the evening star.

> Tum tenuis dare rursus aquas et pascere rursus
> Solis ad occasum, cum frigidus aera vesper
> Temperat, et saltus reficit iam roscida luna
> Litoraque alcyonem resonant. . . .[67]

The Greek pastoral poets, Theocritus [68] and Moschus,[69] had praised the miracle of this bird; and Lucian's Socrates, describing the peace that it brings, asks his friend to observe the halcyon's world "calm and serene even in mid-winter; see how clear the sky, the whole ocean at peace, smooth as a looking-glass." [70] The fact that Mary is given this bird as a heraldic device suggests that she is to be associated with tranquillity and peace, but she is also linked in stanzas LXXXVII–

[67] *Georgics* III.335–38.
[68] VII.57–59.
[69] III.40–41.
[70] *Halcyon* 2.

LXXXVIII with the perfection of those early poetical topics: gardens, woods, meadows, and streams. In stanza LXXX, she has something to do with wisdom of a heavenly kind: "Nor yet that *Wisdome* would affect,/ But as 'tis *Heavens Dialect.*" She is also a war maiden, who stands off the attacks and foils the amorous ambushes of soldier-lovers. We are told that she excels all other women in virtue and knowledge, and that she is the virgin of virgins: "That, as all *Virgins* She preceds." We have left the halcyon for this account of the girl who also brings peace, adds grace to the things of nature, is war-like, and gifted with heavenly wisdom. The bird returns now to tell us in the words of Antipater of Sidon that its mistress is the goddess Pallas Athena: "ἰστῶν Παλλάδος ἀλκυόνα." [71]

It is possibly this goddess, so important in the statecraft of Athens and Rome, whom Marvell hides behind the figure of Mary Fairfax. She was the virgin of virgins, as superior to all goddesses in chastity as she was their superior in wisdom. We hardly need go beyond the *Iliad* and the *Odyssey* to establish her central virtues. She maintained law and order in the state.[72] She can fight against external enemies, but she is not a female counterpart of Ares; [73] for she restrains men from slaughter, reproving and even defeating the great God of War.[74] She has no weapons of her own, but must borrow her armor from Zeus.[75] Through her, men learned the arts of agriculture, for she invented the tools of the field and created the peaceful olive. For these reasons Vergil invokes her as a patroness of his *Georgics:* "Adsis . . . oleaeque Minerva inventrix." [76] It is Athena, or Minerva, who adds her qualities to gardens, woods, meadows and stream, the topics of Marvell's song.

[71] *Anthol. Pal.* VI.160.
[72] *Odyssey* XIII.394ff.
[73] *Iliad* V.736.
[74] *Ibid.*, V.840; XXI.406.
[75] *Ibid.*, I.199.
[76] I.18–19.

It is, however, her heavenly wisdom that accounted for all her other powers. Homer gives her the epithet of "many-counseled," "πολύβουλος Ἀθήνη," [77] the same epithet that he applies to her father, Zeus. But it is the poet Plato to whom we can turn for a full understanding of her powers. Let us listen to a lecture in philology delivered by Socrates to Hermogenes.

That is a weightier matter, my friend, and here the modern explainers of Homer help us to understand the ancient belief about Athene. Most of these in commenting on the poet say that by Athene he meant *mind* (νοῦς) and *intellect* (διάνοια); and the maker of her name seems to have had the same notion about her but he gives her the still grander title of "the mind of God" (ἡ θεοῦ νόησις), as if he would say: "This is she who has the mind of God" (ἁ θεονόα), using here the alpha in a foreign way for eta and eliding the iota and sigma. Perhaps, however, this was not his reason; he may have called her Theonoë to mean "she who knows divine matters" (τὰ θεῖα νοοῦσα). He may, perhaps, have wished to identify her with moral wisdom (ἐν ἤθει νόησις) by calling her Ethonoë, which he, or his successors thought they improved when they called her Athenaa.[78]

The nature of the mistress of the halcyon as "the mind of God" or as "divine wisdom" is here made plain. The Greek position is, of course, not enough, and we may remember the Christian equivalent. The goddess Athena was able to cross frontiers; in the Christian world, she was known as Sophia and there was a poem about her.

In the *Sophia Salomonos* the heroine, like her Greek prototype, is an emanation rather than a creation of God. She is arrayed in a series of epithets; she is finer than a lily of the fields. She is "the vapor of the power of God," "a pure emanation of the glory," "reflection of eternal light," "a spotless mir-

[77] *Iliad* V.260; see also Hesiod *Theogony* 886–900, and the Homeric "Hymn to Athena."
[78] *Cratylus* 407A–C.

ror." [79] When the poet adds that she lives in closeness with
God [80] and is his grand manifestation,[81] he repeats, probably
without knowing it, the sort of praise that the pagans rendered
to Athena. But Sophia is more than Athena, more than that
great golden figure laden with ivory; for she existed, we are
told, before the Creation,[82] and assisted in the making of the
universe.[83] Since then she has not rested because she is the
artificer of all things.[84] Solomon's poem is mainly addressed
to kings who would rule righteously and with justice, but it
can also be read by all men who follow the divine light, men
like Marvell who read in *"Natures mystick Book."* "For she
knows the things of old and conjectures the things to come." [85]

The second half of the *Sophia Salomonos* proclaims the
"great She" as the inspirer of the kings and captains of Israel.
Here Solomon, like his English disciple, makes the story of the
Exodus his chief example of Sophia's gifts. She led the chosen
of God through the deep sea, and "cast them up out of the
depths of the abyss"; [86] she provided quail food and manna for
the starving. She is also a composer of apocalyptic paradoxes,
who takes us back to stanza LX.

> For land creatures were turned into water creatures,
> And swimming creatures migrated on earth.
> Fire had control of its own power in water,
> And water forgot its own power of extinguishing,
> Flames wasted not the flesh of perishable creatures
> That walked among them, nor was melted
> The easily melted ice-like heavenly food.[87]

[79] 7:25-26.
[80] 8:3-4.
[81] 9:9.
[82] 9:1.
[83] 6:14; 9:4.
[84] 7:22.
[85] 8:8.
[86] 10:18-19.
[87] 19:19-21.

Behind the child Mary and her human virtues stands the pagan wisdom of Athena and of Sophia, the graver and more potent daughter of Jehovah.

If there is a solemn conclusion to the poem it is that divine wisdom must come in this moment of half-light to guide the land of Britain, the erstwhile general, and the poet who celebrates both state and man. Through her, Marvell implies, and through her alone will the garden and the wood be restored. Even the world, which was originally created as a smooth sphere, and is now because of the Flood "All negligently overthrown," still is preserved by divine wisdom. As Marvell writes this, darkness comes like a black bowl over the world; it almost seems as if Atlas had come up from the mere with a leather boat hoisted over his head or as if Alastor, the black one, had entered the temple during the gods' absence. This darkness is also known to Sophia. It is that of lawless men, who think to hold a nation in their power: by "one chain of darkness" all are bound so that even if birds sing, and water falls, and hills echo, and all of Nature is bathed in light, "Over them alone heavy night was spread,/ An image of darkness which was to receive them;/ But to themselves they were heavier than darkness." [88] Sophia may be represented in Mary, but Mary is a charming little girl and not Sophia. "Let's in," says the teasing Marvell, "for the dark *Hemisphere*,/ Does now like one of them appear." This is an amusing conclusion and it is typically Vergilian, but it also goes as far beyond Vergil as Divine Wisdom surpasses Athena. In spite of the speculation in the garden and in the wood, dark without but light within, the black clouds hang over the island's fortunes. "Let's in," says the poet, let us come out of the night and seek the light in the house. " 'Twas no Religious House till now."

[88] 17:15–20.

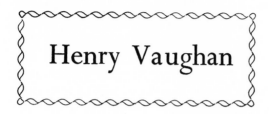

CHAPTER TWELVE

Henry Vaughan

"Cock-Crowing"

Vaughan lived in the narrow space between two worlds: one was a world of crystal translucency and one was of blind darkness. The black world he knew sadly enough and well; the world of light he saw indistinctly because the veil of mortality thwarted his vision: "And onely see through a long night/ Thy edges and thy bordering light." [1] The veil, which Christ alone had penetrated [2] and which Vaughan knew would cover his eyes until Doomsday, [3] becomes a constant symbol of the poet's spiritual frustration. He lives "under veyls here"; [4] he hopes to have "his Curtaines off"; [5] or he awaits the time when his "callous veyl" [6] will be purged away by fire. His realization

[1] *Works*, ed. L. C. Martin (Oxford, 1914), p. 521.
[2] P. 485.
[3] P. 542.
[4] P. 535.
[5] P. 399.
[6] P. 396.

of spiritual insufficiency has, on occasion, a conscious edge of violence:

> Since in these veyls my Ecclips'd Eye
> May not approach thee, (for at night
> Who can have commerce with the light?)
> I'le disapparell, and to buy
> But one half glaunce, most gladly dye.[7]

It is not enough for him that at times he sees the great Light in dreams or in visions that are almost ecstatic; but, fortunately, the failure of spiritual sight is not a prompter of mortal despair. Vaughan remembers his "glimpses" and he is cheered by the knowledge that a candle shines on "some heads," [8] that in him is the seed, the tiny inner warmth, "That Sacred Ray/ Thy Spirit plant." [9] Sometimes his deeds mist within him "and put out that lamp"; [10] sometimes this ray, a star captive in a tomb, cannot blaze with the full ardor of the stars; [11] yet he is blessed when he finds that all creatures, even those lesser than he, possess a glimmering of the secret light.

All creatures, he tells us in "Palm Sunday," have an interior flickering that permits them to recognize their incarnate Creator.[12] Vaughan wishes to share in this gift, to interpret with the birds the splendid doctrine of Providence.[13] He yearns to be a star or a bird; then he "should be/ Shining, or singing still to Thee." [14] The doctrine of the world of light is partially expressed in "The Eagle," [15] but from time to time he recalls

[7] P. 419.
[8] P. 395.
[9] P. 448.
[10] P. 433.
[11] P. 421.
[12] P. 501.
[13] P. 506.
[14] P. 422.
[15] P. 606.

the old contention between light and darkness and knows that he is on the edge of a terrible forest.

> But as these Birds of light make a land glad,
> Chirping their solemn Matins on each tree:
> So in the shades of night some dark fowls be,
> Whose heavy notes make all that hear them, sad.[16]

The rent between the two worlds is here made plain, but Vaughan, while doubtful of satisfaction in the veiled life, seeks constantly to see light in darkness, even though this light is filtered and is not God's "Center and mid-day." In "Cock-Crowing" he selects the bird of light as a commanding symbol. Here he can gloss darkness by light and know his own soul in terms of a lesser creature. Before we trace the history of this symbol, we should read the poem.

> Father of lights! what Sunnie seed,
> What glance of day hast thou confin'd
> Into this bird? To all the breed
> This busie Ray thou hast assign'd;
> Their magnetisme works all night,
> And dreams of Paradise and light.
>
> Their eyes watch for the morning hue,
> Their little grain expelling night
> So shines and sings, as if it knew
> The path unto the house of light.
> It seems their candle, howe'r done,
> Was tinn'd and lighted at the sunne.
>
> If such a tincture, such a touch,
> So firm a longing can impowre
> Shall thy own image think it much
> To watch for thy appearing hour?
> If a meer blast so fill the sail,
> Shall not the breath of God prevail?

[16] P. 497.

O thou immortall light and heat!
Whose hand so shines through all this frame,
That by the beauty of the seat,
We plainly see, who made the same.
Seeing thy seed abides in me,
Dwell thou in it, and I in thee.

To sleep without thee, is to die;
Yea, 'tis a death partakes of hell:
For where thou dost not close the eye
It never opens, I can tell.
In such a dark, Ægyptian border,
The shades of death dwell and disorder.

If joyes, and hopes, and earnest throws,
And hearts, whose Pulse beats still for light
Are given to birds; who, but thee, knows
A love-sick souls exalted flight?
Can souls be track'd by any eye
But his, who gave them wings to flie?

Onely this Veyle which thou hast broke,
And must be broken yet in me,
This veyle, I say, is all the cloke
And cloud which shadows thee from me.
This veyle thy full-ey'd love denies,
And onely gleams and fractions spies.

O take it off! make no delay,
But brush me with thy light, that I
May shine unto a perfect day,
And warme me at thy glorious Eye!
O take it off! or till it flee,
Though with no Lilie, stay with me!

This poem is plainly a minor metaphor in the three larger
images that are the major centers of Vaughan's poetic theology. There is, first, the seed planted by God in the flinty soil
of the human heart, watered by the showers and streams of his

Grace and warmed to growth by the essential light. As the
seed grows, it is whipped by the winds of the world, strangled
by weeds, blighted by the frost of sin. In time it will be a lily,
blossoming to its maker's hand. The growth of the plant from
its green root is likened in a second sense to a great journey
back to the noble, yet "shady City of Palme trees." The traveler often goes, like Nicodemus, by night to find his Lord; and
the way lies through a blasted land, over treacherous rocks
and past dangerous woods. The voyage is sometimes star-
lighted, but often light is shut out by cloud and darkness.
Finally, there is the metaphor of union, when God receives the
flower, and the saved poet returns to the soul-land from
whence he came. "Cock-Crowing" does not overlook any of
these capital topics, but it belongs to the first metaphoric
center, fixing our attention on the seed of light that God, according to Vaughan, has planted in all his creatures. Here the
creature celebrated is the cock, and behind Vaughan's choice
of this bird to expound his doctrine lies the usual tradition,
both pagan and Christian.

In the history of symbols, the mysteries of the cosmos are
frequently suggested by birds that live between heaven and
earth, for wings are necessary to the exploration of celestial
pastures and man must listen to birdsong, as Marvell did, in
order to learn something about celestial harmony. The gods
of the ancients, when not winged themselves, were attended
by significant birds of their own choosing. The eagle accom-
panies Jove as the hawk had once journeyed with Horus; the
peacock is holy to Juno; the dove, to Venus. Though Hades
is a land where no birds sing, the Elysian Fields could not have
been endured or enjoyed without them. Tibullus imagines the
great goddess walking with lovers in the Hereafter and listening to the viols and flutes of choral birds.

> Sed me, quod facilis tenero sum semper Amori,
>   Ipsa Venus compos ducet in Elysios.

> Hic choreae cantusque vigent, passimque vagantes
>   Dulce sonant tenui gutture carmen aves.[17]

The cock, master of the raucous song praised in Vaughan's poem, was to antiquity the most familiar of birds, the *dux et rex* of the yard and doorway; yet, though he was common, he was also a holy bird, sacred to Athena, to Hermes, to Latona, to Demeter, and to the half-gods, Hercules and Aesculapius. It was natural that he was the symbol of the sun; and it was for this reason that Idomeneus, the fighting flame of the *Iliad*, who was descended from Helios, bore an effigy of the bird on his shield.[18] For the Greek and Latin world, the rooster was the "bird of light," and as such he not only expelled the dark but the evils that walked by night.

> Nocte Deae Nocti cristatus caeditur ales,
>   Quod tepidum vigili provocat ore diem.[19]

The sunless hours, as these lines from Ovid imply, are filled with uncertain dread that the cock with his "instinct of light" (so Heliodorus [20] calls it) banishes. The dread that the pagans define with uncertainty is made clear for us when Basil states that the call of the sun-bird puts demons to flight.[21] The fact that the early Church used the rooster as a funereal ornament and that the bird is mentioned in epitaphic verse is, consequently, not surprising; he is not only the bird of light, but a symbol of the eternal light that guides and protects the souls of the dead. The cock's conversion to Christianity was easy,

---

[17] I.3.57–60.

[18] Pausanias *Itinerary* V.25.9.

[19] Ovid *Fasti* I.455–56; see *Met.* XI.597–98 and Lucretius *De. Rer. Nat.* IV.710–14.

[20] *Aethiopicus* I.18.3.

[21] J.-F. Boissonade, *Anecdota Graeca* (Paris, 1829–1833), III, 445. The traditional fear of the lion for the cock is recorded by Pliny (X.48), and this account, repeated in the Middle Ages and Renaissance, is read on the basis of Ps. 21:22 and I Pet. 5:8 as an allegory in which the lion is Satan.

and it was facilitated not only by his pagan repute but also by the special qualities that Christian writers gave to all birds.[22] When Vaughan wrote the first two stanzas of this poem, he was rephrasing in Christian terms what any classical poet might have said. The same classical knowledge helps us read stanzas five, seven, and eight, but we must go to the Scriptures and the tradition of the Church for full comprehension. The cock of St. Peter's denial is supported by an impressive passage in Job (38:36) where the admonishing Jehovah states: "Who placed wisdom in the heart of man, or who gave understanding to the cock?" With this text, men and the bird of dawn are brought together in the benefits of God though their shares are qualitatively different. It is the memory of this fecundating verse and the history of the human symbolism of the cock in

[22] Classical poets sometimes gave birds human characteristics. Propertius makes the cock an author: "Tum queror, in toto non sidere pallia lecto,/ Lucis et auctores non dare carmen aves" (IV.3.31–32), and Ovid makes the crow "auctor aquae" (*Amores* II.6.34). Late Latin and mediaeval poets often turn birds into musical instruments or human musicians. Sedulius makes them little organs: "Tempora veris celebrant crespante sussurro,/ Produnt organulis tempora veris aves" (*Poetae Latini Aevi Carolini*, ed. Traube [Berlin, 1896], III, 227). John of Garland has them playing cithers while the organ plays a requiem (G. Mari, "Poetris magistri Johannis Anglici de arte prosayca metrica et rithmica," *Rom. Forsch.*, XIII [1902], 894). St. Jerome in a prose account of spring describes them as singing psalms (*Epistulae*, ed. Hilberg [Vienna, 1910], XLIII, 3). In the *Carmina Burana*, there is a poem describing the nightingale as a cither-player: "Citharizat cantico dulcis philomena" (eds. Hilka and Schumann [Heidelberg, 1951], poem 138, st. 4, l. 1); elsewhere in the same collection, birds are said to sing to the drum, the psalter, the lyre, and the viol (92.60–64), or "melodia sonant garrule" (151.2). Alanus de Insulis relates them to sirens and gives them many musical duties: "Syrenes nemorum, cytharistae veris, in illum/ Convenere locum, mellitaque carmina sparsim/ Commentantur aves, dum gutturis organa pulsant./ Pingunt ore lyram, dum cantus imbibit istos/ Auditus, dulces effert sonus auribus escas" (*Anticlaudianus, The Minor Anglo-Latin Satirists*, ed. Wright [London, 1872], II, 276). The idea that birds are poets as well as authors is suggested in early Italian literature: "E gli augelletti riprendon lor lena/ E fanno dolci versi in loro usanza" (*Early Italian Literature*, ed. Grillo [London, 1920], I, 213).

the Christian world that effect the transition between the first and last stanzas of Vaughan's poem. The Christian cock is the Christian man; so a poem is produced that is, in all it says, an invocation. What comes from God is thus returned to him.

To bring this about, the pagan symbolism of the cock combines with Biblical expressions to make the Christian symbol. It is St. Ambrose who provided poets with the text on the cock that filled their imaginations with crowing metaphors.

> When this bird sings, the highwayman leaves his ambush, for the morning star, called forth, rises and lights the heaven. With this singing, the anxious sailor puts aside sorrow, for the tempests and storms stirred up by the strong night winds are quieted. The devout man, moved by this singing, rises to pray and to read the offices. Finally, with this song, the cornerstone of the Church himself washes away his sin contracted by denying when once before the cock crowed. With this song hope returns to all. The tedium of sickness is lightened; the pain of wounds lessens; the heat of fevers lowers; faith returns to the fallen; Jesus regards the hesitant and corrects the wanderers.[23]

With these praises, the cock becomes a Christian bird, for the references in both Testaments have made him the angel at the door, or, as Cassiodorus calls him, "spiritualis gallus." [24] But he is more commonly recognized in the beginning as one of those minor saints, "qui in nocte saeculi per fidem clamant in Dominum," [25] and this is a figuration that would have pleased Vaughan. Once Gregory had written his *Moralia in Job*, the cock became the personal analogue of the priest,[26] a

---

[23] *Hexameron* (PL, XIV, 255).

[24] *Expositio in Psalterium* (PL, CXX, 817).

[25] Pseudo-Jerome, *Expositio* (PL, XXIII, 1529).

[26] PL, LXXVI, 527-28. This account is followed with expansions by Hugo of St. Victor in *De Bestis Aliis et Rebus* (PL, CLXXVII, 33-35); see also St. Eucherius, *Formulae Spiritalis* (PL, L, 750); Rupertus, *Commentarius in*

man divinely moved, who has a special understanding of God's ways and whose duty, like that of the cock, is not only to bring light to men but to warn those who sleep in darkness of the imminent coming of God. The responsibilities of these instructed men on the eve of Doomsday are described by Rupertus with the metaphor of the cock: "And just as the rooster by crowing shakes off with his notes the sleep of sloth, announcing the coming light, the priest . . . ." In Vaughan's final four stanzas, the Christian cock becomes, as tradition will have it, the sign of the Last Judgment.

All of these texts are nonpoetical, and we must turn to the Latin poetry of the Middle Ages to find the literary way to Vaughan. In his great hymn, "Aeterne rerum conditor," Ambrose brought the cock into the liturgy.

> Surgemus ergo strenue,
>   Gallus jactantes excitat,
> Et somnolentes increpat,
>   Gallus negantes arguit.
> Gallo canente, spes redit,
>   Ægris salus refunditur,
> Mucro latronis conditur
>   Lapsis fides revertitur.[27]

Prudentius, the successor of Ambrose, made the bird's place sure when he put him at the entrance of the *Liber Cathemerinon;* here in the "Hymnus ad Galli Cantum," the singing cock awakens men from spiritual slumber, warning them of the coming splendour. "Nostri figura est iudicis," says the poet and then solemnly expands the idea.

> Hic somnus ad tempus datus
>   Est forma mortis perpetis:

Job (PL, CLXVIII, 1163); and *Le Bestiare,* ed. Walberg (Paris, 1900), ll. 230–313.
  [27] *PL,* XVI, 1473.

Peccata, ceu nox horrida,
  Cogunt iacere ac stertere.

Sed vox ab alto culmine
  Christi docentis praemonet
Adesse iam lucem prope,
  Ne mens sopori serviat.

Ne somnus usque ad terminos
  Vitae socordis opprimat
Pectus sepultum crimine
  Et lucis oblitum suae.

Vaughan almost says this in English: "To sleep without thee, is to die;/ Yea, 'tis a death partakes of hell." [28] Prudentius, who strives for the fullest interpretation, continues, reminding his readers that Peter's denial came as Christ conquered Hell and Death. His bird, too, has further lessons for those who sleep in darkness and dream vainly of gold, glory, and pleasure. "Fit mane, nil sunt omnia." For the cock, we are then assured, is not only the herald of God's light, the resonant shout of Doomsday, but also the grave Judge.

Tu, Christe, somnium dissice,
  Tu rumpe noctis vincula,
Tu solve peccatum vetus
  Novumque lumen ingere.[29]

The hymns of Ambrose and Prudentius made the cock a divine analogue, and thereafter he finds a sure place in the ritual. The Mozarabic hymns included one song for matins, "Gallo canente venimus" [30] and in two other hymns—"Gallus

---

[28] Vaughan's "dark Ægyptian border," which also appears in "The Relapse" as "a thick, Egyptian damp" (p. 433) has a symbolism of sin and sinners; see Tertullian, *De Spectaculis* (PL, I, 635); and St. Prosper, *Psalmorum . . . Expositio* (PL, LI, 326).

[29] *Carmina*, ed. Dressel (Leipzig, 1860), pp. 4–9.

[30] *PL*, LXXXVI, 935.

diei nuntius" [31] and "Gallus auroram resonis/ Salutans canti-
bus" [32]—the bird has a symbolic rôle. The poets of the age of
Charlemagne naturally celebrated the priestly rooster who
called men to worship [33] and who predicted the day of God's
Coming.[34] The latter theme is handsomely embroidered in
the *Carmina Centulensis*, where the poet presents the cock
and the thrush singing a doomsong together after the morning
choir; a relatively somber hymn it is, in which they urge the
righteous to prepare immediately for the new age of gold.[35] But
all of these poems are minor compared to the fourteenth-
century, "Multi sunt presbyteri qui ignorant, quare/ Super
domum domini gallus solet stare."

By the time this poem was written the cock had obviously
taken a firm perch on spires, and this poem attempts to tell us
why he is so honored. Throughout this poem, the mutual
duties of priest and layman are carefully annotated in terms of
the symbolic legend of the cock; for though the cock is a
priest in analogy—"si bonus presbyter eius fit figura"—the
secular can also take instruction from the bird. Actually, the
poem is a series of contrasts. The care of the bird for his flock
is balanced against the fact that the hellish basilisk is hatched
from his eggs. "Sic crescit diabolus ex presbyterorum/ Magna
negligentia." Once more we hear of the cock as a mighty
ward against evil, of his strict warnings in God's service, of
his premonitions of the Day of Judgment.

> Sic et bonus presbyter, respuens terrena,
>   Ducat suos subditos ex inferni poena,

[31] J.-F. Gergier, *Lyricus Sacer* (Bensaçon, 1889), R, poem 21.
[32] J. Santolius, *Hymni Sacri et Novi* (Paris, 1698), p. 192.
[33] Paulus Albarus, *Carmina*, ed. Traube, *PLAC* (Berlin, 1896), III, 128.
[34] Milo, *Carmina*, *PLAC*, III, 582–84, 661.
[35] III.332. There is an enigma on the cock by Tatwin (Wright, II, 543)
in which the bird is associated with adventual prophecies.

> Praebens iter caelicum caeli per amoena
> Ut cum Christus venerit, turba sit serena.[36]

Without this tradition, Vaughan's poem might not have come into being in the text that we have; with the tradition, it is richer and fuller in all its implications. For centuries before Vaughan saw visions by the Usk, the cock had been famed for his instinctive knowledge of light, not only that of the lesser light of the sun but also of the divine light. For this reason he was associated with the priest as an expeller of spiritual darkness and of evil. In the natural world he made lions afraid; in the higher world, he was victor over the lions of Hell. While he reminded men of their duties to God and roused them from their worldly slumber, he also warned them of Christ's Second Coming and urged them to prepare for the Day of Judgment. These traditions make the fabric of the early and late stanzas of "Cock-Crowing," but there is another connection that must be established because Vaughan says that the bird has within him a "busie Ray," "a little grain expelling night," whereas man, "thy own image," has a soul that is far broader in its comprehension of the divine. Hence, if the rooster can dream "of Paradise and light,"

> Shall thy own image think it much
> To watch for thy appearing hour?

The difference between man and the cock implies the difference between "sapientia" and "intelligentia." For Vaughan this difference is expressed by the breeze that fills a sail and that which fills the soul of the poet, the very breath of God. But as the poem proceeds, the soul becomes like a bird.

> If joyes, and hopes, and earnest throws
> And hearts, whose Pulse beats still for light

[36] *The Oxford Book of Medieval Latin Verse*, ed. Gaslee (Oxford, 1925), pp. 178–80.

>   Are given to birds; who, but thee, knows
>   A love-sick souls exalted flight?
>   Can souls be track'd by any eye
>   But his, who gave them wings to flie?

The translation of soul into bird is also part of a long poetic process.

Drawing on the bank of pagan symbolism, the early Christians associated the soul with flying things. The Greeks had represented the soul as a winged replica of the person who was dead, and Psyche, the soul-butterfly, set the pattern for the iconographical description of the Christian soul with her colored wings.[37] The relationship between the soul or mind of man, and birds, was strongly perceived by the Greeks, and it is not surprising to find that Plato compares the mind to an aviary,[38] or that Plotinus discovers three kinds of souls among men and compares them to three classes of birds.[39] This decorous symbol was appropriated by the Fathers of Christian belief because it was also authorized by the Scriptures.

As we stand at the deathbeds of the saints of antiquity, we see, if we believe their chroniclers, their souls ascending to heaven as birds. St. Benedict saw the soul of his sister, leaving her body in the form of a dove; [40] and St. Gregory in his record of the death of Abbot Spes says that the soul of that devout man was seen "in columbae specie." [41] In the *Peristephanon*, Prudentius turns his experience into poetry.

>   Emicat inde columba repens
>   Martyris os nive candidior
>   Visa relinquere et astra sequi;
>   Spiritus hic erat Eulaliae
>   Lacteolus, celer, innocuus.

[37] See Chapter Two.
[38] *Theaetetus* 197C.
[39] *Enneads* V.9.1, 6–21.
[40] *Prolegomena* (PL, LXVI, 196).
[41] *Dialogi* (PL, LXXVII, 336).

Colla fluunt abeunte anima
Et rogus igneus emoritur,
Pax datur artubus exanimis,
Flatus in aethere plaudit ovans
Templaque celsa petit volucer.

Vidit et ipse satelles avem
Feminae ab ore meare palam,
Obstupefactus et attonitus
Prosilit et sua gesta fugit,
Lictor et ipse fugit pavidus.[42]

Though for most early Christian poets the soul assumes the form of a dove or a nameless bird,[43] the Renaissance was also able to associate the soul with the cock. The translation is due not to Christian tradition, but once again, to Plato.

"I owe, Crito," says the dying Socrates, "a cock to Aesculapius; do not forget to pay it." The interpretation of this final request of the great philosopher has caused men of all times to whip their minds. The irreverent Lucian observes that the remark shows what little regard Socrates had for Zeus.[44] The testimony of this scoffer was hardly acceptable to early Christians; yet, in this case, Tertullian agrees with the pagan and observes that Socrates, the atheist, ordered the sacrifice out of filial consideration for his father.[45] Origen thinks the demand shows that Socrates, in spite of his wisdom, abandoned eminent principles for the trivial and unimportant.[46] Chrysostom [47] and Theodoret [48] smell idolatry. Lactantius is more brutal: Socrates feared the judge of the dead, stern Rhadamanthus.[49]

[42] *Op. cit.*, p. 338.
[43] See Rabanus Maurus (*PL*, CXII, 871); Rupertus (*PL*, CLXVIII, 294); Garnerus de St. Victor (*PL*, CXCIII, 65).
[44] *Bis. Accus.* 5.
[45] *Ad Nationes* (*PL*, I, 589).
[46] *Contra Celsum* (*PG*, XI, 1294).
[47] *Commentarius in Epistolam ad Romanos* (*PG*, LX, 414).
[48] *Graecorum Affectionum Curatio* (*PG*, LXXXIII, 1006).
[49] *Institutiones Divinae* (*PL*, VI, 417).

The humanists, to whom Plato was the master that Aristotle was to the scholastics, rose to the defence of their philosopher. Ficino saw in the dying request of Socrates a statement of Christian intent. Socrates, he insists, sought among the gods for a physician who could cure the diseases of the soul; and when at last he had resolved his own diseases (doubts and fears), he was eager to thank God.[50] Pico della Mirandola fully agrees with his friend and extends the allegory. The cock, he states, is the soul of man; this is the reason that Socrates said he owed a cock to Aesculapius. By this ultimate statement he meant that he owed his own soul to the great doctor of souls.[51] So for the Florentine Platonists the cock of the *Phaedo* was the soul of the philosopher, but their concept was strengthened by another citation in the books of the past.

As every educated man of the seventeenth century knew, there is among the cryptic and almost mystical sayings of Pythagoras the strict advice: "Feed the cock." The baffling command was explained by the sixteenth-century editor, Lilius Gyraldus—a great explainer of enigmas—as golden doctrine. Pythagoras, he tells us, was encouraging his disciples to feed the divine part of the soul (the cock) with celestial knowledge just as they fed their bodies with more mundane food.[52] So the cock of Erasmus' St. Socrates and the cock of Milton's St. Pythagoras become in the sixteenth century the immortal soul of man. The symbol of solar light arrives with pagan help at a greater definition, for it changes into the "seed," the created light that dwells in all humankind.

With this alteration we can better understand how Vaughan could move from the allegory of the cock to the Christian desires of his inner self. Behind much of the transformation

[50] Plato, *Opera* (Lyons, 1548), p. 333.

[51] *Commentationes* (Bologna, 1496), p. 134r.

[52] *Pythagorae Symbolorum Interpretatio*, in *Opera* (Leyden, 1696), II, 659–60.

may rest his philosophical belief in the mysterious doctrines of the universe that he shared with his brother,[53] but enforcing these and making them real is the poetical result of the long struggle of men to express in terms of the lower world what their hearts tell them about the unknowable. In the darkness, the heart of flint sparks, and from its little lights the poet gains courage to await the rending of the veil. The seed has grown into a plant though the plant may not yet have brought forth a bright flower.

> O take it off! make no delay,
> But brush me with thy light, that I
> May shine unto a perfect day,
> And warme me at thy glorious Eye!
> O take it off! or till it flee,
> Though with no Lilie, stay with me!

In this last stanza, reminded by the cock, Vaughan writes his own "Venite rerum Conditor"; but as he writes it, he also realizes that the time may be far away, that he may have to visit with the night before he sees the eternal brightness of God. He draws his comfort and he frames his prayer according to the text of the creature instinct with light. This symbol remains with us, for Vaughan's cock crows again for Masefield.

> But in the darkest hour of night
> When even the foxes peer for light
> The byre-cock crows; he feels the light.
>
> So, in this water mixed with dust
> The byre-cock spirit crows from trust
> That death will change because it must.

[53] See *The Works of Thomas Vaughan*, ed. Waite (London, 1919), pp. 81–82, 266–67.

Index of Authors and Editors

DATE DUE

MAR 19 71			
MAY 5 75			
MAY			
APR 0 3			
MAY 1 2 2001			
GAYLORD			PRINTED IN U.S.A.